Carol S. Anderson

LINGUISTICA EXTRANEA

Studia, 14

THE INDO-EUROPEANS

IN THE FOURTH AND THIRD MILLENNIA

Edited by Edgar C. Polomé

1982

KAROMA PUBLISHERS, INC.   ANN ARBOR

CONTENTS

PREFACE

Edgar C. Polomé

In the course of recent decades, a number of important new perspectives have been opened in the study of Indo-European. In the field of linguistics, syntax— which had remained the stepchild of the Neogrammarians and the structuralists— has received increased attention under the influence of recent developments in linguistic theory. Combining the results of the investigations in transformational grammar and typology with the well-established scholarship of previous genera- tions, W. P. Lehmann ventured to produce a *Proto-Indo-European Syntax* (Austin: University of Texas Press, 1974), and this attempt at an explanatory syntax of the parent language soon became an incentive for further scrutiny into the syntactic categories of Indo-European and their development in the various dialects. The issue of the original word order became an object of lively discussion, triggering the writing of numerous articles and valuable monographs such as Paul Friedrich's *Proto-Indo-European Syntax: The Order of Meaningful Elements* (Butte, Montana: The Journal of Indo-European Studies, 1975). The correlation between syntactic features and morphology was often emphasized in these studies and led to a num- ber of searching *Einzeluntersuchungen* such as Dorothy Disterheft's doctoral dissertation on *The Syntactic Development of the Infinitive in Indo-European* (Columbus, Ohio: Slavica Publishers, 1980), or the work of Carol Justus on Hittite relative clauses and related items. The importance and vitality of such problems is well illustrated by the recent Colloquium of the Indogermanische Gesellschaft, the proceedings of which were edited by Paolo Ramat under the title *Linguistic Reconstruction and Indo-European Syntax* (Amsterdam: John Benjamins, 1980). An assessment of recent developments in a broader framework is given by Henrik Birnbaum in his *Linguistic Reconstruction: Its Potentials and Limitations in New Perspective* (Washington, DC: Journal of Indo-European Studies, 1977). These include in particular the efforts of T. Gamkrelidze and V. V. Ivanov, on the one hand, and Paul Hopper, on the other, to propose a typologically more acceptable alternative for the usually reconstructed subsystem of Proto-Indo-European obstruents—a topic discussed in detail by Paul Hopper in his contribution to this volume. To the suggested revision of the reconstructed phonological system—the most radical change proposed since the "laryngeal theory"—we might add the renewal of studies on Indo-European accentuation, especially under the influence of V. A. Dybo and V. M. Illič-Svityč, illustrated, for example, by Frederik Kortlandt's concise but most substantial *Slavic Accentuation: A Study in Relative Chronology* (Lisse, The Netherlands: Peter de Ridder Press, 1975), as well as the work done on morphology since the publication of Calvert Watkins' volume on the Indo-European verb in Jerzy Kuryłowicz' *Indogermanische Grammatik* (Bd. III, *Formenlehre* I, Teil: *Geschichte der Indogermanischen Verbalflexion,* Heidelberg: Carl Winter, 1969). The better part of William R. Schmalstieg's "new synthesis" on *Indo-European Linguistics* (University Park: University of Pennsylvania Press, 1980) is devoted to a thorough analysis of verb morphology, and his chapter on noun morphology provides an interesting background for further investigation in correlation with W. P. Lehmann's stimulating contribution on the same subject in this volume.

Indo-European poetic language, illustrated by the collection of papers published by Rüdiger Schmitt (*Indogermanische Dichtersprache,* Darmstadt: Wissenschaftliche Buchgesellschaft, 1968), as well as by his own work (*Dichtung und Dichtersprache in indogermanischer Zeit,* Wiesbaden: O. Harrassowitz, 1967), has become a major subject of investigation, as the recent *Ricerche di Cultura Poetica Indoeuropea* of Enrico Campanile (Pisa: Giardini, 1977) shows and Calvert Watkins further emphasizes in his contribution to this volume.

In the field of archaeology, new methods of dating by calibration of the carbon-14 determinations with dendrochronological controls have led to a thorough revision of all previous chronologies. On this basis, Homer L. Thomas reviews the archaeological evidence relevant to the Indo-European migration and attempts here a new comparative chronology. This study may answer some of the queries of British archaeologists who contest Marija Gimbutas' ethnic identification of the Indo-Europeans with the late Neolithic Pit Grave (i.e., *Kurgan*) culture, e.g., J. M. Coles and A. F. Harding, *The Bronze in Europe* (New York: St. Martin's Press, 1979), who point out (p. 7) that "the supposedly derivative groups in Europe are in fact *contemporaneous* with the Pit Graves in south Russia, and not appreciably *later* than them." Marija Gimbutas' contribution to this volume focuses, however, on the civilization that the Indo-European invaders encountered in Europe and with which they ultimately merged after three successive waves, producing thorough social and cultural changes reflected by the archaeological material. Whatever artistic endeavors resulted from the new cultures that emerged after the Indo-Europeanization are reviewed by Shirley Alexander.

Finally, in the field of culture and religion, where the contributions of Emile Benveniste and Georges Dumézil have completely renewed the content and scope of the investigations, Edgar C. Polomé tries to give a "state of the art" report, indicating how a multidisciplinary approach has put cultural and religious studies on a much more solid basis than in previous generations of scholarship.

The papers published here are revised versions of oral presentations made at a symposium organized at the University of Texas at Austin in February 1980 to commemorate the tenth anniversary of the foundation of the Department of Oriental and African Languages and Literatures and to honor Professor Raja Rao upon his retirement because of his constant, active support of and encouragement to Indo-European studies. A number of distinguished scholars participated in the discussion of these papers, and their contributions to the argument have been most valued by the speakers and taken into account in their final texts. We are therefore particularly grateful to Professors Eric Hamp (University of Chicago), Carol Justus (University of California at Berkeley), Bruce Lincoln (University of Minnesota), Thomas Markey (University of Michigan), and Ladislas Zgusta (University of Illinois) for their share in the success of the symposium and for the valuable help and information their comments brought to the contributors as well as to the audience.

We want to convey our special thanks to Dean Robert King of the College of Liberal Arts for presiding at our first meeting and for addressing our symposium. Without his moral and financial support, our conference would never have been possible. We also want to include Vice-President William Livingston, Dean of the Graduate School, in our expressions of deep gratitude for the grant which helped us bring to Austin some of the most active scholars in Indo-European studies to discuss together the major problems facing our discipline in the eighties.

OLD EUROPE IN THE FIFTH MILLENNIUM B.C.:
The European Situation on the Arrival of Indo-Europeans

Marija Gimbutas
University of California, Los Angeles

With the growing realization of the necessity to distinguish the Neolithic and Copper Age pre-Indo-European civilization from the "Indo-Europeanized" Europe of the Bronze Age, I coined, ten years ago, the new term "Old Europe." This term covers, in a broad sense, all Europe west of the Pontic Steppe before the series of incursions of the steppe (or "Kurgan") pastoralists in the second half of the fifth, of the fourth, and the beginning of the third millennium B.C., for in my view Europe is not the homeland of the Indo-European speakers. In a narrower sense, the term Old Europe applies to Europe's first civilization, i.e., the highest Neolithic and Copper Age culture focused in the southeast and the Danubian basin, gradually destroyed by repeated Kurgan infiltrations.

My purpose here will be to present the basic features of Old Europe in southeast and east-central Europe—its rapidly developing arts and crafts, architecture, economic and social structure, its sophistication of worship and religious institutions, and sacred script. All these features are in sharp contradistinction to those of the steppe pastoralist culture, *Kurgan*, most likely Proto-Indo-European.

The two cultural systems are very different: the first is sedentary, matrifocal, peaceful, art-loving, earth- and sea-bound; the second is patrifocal, mobile, warlike, ideologically sky-oriented, and indifferent to art. The two systems can best be understood if studied before the period of their clash and mélange, i.e., before ca. 4500-4000 B.C. Because of their high chronology, the study of these cultural systems must remain in the hands of the prehistorians. Nevertheless, it is a study essential to all Indo-Europeanists, linguists, and mythologists alike, for the continuous remnants of the pre-Indo-European substratum, persisting to the present time, are a significant part of that with which they deal.

Chronological Outline of Major Events

Archaeological recognition of the very ancient and rich heritage of European civilization is due to new dating methods—radiocarbon and dendrochronology. New dating techniques have provided new dimensions for the time span of the earliest agriculturalists and metallurgists of southeast Europe. In using the radiocarbon dates corrected to the dates of samples of dendrochronologically known age, archaeologists can now speak of historical age for the last 8,000 years—as far back as ca. 6200 B.C.

The roots of Old Europe go back to the period of great transformation from the Paleolithic to the Neolithic. Increased mutual contacts and rising navigational skills enabled the spread of trade among the east and central Mediterranean, the Aegean area, and Anatolia. This in turn influenced material progress and social development. Southeastern Europe developed a full-fledged neolithic economy with the knowledge of agriculture (wheat, barley, peas, lentils, sheep, goats, cattle, pigs, pottery, and polished stone) several millennia earlier than northern Europe (see Figure 1, p. 26).*

Ca. 6500-6000 B.C.

A consistent increase in the size and number of settled communities is observable. Agricultural settlements are known in Crete and the Balkan Peninsula; in the Danubian Plain; and in the circum-Adriatic region, including Yugoslavia and southern Italy. The gracile Mediterranean people dispersed up to the Danube and the Carpathians.

Hard-baked ceramic wares came into general use. No later than 6500-6300 B.C., the painting of pottery began in the Aegean region. This technique soon became one of the major media of artistic creativity as well as a medium of symbolic language.

Ca. 6000-5500 B.C.

A population increase is shown in the Mediterranean and Aegean regions, the central Balkans, and central Bulgaria by agglomerations of houses built of bricks on stone foundations (in the Aegean), and of timber uprights and clay daub (in the temperate zone).

Ca. 5500-5000 B.C.

Copper metallurgy began in the Danubian basin, notably in Bulgaria, Romania, Yugoslavia, and Hungary; it was an indigenous Old European discovery; there was no break in the cultural continuum between the Neolithic and the Chalcolithic ("copper-and-stone") periods.

---

*All figures are located at the end of this article, pp. 26-55 (captions are on pp. 22-24).

This period is the zenith of Old European civilization, characterized by exquisite polychrome, graphite, and gold-painted pottery, plastic art, and highly sophisticated religious objects and ceremonial costume. Two-story temples with wall paintings and monumental building complexes were built. Around 4500 B.C. a dramatic increase of copper and gold ornaments and tools is evidenced, thus the emergence of large-scale copper mines in central Bulgaria and northern Yugoslavia, wide-reaching trade accompanied by general sophistication of life-style due to the material abundance and leisure time. The recently excavated cemetery at Varna on the Black Sea coast of Bulgaria includes graves equipped with hundreds of gold and copper items, thousands of Aegean shells, marble vases, and rhyta, graphite and gold-painted pottery, and cultic objects (Gimbutas 1977a, 1977b; Ivanov 1978).[1] They are witness to a rising middle class with a life-style reminiscent of that in Bronze Age Thera and Crete some 3,000 years later.

From the relatively homogeneous Neolithic culture, there developed increasingly differentiated regional traditions characterized by diverse art styles, by accelerating socioeconomic complexity, and by increased specialization and development of metallurgical and other crafts. Some villages of this period amount to small townships. Larger than the habitation sites of the preceding period, they reflect an increased population and refinement of social organization.

The complexes of new traits which appeared during this period have in the past led scholars to assume that a tide of colonization burst through the Balkans either from Anatolia or from the eastern Mediterranean. However, the physical anthropological evidence indicates that most of the Chalcolithic population of the Balkans persisted from earlier times, and in my view the cultural efflorescence was essentially the product of local development. The growing individuality of various geographic units, manifested by an unprecedented diversity and creativity in ceramic art, is a phenomenon precisely opposite to that which normally results from the impact of a substantial ethnic movement.

Within the broad geographic regions of the Balkans and east-central Europe, a multiplicity of cultures developed, each marked by habitation patterns and individuality of ceramic art. These are briefly listed below:

1. The *Hamangia* culture developed in the West Pontic region (Dobruja).
2. The *Karanovo* culture, a continuum from the Neolithic, expanded eastward and northward:
   a. replacing the Hamangia culture in Dobruja in the mid-fifth millennium;
   b. amalgamating with the local culture in eastern Bulgaria to become "Sava";
   c. developing in the lower Danube region into a variant "Boian" and subsequently "Gumelniţa."
3. The *Vinča* culture arose in the Central Balkans. It extended from Bosnia to western Romania, concentrating primarily in the Vardar-Morava and Danube river basins.

4. The *Tisza* culture in the valley of the Tisza River was eventually superseded by the Lengyel (Polgár) culture.
5. The *Danilo-Hvar* culture occupied the western area of Dalmatia along the Adriatic.
6. The *Butmir* culture of Bosnia, a development from the late Starčevo (or Kakanj) complex, was related to Vinča and the Adriatic Danilo groups.
7. The *Lengyel* culture covered the Middle Danube area including western Hungary, eastern Austria, Moravia, Slovakia, and southern Poland.
8. The *Petreşti* group of Karanovo background replaced the Early Vinča complex in Transylvania.
9. The *Cucuteni* culture (*Tripolye* in Russian, *Tripilye* in Ukrainian) of Karanovo background succeeded the Linear Pottery culture in Moldavia and the western Ukraine.
10. The cultures of the Aegean area are collectively known as the *Aegean Late Neolithic*. The Late Neolithic and Chalcolithic of Thessaly includes the four *Dimini* subphases and the *Larisa* and *Rakhmani* phases.

(See Figure 2, p. 27.)

1. Settlement Pattern and Subsistence

The villages were mainly of two types: either extended on large terraces, or relatively small in area situated on compact tells of neolithic origin. The latter type covers about 5,000 square meters, the former up to 200,000 or more square meters. Spacious villages conforming to the terrain of river terraces are encountered in the Danilo, Butmir, Lengyel, Vinča, Petreşti, and Cucuteni areas; compact villages are found in the areas of the Karanovo and Aegean culture.

The large extended villages differ in plan from area to area. Three basic types can be distinguished: (1) houses in rows along parallel streets, characteristic of Vinča and Butmir cultures; (2) houses randomly placed, typical of Lengyel, Petreşti, and earlier Cucuteni cultures; and (3) houses in a circle or ellipse on wide terraces. These are Late Cucutenian towns.

The Karanovian villages (Figures 3-5, pp. 28-30) on the contrary present an almost honeycomb pattern, house next to house, separated if at all by very narrow streets or pathways. Extant houses were renewed, or razed and rebuilt on the same spot. In some habitations, the floors and ovens had been replastered 15 to 20 times.

Danilo and Hvar people along the Adriatic coast and on the Adriatic islands lived not only in open villages but also in caves conveniently located near adjoining fertile land. The possibility that caves were inhabited year-round is substantiated by botanical specimens recovered from nearby areas where the terrain was flat enough for small-scale farming.

Old Europeans never chose to live in inconvenient places such as the high, steep hills favored by the Indo-Europeans who built hill-forts in inaccessible locations and frequently surrounded them with cyclopean stone walls. Old European site locations are notable for their beautiful setting, good water and soil, and the availability of animal pasture. Vinča, Butmir, Petreşti, and Cucutenian settlement locales are remarkable for an excellent view of the environs but not for their defensive positioning. The characteristic absence of heavy fortifications and of weapons speaks for the peaceful character of most of these art-loving peoples. Some defensive measures—usually ditches or palisades—however, were taken to protect the villages from animal or human intruders, or—in the marginal areas in the east— from possibly hostile neighbors. The Karanovo sites in northeastern Bulgaria were protected by palisades. Recent excavations at Goljamo Delčevo have shown such defensive structures. The early village (Karanovo III-IV) was protected by three palisades. In later times (Karanovo VI) the site was surrounded on three sides by a rampart with an emplacement of two parallel clay fences approximately 80 cm apart. In the terminal occupation of the tell, the base of the palisade was reinforced with stones (Todorova et al. 1975).[2] Cucuteni A settlements were protected inland by funnel-shaped trenches (at Cucuteni, Truşeşti, and Habaşeşti in Moldavia) (Florescu 1969).[3] AB phase sites are in lower, more open spaces, usually very wide terraces; there deep, wide ditches encircled the settlements. At Traian, the funnel-shaped ditch was 2.5 to 4 m deep and 4 to 7 m wide. B phase settlements, possibly under threat of incursions from the steppe area, were in naturally protected locations. The defense systems of the B phase are more elaborate than former ones.

The normal dwelling in Butmir, Vinča, Tisza, Lengyel, Petreşti, Cucuteni, and Karanovo cultures (Figures 6 and 7, pp. 31-32) was a rectangular two- or three-room house 8 to 20 m long and 5 to 6 m wide with clay daub walls on a framework of timber uprights, the gabled roof supported by a row of heavy posts down the middle of the interior. Rarely, houses of 3 or 4 rooms were up to 30 m in length.

In every house, one room contained a bread oven built of branches and covered by a beehive-shaped roof of clay. Its clay floor covered a foundation of flat stones and formed a platform in front of the oven. Pits filled with clean ashes (perhaps collected to be used as detergent) were found at the side of the platform. Groups of loom weights often found nearby suggest that a vertical loom usually stood beside the oven. Probably spinning and other domestic tasks were also performed in this room since quern stones, spindle-whorls, bone, and flint tools are commonly concentrated near the oven. Along the wall, opposite the oven, was an area covered with wooden boards. Groups of vases, braziers with horizontally pierced holes, and storage jars stood on the floor.

Interior ovens were not used for cooking. Cooking was done at the open hearths outside the house, near which grinding places have been identified. Stone working areas for tools (blades, knives, scrapers, borers, awls, and arrowheads) were also outside the houses.

Vinča and Karanovo houses usually consisted of a main room and an ante-chamber, with the entrance at the narrow end. Split-plank floor and wall construction is characteristic. Cucuteni houses consisting of one to four rooms, each including an oven with a narrow chimney in the center, built up against a wall, had floors of split log plastered with a thick layer of clay. A raised clay platform next to the oven was probably used for sleeping.

Economic patterns with gradual improvement of agriculture and animal-raising techniques continued from Neolithic times. The subsistence economy was predicated on the usual crops and domesticates: emmer and einkorn wheat, six-row barley, peas, and lentils; cattle, pigs, sheep/goats, and dogs. Local environmental conditions account for regional variabilities in the several geographical zones, but everywhere there is a significant numerical increase of cattle and pigs, and a decrease of sheep. Hunting, fishing, and other exploitation of food resources of the local environment accompanied the spread of forestation during the Atlantic climatic condition which prevailed.

The rise in the number of cattle is shown statistically in all sites of east-central Europe. Between the end of the Neolithic and the Copper Ages there was an increase of 20 percent. The Neolithic Starčevo site at Divostin in central Yugoslavia yielded 45 percent cattle bones of the total number of domesticated animal bones, and the Copper Age Vinča assemblage contained 65 percent. In Bosnia, at Obre, the percentage of cattle bones of the late Starčevo (Obre I) period was 47.90, that of the Butmir period (Obre II) was 67.16.

Local forests apparently abounded in game. In some areas, such as Hungary, Moldavia, the western Ukraine, and northeastern Bulgaria, about 40 percent of the animal bones recovered from settlements are from wild species; the aurochs, because of its heavy yield of meat, was of prime importance, followed by wild swine, red deer, and roe deer. Fruit, berries, and nuts were collected where available in the forested uplands. Crabapples, hazelnuts, and acorns have been found in a number of sites.

Fishing activities were intensified; numbers of barbed harpoons, fish hooks, and spear points of bone and antler in the Tisza, Vinča, and Karanovo settlements attest to the importance of the river. Large fish, such as carp, catfish, and sturgeon, must have contributed greatly to the subsistence. In the coastal regions snails and mussels figured in the diet, and deep-sea fishing for the *aurata aurata* was important to the Hamangia people living on the shores of the Black Sea.

2. Metallurgy and Trade

Copper metallurgy developed autonomously in east-central Europe after the middle of the sixth millennium B.C., its origin probably linked to the advanced technology of pottery firing. Early copper artifacts were hammered. From around the middle of the fifth millennium B.C., the exploitation of copper mines became systematic (Jovanović 1980; Chernykh 1978).[4] The production of tools and ornaments increased. Smelting developed, but the alloying of copper with arsenic or tin was not practiced. Old Europeans did not produce hard metal. The pure copper they used was too soft for weapons. The period of 4500-4200 B.C. also saw the emergence of gold manufacture, as well as the production of gold- and graphite-decorated pottery (see Figure 8, p. 33).

The unprecedented wealth of copper, gold, Aegean shells (spondylus and dentalium), and marble, Carpathian obsidian, and central Bulgarian graphite recovered from the cemetery of Varna on the Black Sea coast of Bulgaria in 1972-78 bears witness to the importance of Varna as a harbor and trading center. Its graves yielded over 3,000 objects of gold (see Figure 9, p. 34).

Trade in copper and gold extended for thousands of kilometers. Central Bulgarian copper from the mines at Ai-bunar spread as far east as the Lower Volga. Horse-riding semi-nomads of the south Russian steppe must be credited for the diffusion of copper over the steppe. The shining metal of Old Europe certainly was a great attraction for the steppe inhabitants. After the middle of the fifth millennium B.C., contacts between Old Europe and steppe pastoralists increased. The wheel (and vehicle) also emerged at this time, which contributed to mobility and trade. Miniature models of wheels in clay are known from the Karanovo and Cucuteni cultures of the mid-fifth millennium B.C. (Karanovo VI and Cucuteni A_2 phases) (Dinu 1979).[5]

3. Social Organization

a. *Theocratic Monarchies?* Old European societies were unstratified: there were no contrasting classes of rulers and laborers, but there was a rich middle class which rose as a consequence of metallurgy and expansion of trade. Neither royal tombs, distinct in burial rites from those of the rest of the population, nor royal quarters, distinguished by extravagance, have been discovered. I see no evidence of the existence of a patriarchal chieftain system with pronounced ranking of the Indo-European type. Instead, there are in Old Europe a multitude of temples with accumulations of wealth—gold, copper, marble, shells, and exquisite ceramics. The goods of highest quality, produced by the best craftsmen, belonged not to the chief, as is customary in chiefdoms, but to the Goddess and to her representative, the queen-priestess. The social organization represented by the rise of temples was a primary centrifugal social force.

The question of government organization is as yet difficult to answer. Central areas and secondary provinces can be observed in each culture group. Some of the foci were clearly more influential than others, but whether centralized government existed we do not know. I favor the theory of small theocratic kingdoms or city-states, analogous to Etruscan *lucomonies* and Minoan palaces, with a queen-priestess as ruler, and her brother or husband as supervisor of agriculture and trade.

The basis of such a structure was more social and religious in character than civil, political, or military.

b. *The Matrilinear Society.* There is absolutely no indication that Old European society was patrilinear or patriarchal. Evidence from the cemeteries does not indicate a subordinate position of women. There was no ranking along a patriarchal masculine-feminine value scale as there was in Europe after the infiltration of steppe pastoralists who introduced the patriarchal and the patrilinear systems. The study of grave equipment in each culture group suggests an egalitarian society. A division of labor between the sexes is demonstrated by grave goods, but not a superiority of either. The richest graves belong to both men and women. Age was a determining factor; children had the lowest number of objects.

A strong support for the existence of matrilinearity in Old Europe is the historic continuity of matrilinear succession in the non-Indo-European societies of Europe and Asia Minor, such as the Etruscan, Pelasgian, Lydian, Carian, and Basque. Even in Rome during the monarchy, royal office passed regularly through the female line—clearly a non-Indo-European tradition most probably inherited from Old Europe. Polybius, in the second century B.C., speaking of the Greek colony, Lokroi, on the toe of Italy, says, "all their ancestral honors are traced through women." Furthermore, we hear from Greek historians that the Etruscans and prehistoric Athenians had "wives in common" and "their children did not know their own fathers." The woman in such a system is free to marry the man of her choice, and as many as she pleases (there is no question of adultery—that was a male invention), and she retains control of her children with regard to their paternity. This evidence led George Thomson to the assumption that group marriage was combined with common ownership in prehistoric Aegean societies (Thomson 1978).[6] Matrilinear succession on some Aegean islands (e.g., Lesbos, Skyros) is reported by written records in the eighteenth century and continues in partial form to this very day. Matrilinear succession to real property and prenuptial promiscuity were practiced in isolated mountainous regions of southwestern Yugoslavia up to the twentieth century (personal communication from Dj. Basler, Sarajevo 1968).[7] Such customs are certainly unthinkable in present patriarchal society; only a very deeply rooted tradition could have survived for millennia the counter-influence of the patrilinearity of surrounding tribes.

A matrifocal society is reflected by the types of Old European goddesses and their worship. It is obvious that goddesses, not gods, dominated the Old European pantheon. Goddesses ruled absolutely over human, animal, and plant life. Goddesses, not male gods, spontaneously generated the life-force and created the universe. As demonstrated by the thousands of figurines and temples from the Neolithic through the Copper Ages, the male god was an adjunct of the female goddess, as consort or son. In the models of house-shrines and temples, and in actual temple remains, females are shown as supervising the preparation and performance of rituals dedicated to the various aspects and functions of the Goddess. Enormous energy was expended in the production of cult equipment and votive gifts. Some temple models show the grinding of grain and the baking of sacred bread. The routine acts of daily existence were religious rituals by virtue of replicating the sacred models. In the temple workshops, which usually constitute half the building or occupy the floor below the temple proper, females made and decorated quantities of the various pots appropriate to different rites. Next to the altar of the temple stood a vertical loom on which were probably woven the sacred garments and temple appurtenances. The most sophisticated creations of Old Europe—the most exquisite vases, sculptures, etc., now extant—were women's work (the equipment for decoration of vases so far is known only from female graves). Since the requirements of the temple were of primary importance, production for the temple must have doubled or tripled the general level of productivity, both stimulating and maintaining the level of feminine craftsmanship.

4. Religion

a. *Temples.* The tradition of temple building begins in the seventh millennium B.C. A remarkable series of temple models and actual rectangular temples from the sixth and fifth millennia B.C. bear witness to a great architectural tradition.

At present about 50 models from various culture groups and phases are known. They are more informative than the actual temple remains, since they present details of architecture, decoration, and furnishings otherwise unavailable to prehistoric archaeology. Actual remains of sanctuaries suggest that miniature models in clay were replicas of the real temples. They almost always were found at the altars, probably as gifts to the goddess.

The seventh and sixth millennia temple models seemed to have conceived of the temple as literally the body or the house of the deity. Shrine models from Porodin near Bitola in Macedonia, for instance, have a cylindrical "chimney" in the middle of the roof upon which is modeled the masked features of a large-eyed Bird Goddess, a necklace encircling her neck ("chimney"). Other models have round openings fit for the goddess to enter in the shape of a bird or are made in the form of a bird's nest. The fifth millennium models are replicas of complex buildings, usually two-storied, consisting of a large substructure and an actual temple (or several temples) on the top floor. We shall illustrate here several of such exquisite models. First is the outstanding, large model from Căscioarele, the Danube island settlement, southern Romania, dated to ca. 4500 B.C. (Karanovo VI period) (see Figure 10, p. 35). The model consists of a large substructure which supports four individual temples. Each temple has a wide-arched portal, and is crowned with horns on the gable and over the four corners. The second is from Rozsokhuvatka near Cherkassy in the Ukraine, from a Cucuteni (Tripolye) settlement dating from about the second half of the fifth millennium B.C. (see Figure 11,

p. 36). It portrays a two-story temple standing on four legs, the second floor comprising the temple of two rooms and a platform in front of the large portal. Wide entrances are shown on both floors. The actual temple discovered recently at Radingrad near Razgrad, northeastern Bulgaria (excavation by Totju Ivanov, 1974-78) resembles the above-mentioned model from Rozsokhuvatka. It was a two-story building. On the first floor was a ceramic workshop which contained a large oven and finished and unfinished vases and tools for the production and decoration of pots. On the second floor was the temple proper, with a large rectangular clay altar, 75 cm high. Figurines and clay models of temples were found to the left of the altar and also a vertical loom (for weaving sacred garments?). Vases found near the altar were filled with clay beads (gifts to the Goddess). The temple of Radingrad was built before 5000 B.C. (Karanovo IV period) and was used in the early part of the fifth millennium B.C. (Karanovo V period).

Some shrine models are roofless; they illustrate cult activities and interior arrangement, a large bread oven, and an altar. The walls are painted with symbolic design. The model from Popudnia, a late Cucuteni (Tripolye) settlement north of Uman in the western Ukraine dating from the first half of the fourth millennium B.C., consisted of a main room and a vestibule. In the main room are benches and an oven on a raised platform. On the bench to the right of the oven is a female figurine with hands on breasts; near the other wall a female figurine is grinding grain. Further along the same wall stand three large pear-shaped vases. In the center of the shrine is a raised cloverleaf-shaped platform, probably an offering place. The interior walls of the Popudnia model are decorated with bands of black-painted diamonds flanked by chevrons. The actual temple of Căscioarele from the early part of the fifth millennium B.C. (Karanovo V to late Boian period) had two rooms, one of which had painted walls of curvilinear design in cream on red. A terracotta medallion painted with a red snake-coil outlined in cream decorated the western wall. Two hollow pillars about 2 m high were found in this room. The thinner pillar was painted in cream ribbons on a reddish-brown background. Next to it an altar, about 40 cm high, was also painted with curvilinear ribbons of cream. Pithoi and beautifully painted vases were found standing nearby (Dumitrescu 1970; Gimbutas 1980).[8]

The figurines portrayed (in clay models) and found in actual shrines are shown to perform various cult activities—ritual grinding, baking of sacred bread, attending sacrifices—or are seated on the altar, apparently used for the reenactment of a particular religious ceremony. In the mid-fifth millennium Cucuteni (Early Tripolye) shrine at Sabatinivka in the valley of Southern Bug in the Ukraine, 16 figurines were sitting on chairs on the altar, all with snake-shaped heads and massive thighs. One held a baby snake. The other group of 15 were in action—baking, grinding, or standing at the dish containing remains of a bull sacrifice. In the corner next to the altar stood a life-size clay throne with horned back support, perhaps for a priestess to supervise the ceremony (Makarevich 1960)[9] (see Figure 12, p. 37). At Ovčarovo near Trgovište, northeastern Bulgaria, 26 miniature cult objects were found within the remains of a burned shrine. They included four figurines with upraised arms, three altar screens (or temple facades) decorated with symbols, nine chairs, three tables, three lidded vessels, three drums, and several dishes larger than figurines. Such objects vividly suggest ceremonies with music and dances, lustrations, and offerings (Todorova 1976).[10]

The production of an enormous variety of cult paraphernalia—exquisite anthropomorphic, zoomorphic, and ornithomorphic vases, sacrificial containers, lamps, ladles, etc.—is one of the very characteristic features of this culture and may be viewed as a response to the demands of a theocentric culture where most production centered around the temple. The consideration of these creations is unfortunately beyond the scope of this article. Regarding the technological and aesthetic skills, nothing similar was created in the millennia that followed the demise of Old Europe.

b. *Ceremonial Costume and Mask.* A wealth of costume details is preserved on the clay figurines. Deep incisions encrusted with white paste or red ochre affirm the presence of hip-belts, fringe, aprons, narrow skirts, blouses, stoles, a variety of hair styles, and the use of caps, necklaces, bracelets, and medallions. Whether these fashions were commonly worn, or were traditional garb for priestesses or other participants in ritual celebrations, can only be conjectured. The latter was probably the case; most of the figurines seem to have been characters in tableaux of ritual. But, ritual or not, the costumes reflect stylistic conventions of dress and taste characteristic of the period.

In the female costume several dress combinations recur persistently: partly dressed figures wear only a hip-belt, or a hip-belt from which hangs an apron or panels of an entire skirt of fringe, resembling a hula skirt; others wear a tight skirt with shoulder straps or a blouse (see Figures 13a and 13b, pp. 38-39).

A number of figurines show incised or painted stoles over the shoulders and in front and back. The skirt, which generally begins below the waist and hugs the hips, has a decorative texture of white encrusted incisions, showing net-pattern, zigzags, checkerboard, or dots. The skirt narrows below the knees, and on some figurines wrappings around the legs are indicated. It may be that the skirt was slit in front below the knees and fastened between the legs with woven bands. This type of skirt gives the impression of constraining movement and quite likely had a ritualistic purpose.

The figurines tell little about male attire; males are usually portrayed nude, except for a large V-shaped collar and a belt. In the last phase of the Cucuteni culture male figures wear a hip-belt and a strap passing diagonally across the chest and back over one of the shoulders.

The Copper Age Cucuteni and Karanovo figurines appear to be wearing shoes rendered by incision, painting, or modeling. They seem to be of soft leather; some are decorated in front or around the edges (see Figure 14, p. 40).

Special attention to coiffure and headgear is evidenced. The Bird and Snake Goddesses in particular, or devotees associated with their images, had beautiful coiffures, a crown, or decorative headbands. Vinča and Butmir figurines have hair neatly combed and divided symmetrically in the center, the two panels perhaps separated by a central ribbon. Late Cucutenian figurines, primarily nude, but some wearing hip-belt and necklace, have a long, thick coil of hair hanging down the back and ending in a large, circular bun or with an attached disc, reminiscent of the style favored by Egyptian ritual dancers of the third millennium B.C. A typical item of dress is a conical cap on which radial or horizontal parallel incisions perhaps represent its construction of narrow ribbon-like bands (see Figures 15a and 15b, pp. 41-42).

Figurines were portrayed wearing masks representing certain goddesses, gods, or their sacred animals, or else they were simply shown as bird-headed (with beaked faces on a cylindrical neck), snake-headed (with a long mouth, round eyes, and no nose), or ram- or other animal-headed. Frequently-occurring perforations of the mask were obviously intended to carry some sort of organic attachment. Plumes, flowers, fruits, and other materials could have been employed in this way.

The mask was most notably the preoccupation of the Vinča artist. The types of mask sculpted through time range from rough triangular, through pentagonal, to oval and lozenge-shaped having incised or painted symbolic signs.

c. *Deities Worshipped.* In the literature on prehistoric religion the female figures of clay, bone, and stone are usually considered to be the "Mother Goddess." Is she indeed nothing more than an image of motherhood? The term is not entirely a misnomer if we understand her as a creatress or as a cosmogenic woman. It must be emphasized that from the Upper Paleolithic onward the persona of the Goddess splintered the response to the developing economy, and the images of deities portray not only the single maternal metaphor of the deity. Study of the several stereotypical shapes and postures of the figurines and of the associated symbolism of the signs incised upon them clearly shows that the figurines intend to project a multiplicity of divine aspects and a variety of divine functions.

There are, in my opinion, two primary aspects of the Goddess (not necessarily two Goddesses) presented by the effigies. The first is, "She who is the Giver of All"—Giver of Life, Giver of Moisture, of Food, of Happiness; she is also "Taker of All," i.e., Death. The second aspect of the Goddess is connected with the periodic awakening of nature: she is springtime, the new moon, rebirth, regeneration, and metamorphosis. Both go back to the Upper Paleolithic. The significance of each aspect is visually supported on the figurines by appropriate symbols and signs. The first aspect of the Goddess as Giver and Taker of All, that is, as both beginning and end of life, is accompanied by aquatic symbols—water birds, snakes, fish, frogs, all animals associated with water—and representations of water itself in the form of zigzag bands, groups of parallel lines, meanders, nets, checkerboards, and running spirals. The second aspect of the Goddess as Rebirth, Renewal, and Transcendance is accompanied by the symbols of "becoming": eggs, uteri, phalluses, whirls, crescents, and horns which resemble cornucopias. The Goddess often appears in the form of a bee, a butterfly, or a caterpillar. This second group involves male animals such as bulls and dogs.

The Giver of All, The Fish, Water Bird, and Snake Goddess

Hybrids of the human female with bird or snake dominated mythical imagery throughout the Upper Paleolithic, Neolithic, Chalcolithic, and Copper Ages from ca. 26,000 to the end of Old Europe at ca. 3000 B.C., but lingered in the Aegean and Mediterranean regions through the Bronze Age and later—at least 40 percent of the total number of figurines belong to this type. The Fish, Bird, and Snake Goddesses were interrelated in meaning and function. Each is Creatress and Giver. They are, therefore, inseparable from cosmogonic and cosmogenic myths such as water birds carrying cosmic eggs. She as the Mother or *Source* is the giver of rain, water, milk, and meat (sheep, their skin and wool). Her portrayals usually show exaggerated breasts marked with parallel lines, or a wide-open beak or round hole for a mouth. Her large eyes are a magical source, and are surrounded by aquatic symbolism (usually groups of parallel lines). Beginning in the Neolithic, the ram (the earliest domesticated animal, a vital source of food and clothing) became her sacred animal. The symbols of this goddess on spindle whorls and loom weights suggest that she was the originator or guardian of the crafts of spinning and weaving. Metaphorically, as "the spinner and weaver of human life," she became the Goddess of Fate.

Along with the life-giving aspect of the Goddess, her life-taking or death-giving aspect must have developed in preagricultural times. The images of vultures and owls are known from the Upper Paleolithic and from the earliest Neolithic (in the frescoes of Çatal Hüyük, in central Anatolia, vultures appear above headless human beings). The figurine type of the nude goddess with large pubic triangle, folded arms, and face of an owl, well known from Old European graves, may be representative of the Goddess in the aspect of night and death.

In early agricultural times, the Giver of All developed another function, a function vital to tillers of the soil—namely, that of "Giver of Bread." Her images were deposited in grain silos or in egg-shaped vases, where they were indispensable insurance for the resurgence of plant life. She also appears as a pregnant woman, her ripe body a metaphor of the fertile field. She was worshipped with her sacred animal, the pig. The fattening of the pig encouraged the growth and ripening of crops or fertility in general.

Richly represented throughout the Neolithic, Chalcolithic, and Copper Ages, still another aspect of the Goddess is, by natural association, that of "Birth-giving Goddess." She is portrayed with outstretched legs and upraised arms in a naturalistic birth-giving posture. This stereotypic image appears in relief on large vases and on temple walls; carved in black and green stone or alabaster, it was worn as an amulet.

The "Periodic Regeneration" aspect of the Goddess may be as ancient as the Giver of All aspect, since symbols of "becoming" are present in the Upper Paleolithic: crescents and horns appear in association with Paleolithic nudes. To regenerate the life-force was her main function; therefore, the Goddess was flanked by male animals noted for physical strength—bulls, he-goats, dogs. In her incarnation as a crescent, caterpillar, bee, or butterfly, she was a symbol of new life; she emerged from the body or horns of the bull as a bee or butterfly.

The female principle was conceived as creative and eternal, the male as spontaneous and ephemeral. The male principle was represented symbolically by male animals and by phalluses and ithyphallic animal-masked men—goat-men or bull-men. They appear as adjuncts of the Goddess. The figurines of ecstatic dancers, goat- or bull-masked, may represent worshippers of the Goddess in rituals enacting the dance of life (see Plate 1, p. 56).*

5. The Symbols and the Sacred Script

Symbolic signs consistently recur—singly or in combination with the linear signs—in all cultural regions and throughout all phases. They are found on vases, temple models, altars, thrones, chairs, sacrificial containers, ladles, figurines, pendants, lamps, plaques, seals, breadloaf-shaped objects, spindle whorls, and loom weights.

Hand-stamp seals with conventionalized signs of the seventh and sixth millennia B.C. were used to mark ceramic, and probably more perishable, objects. The marks occurring on clay or stone seals consist of the following signs: multiple chevrons, X with Vs between the arms, zigzags, Ms, Ns, whirls, crosses, filled crosses, concentric circles and squares, triangles with a dot, parallel lines; two lines and three lines, tri-line joined by horizontal bar, "brushes," four and multiple lines, alone or joined by a line. There are also meanders, snake coils, spirals, nets, and checkerboards, and snake-skin symbols (dotted bands, interconnected lozenges). When cylindrical seals came into use in the fifth millennium B.C., they continued to be engraved with such symbols (see Figure 16, p. 43).

The motifs of decorated pottery from as early as the middle of the seventh millennium B.C. are clearly symbolic chevrons, triangles, and nets. In the sixth millennium B.C., Vs, chevrons, Xs, and parallel lines appear in bands, in rectangles,

---

*All plates appear at the end of this article, pp. 56-60 (captions, p. 25).

or in discs to distinguish them as symbols or ideograms from the rest of the decorative design which accompanies them. The presentation of the symbols in panels and compartments increased toward the end of the sixth millennium B.C. and continued in the fifth millennium B.C. and later (see Figure 17, p. 44).

If a sign appears on articulate figurines, for instance, a deity identifiable by symbolic form—such as the Snake Goddess (with snake limbs) or the Bird Goddess (with beaked mask and arm stumps for wings) or on objects of known function such as spindle whorls or loom weights with known associations (spinning, weaving, sheep, wool)—we may attempt to glimpse the meaning of the hieroglyph through the association.

From the Upper Paleolithic to the Bronze Age, figurines of bird-woman hybrids and of water birds were incised with meanders, Vs, chevrons, two lines, three lines, four lines, and multiple parallel lines. Breasts of figurines and breast amulets were incised with parallel lines. The consistent use of the same signs throughout some 20,000 years suggests that those signs have specific symbolic connotation. Neolithic and Chalcolithic Bird Goddess effigies with beaked masks are usually marked below the neck, above the breasts, or at the pubic triangle with a V or chevron sign. The image marked with chevrons may be totally schematized, relying for identification on the symbolic mark. We may therefore assume that the V glyph represents the Bird Goddess, and that objects so marked are dedicated to her cult. Vs, multiple Vs (chevron), incised alone or in combination with an X sign or a meander, consistently appear on both articulate and schematic effigies of the Bird Goddess, and on objects associated with her cult. The V/chevron sign is also commonly associated with two, three, and four lines.

The catalog of symbols (ideograms with some possible phonograms) assembled from the totality of three hundred figurines and anthropomorphic lidded vases which bear features of the Bird Goddess from the Vinča, Cucuteni, Karanovo, Tisza, Bükk, Butmir, Lengyel, and Petreşti cultures is illustrated in Figure 18, p. 45. Examination of the full repertory leads this author to the following observations. The symbolic signs surrounding the image of the Bird Goddess: 1) identify the Goddess (V, X, meander); 2) stress her intimacy with the aquatic, life-giving sphere (V or X connected or associated with meanders, running spirals, M sign, net, and checkerboard); 3) indicate her function as a Giver of rain, milk, bread, meat, fleece, or general fertility and abundance. This last category comprises four, or multiple, dashes or parallel lines, multiple stabbings, brush and fleece signs, consistently associated with the body, neck, mouth, eyes, arms, or feet of the Goddess; and with the ram (sacred animal of the Goddess), on spouted vases, spindle whorls, and loom weights.

Such duplication, multiplication, and juxtaposition of symbolic signs had perhaps invocational intent. A combination of two signs, such as:

V and ⊔⊔ forming ⩔̲

was obviously devised to express a more complicated concept, in this case perhaps the name of the Goddess with the epithet "The Bountiful" or the like (see Figure 19, p. 46).

The assignment of certain glyphs to certain aspects of the deity, as above, offers a possible beginning toward a tentative decipherment. When additional signs—single or double lines, curves and dots—begin to be attached to single or multiplied ones, difficulties are compounded.

Combinations of several or more signs in groups or in lines, particularly of *V*, *M*, *X* signs and one, three, or four straight lines, make their appearance on seals and cult vessels during the first half of the sixth millennium B.C. on the Starčevo and Karanovo culture groups.

If signs on seals, such as parallel zigzags, whirl, snake coil, etc., symbolize a concept ("water," "good luck," "Snake Goddess"), rows or groups of abstract linear signs obviously bear a more complex meaning. This stage can be regarded as an actual beginning of the script. From the middle of the sixth millennium B.C., such combinations increased.

The script which emerged after the middle of the sixth millennium B.C. was created by modification of symbols by lines, curves, and dots. The following combinations appear: *V*s in various sizes with the addition of a dash or line at the side, across, or above; *V* connected to an inverted *V*; *V* connected to an arm of a meander; *V* filled with one, two, or three lines, amplified by two or three parallel lines; *V* joined with *M*; and *V* extended by a curved line. The most frequent combinations are of one or two lines with a *V*, *X*, and *M*. Some inscriptions demonstrate a maze of repetitive *V*s, or *V*s and *M*s or *V*s and *Y*s. Such repetitive clusters of signs are seen on the Karanovo seal with four divisions, on figurines, spindle whorls, vases, and other objects; they might be epithets, vows, prayers, or assignment of a gift to the Goddess (see Figure 20, p. 47).

The inscriptions which appear in rows or groups include a considerable number of signs classifiable as basic or core signs: *V*, *X*, *I*, *II*, *III*, *M*, and the meander. In addition, there are also duplicated, inverted, juxtaposed *V*s, and combinations of *V*s, *X*s, and *M*s. I assume, therefore, that the Old European script arose as an outgrowth of the signs used in the worship of the Goddess, primarily in her epiphany as Bird Goddess. It would be difficult to prove that the inscriptions are not related to the cult. Even those on spindle whorls were not unconnected with the worship of the Goddess in her aspect as patroness of crafts. The sudden emergence of the script corresponds to the sophistication of the Goddess cult as shown by the great quantities of cultic equipment and the large number of temple models and actual temples dedicated to her.

Inscriptions appear in horizontal or vertical rows, in circles, or in randomly placed groups. On figurines there are bands front and back, across the chest, or under the abdomen. On vessels the bands occur on the wall near the base or rim, or around the central portion, or they occur in panels on temple models—on both sides or above the entrance; on plaques they are often in four or more compartments; on spindle whorls inscriptions occur in a circle around the hole. Inscriptions appear in isolated bands, in clusters, or in association with signs placed in other compartments, seeming to stress and strengthen the contact with the Goddess by emphasis of certain aspects of her powers (see Figure 21, and Figures 22a and 22b, pp. 48-50).

At present, over sixty sites are known to have yielded inscribed objects, the material ranging from over 300 objects to single examples. Most of the sites are those of Vinča and Tisza culture groups in the Morava, Danube, and Tisza basins of Yugoslavia, eastern Hungary, northwestern Bulgaria, and western Romania, and of the Karanovo culture in central Bulgaria and southern Romania. Inscribed or painted signs, unnoticed earlier, are now being recognized on Dimini, Cucuteni, Petreşti, Lengyel, Butmir, Bükk, and Linear Pottery ceramics. It is no longer appropriate to speak of "Vinča script," or of the Tartaria plaques as sole examples of this phenomenon. It is now clear that the script was a universal feature of the Old European civilization; therefore, this author advocates the term "Script of Old Europe."

One of the best examples of artifacts with the Old European script was found at Gradešniça, a Vinča site near Vraca, northwestern Bulgaria. This was a shallow dish inscribed on both sides. The face is divided by four horizontal lines into four registers, each containing three or more signs. A schematic human figure made up of *V*s or triangles encircled by linear signs is incised on the back. This settlement also yielded temple models and anthropomorphic vases with inscriptions (see Figure 23, p. 51).

Inscriptions have also been found on cave entrance walls. At Sitovo in the central Rodopi Mountains of Bulgaria, an inscription 3.4 m long with characters 13 to 16 cm high was discovered. The Karanovo pottery found inside the cave dates the inscription to the first half of the fifth millennium B.C. (see Figure 24, p. 52).

The Old European script virtually disappeared at the time of the disintegration of the Karanovo, Vinča, and other Old European cultures around 4000 B.C., following the infiltration of horse-riding pastoralists from the steppes of southern Russia. It survived, however, in the Aegean area, where the Old European civilization endured for over two millennia longer than in the Danubian part of Europe. It is not surprising, therefore, to perceive similarities between it and the script signs of Early Bronze Age Aegean, Minoan, and Cypriot scripts. The analogies between the Old European characters and those of the classical Cypriot syllabary are intriguing, suggesting that the Old European script, devised some 4,000 years before Linear A on Crete and Cypro-Minoan on Cyprus, could have been a syllabic script developed by non-Indo-European speakers probably ancestral to the Cypriot and Minoan.

6. Conclusion: The Kurgan Penetration

Old Europe was rapidly developing into an urban culture, but its growth was interrupted and eventually stopped by destructive forces from the east—the steadily increasing infiltration of the semi-nomadic, horse-riding pastoralists from the Pontic steppes. Periodic waves of infiltration into civilized Europe effected the disintegration of the first European civilization. Only on the islands, like Crete, Thera, and Malta, did the traditions of Old Europe survive for almost two millennia. The Bronze Age culture that followed north of the Aegean was an amalgam of the substrate and totally different elements of an eastern culture.

Thanks to a growing number of radiocarbon dates, archaeologists can ascertain the periods of Kurgan penetration into Europe. There was no single massive invasion, but a series of repeated incursions concentrated into three major thrusts:

Wave No. 1, ca. 4400-4200 B.C. (Figure 25, p. 53)
Wave No. 2, ca. 3400-3200 B.C. (Figure 26, p. 54)
Wave No. 3, ca. 3000-2800 B.C. (Figure 27, p. 55)

(Gimbutas 1978; 1980)[11]

The steppe (or "Kurgan") people were, above all, pastoralists. As such, their social system was composed of small patrilinear units that were socially stratified according to the strategic services performed by its male members. The grazing of large herds over vast expanses of land necessitated a living pattern of seasonal settlements or small villages affording sufficient pasturage for animals. The chief tasks of a pastoral economy were executed by men, not by women as was characteristic of the indigenous agricultural system.

It was inevitable that an economy based on farming and another which relied on stock breeding would produce unrelated ideologies. The upheaval of the Old European civilization is registered in the abrupt cessation of painted pottery and figurines, the disappearance of shrines, the termination of symbols and signs.

Old European ceramics are readily identified with the rich symbolic signs and decorative motifs that reflect an ideology concerned with cosmogony, generation, birth, and regeneration. Symbols were compartmentalized or interwoven in a myriad combination—meanders and spirals, chevrons and zigzags, circles, eggs, horns, etc. There were a multitude of pictorial and sculptural representations of goddesses and gods, of worshippers, and sacred animals. Kurgan pottery is devoid of symbolic language and of aesthetic treatment in general because it obviously did not serve the same ceremonial purposes as that of Old Europe. The stabbing and impressing technique is quite primitive and seems to focus on only one symbol, the sun. Occasionally, a schematized fir tree occurs which may symbolize a "tree-of-life."

Mythical images that were in existence on the Eurasiatic steppe dispersed now over a large part of Europe, and continued to the beginning of Christianity and beyond. The new ideology was an apotheosis of the horseman and warrior. The principal gods carry weapons and ride horses or chariots; they are figures of inexhaustible energy, physical power, and fecundity. In contrast to the pre-Indo-European cultures whose myths centered around the moon, water, and the female, the religion of pastoral, semi-sedentary Indo-European peoples was oriented toward the rotating sky, the sun, stars, planets, and other sky phenomena such as thunder and lightning. Their sky and sun gods were shining, "bright as the sky"; they wore starry cloaks adorned with glittering gold, copper, or amber pendants, torques, chest plates, belts. They carried shining daggers, swords, and shields. The Indo-Europeans glorified the magical swiftness of arrow and javelin and the sharpness of the blade. Throughout the millennia, the Indo-Europeans exulted in the making of weapons, not pottery or sculpture. The touch of the ax blade awakened the powers of nature and transmitted the fecundity of the Thunder God; by the touch of his spear tip, the god of war and the underworld marked the hero for glorious death.

NOTES

1. M. Gimbutas, "Gold Treasure at Varna," *Archaeology* 30,1 (New York 1977):44-51. *Id.* "Varna, a sensationally rich cemetery of the Karanovo Civilization, about 4500 B.C.," *Expedition* 19,4 (Philadelphia 1977):39-47.

Ivan Ivanov, *Sakroviščata na Varnenskija khalkoliten nekropol.* Sofia 1978.

2. H. Todorova, V. Vasilev, S. Ivanov, M. Kopf, H. Quitta, and G. Kohl, *Seliščnata mogila pri Goljamo Delčevo.* Sofia 1975.

3. Adrian C. Florescu, "Befestigungsanlagen der spätneolithischen Siedungen im Donau-Karpatenraum," *Študijné Zvesti* 17 (Bratislava 1969):111-24.

4. A. C. Renfrew, "The Autonomy of the Southeast European Copper Age," *Proceedings of the Prehistoric Society* 35,1 (London 1969):12-47; B. Jovanović, "The Origins of Copper Mining in Europe," *Scientific American,* May 1980, 242.5: 152-67; E. N. Chernykh, *Gornoe delo i metallurgija v drevnejshej Bolgarii,* Sofia 1978.

5. M. Dinu, *Contacts Between the Late Cucuteni B Tribes and the Ponto-Danubian Steppe Tribes.* Lecture delivered at Dubrovnik Conference on "The Transformation of Europe and Anatolia at 4500-2500 B.C.," 1979.

6. G. Thomson, *The Prehistoric Aegean. Studies in Ancient Greek Society.* London, 1978 edition.

7. Personal communication from Djuro Basler, Sarajevo, 1968.

8. Vladimir Dumitrescu, "Edifice destiné au culte découvert dans la couche Boian-Spanţov de la station-tell de Căscioarele," *Dacia* 14 N.S. (Bucharest 1970): 5-24. Marija Gimbutas, "The Temples of Old Europe," *Archaeology,* December 1980 (New York).

9. M. L. Makarevich, "Ob ideologicheskikh predstavleniyakh u tripol'skikh plemen'," *Zapiski Odesskogo Arkheologicheskogo Obshchestva* (Odessa 1960).

10. Henrietta Todorova, *Ovčarovo,* Sofia 1976; *Id.* "Kultszene und Hausmodell aus Ovčarovo, Bez. Tărgovište," *Thracia* III (Sofia):39-46.

11. Marija Gimbutas, "La fin de l'Europe Ancienne," *La Recherche* No. 87, March 1978 (Paris):227-35; *Id.* "The Three Waves of the Steppe People into East Central Europe," *Actes Suisses d'Anthropologie* 43.2 (Geneva 1980).

SOURCES OF ILLUSTRATIONS

Benac, Alojz. 1973. A Neolithic Settlement of the Butmir Group at Obre, Gornje Polje. *Wissenschaftliche Mitteilungen des Bosnisch-Herzegowinischen Landesmuseums* IIIA (Sarajevo).

Berciu, D. 1961. *Contribuţii la problemele neoliticului în Romînia în lumina noilor cercetări.* (Bucharest: Academy of Sciences, Romanian P.R.)

Dumitrescu, Hortensia. 1968. Un modèle de sanctuaire découvert dans la station énéolitique de Căscioarele. *Dacia* N.S. 12 (Bucharest: Institute of Archaeology, Academy of Sciences, Romanian P.R.):381-94.

Dumitrescu, Vladimir. 1970. Edifice destiné au culte découvert dans la couche Boian-Spanţov de la station-tell de Căscioarele. *Dacia* N.S. 15:5-24.

———. 1974. *Arta preistorică în România.* (Bucharest: Editura Meridiane.)

Gimbutas, Marija. 1974. *The Gods and Goddesses of Old Europe, 7000-3500 B.C. Myths, Legends and Cult Images* (London: Thames and Hudson).

Kalicz, Nándor and János Makkay. 1977. *Die Linienbandkeramik in der grossen ungarischen Tiefebene* (Budapest: Akadémiai Kiádo).

Kutzián, I. Bognár. 1976. On the Origins of Early Copper-Processing in Europe. *To Illustrate the Monuments, Essays on Archaeology Presented to Stuart Piggott* (London: Thames and Hudson):69-77.

Makarevich, M. L. 1960. Ob ideologicheskikh predstavleniyakh u tripol'skikh plemen'. *Zapiski Odesskogo Archeol. Obshchestva* (Odessa).

Marinescu Bîlcu, Silvia. 1974. *Culture Precucuteni pe teritoriul Romaniei.* Bucharest: Academy of Sciences, Romanian P.R.)

Nikolov, Bogdan. 1974. *Gradechnitza* (Sofia: Editions Naouka i Izkoustvo).

Passek, T. S. 1949. *Periodizatsija tripol'skikh poselenii.* Materialy i Issledovanija po Arkheologii SSSR, No. 10 (Moscow and Leningrad: Academy of Sciences, USSR).

Prendi, Frano. 1966. La civilisation préhistorique de Maliq. *Studia Albanica* 1 (Tirana):255-72.

Rosetti, D. 1938. Steinkupferzeitliche Plastik aus einem Wohnhügel bei Bukarest. *IPEK* 12 (Berlin):29-50.

Roska, Márton. 1941. *Die Sammlung Zsófia von Torma in der numismatisch-archaeologischen Abteilung des Siebenbürgschen National-Musems* (Cluj-Koloszvár).

Shmaglij, M. M., V. P. Dudkin and K. V. Zin'kovs'kij. 1973. Pro kompleksne vivchennja tripil'skikh poselen'. *Arkheologija* 8 (Kiev):23-39.

Tasić, N. and E. Tomić. 1969. *Crnokalačka Bara, naselje starčevačke i vinčanske kulture.* Disserationes VIII (Narodni Muzej Kruševac).

Todorova, Henrieta. 1976. *Ovčarovo* (Sofia: Izdatelstvo "Septemvri").

Vasić, Miloje M. 1932-36. *Preistoriska Vinča* I-IV. (Belgrade: University.)

Winn, Milton M. 1973. *The Signs of the Vinča Culture: An Internal Analysis; Their Role, Chronology and Independence from Mesopotamia.* University of California, Los Angeles, Ph.D. History, archaeology. Ann Arbor: University Microfilms.

FIGURE CAPTIONS

Figure 1. The first European civilization: southeast Europe plus Danubian and Carpathian basins. Arrows indicate routes of maritime communication and influences.

Figure 2. Culture groups of Old Europe in the fifth millennium B.C.

Figure 3. Cucuteni settlement plan. Habaşeşti, Moldavia. Cucuteni A_3 phase, ca. 4400-4200 B.C. (After Dumitrescu 1954.)

Figure 4. A Late Cucuteni (Tripolye) town at Majdan, district of Uman', western Ukraine. Houses in twelve concentric rows were identified by magnetometer study and remains of burnt-clay house floors. Houses are ca. 30 m long. The area of the settlement covers over 300 hectares. (After Shmaglij, Dudkin, and Zin'kovs'kij 1973.)

Figure 5. A plan of a compact Karanovo village with two main streets and only narrow paths between the houses. Poljanica near Trgovište, northeastern Bulgaria. Karanovo V phase, early fifth millennium B.C. (After Todorova 1976.)

Figure 6. Butmir II house from Obre near Kakanj in Bosnia, ca. 49-48th century B.C. The house has two rooms with a bread oven in the smaller room. Walls are built of timber posts and horizontal lines of twigs coated with clay 5-8 cm thick on each side. Activity areas (weaving, bone and flint working) on both sides of the oven. A wooden platform in front of the oven perhaps was a sacred corner. A small dish on the platform was filled with wheat grains. Groups of large storage jars in both rooms. (After Benac 1973.)

Figure 7. Cucuteni (Tripolye) house from the settlement of Vladimirovka on the Siniukha river, the tributary of the Southern Bug, western Ukraine, ca. 4500-4300 B.C. The house has two rooms with a separate entrance, oven, a cloverleaf-shaped platform, and a large number of vases standing on the floor. Clay floors are built over the layer of split planks. The walls are of wattle and daub. The roof is supported by a central row of posts. (After Passek 1949.)

Figure 8. Copper axes, typical of east-central European metallurgy. 1: Tibava, western Slovakia. 2: Pločnik, southern Yugoslavia. 3: Gabarevo, central Bulgaria. 4: Jászladány type from Mezötúr, northeastern Hungary. 5: Vésztö, eastern Hungary. (After Kutzián 1976.)

Figure 9. The metallurgical province of Old Europe (solid line) and foci (criss-crossed areas) during the fifth millennium B.C. I: Central Bulgarian. II: Vinča. III: Carpathian-Polgár. The arrows indicate the distribution of copper artifacts from the east-central European foci. Copper items were imported by the Kurgan I (Srednij Stog II-Khvalynsk) people in the Dnieper-Volga steppe (dotted line).

Figure 10. Four temples standing on a large substructure with round windows. L. 51 cm. Clay model from Căscioarele, southern Romania. Karanovo VI (Gumel-niţa) phase, 4500-4200 B.C. (After Dumitrescu 1968.)

Figure 11. Clay model of a two-storied temple found in a Cucuteni (Tripolye) settlement at Rozsokhuvatka, district of Cherkassy, western Ukraine. (After Arkhe-ologija Ukrainskij RST, ed. Telegin et al. 1971.)

Figure 12. The shrine of Sabatinivka, Southern Bug valley. Early Cucuteni (Tri-polye A) phase, middle of the fifth millennium B.C. 1: stone pavement; 2: clay oven; 3: altar of clay covered with wooden boards; 4: clay throne; 5: clay figurines with snake-shaped arms or no arms and tiny heads, probably representing Snake Goddess; 6: groups of vases including a dish filled with burned bones of a bull. (After Makarevich 1960.)

Figures 13a & b. Vinča and Karanovo figurines from ca. 4500-4000 B.C. with inci-sions and white paste encrustation indicating costume details: blouse and skirt (a) and hip-belt with fringe (b). a: Late Vinča terracotta figurine with perforated arm stumps and wearing a mask from Vinča near Belgrade; b: Karanovo VI terracotta figurine from Sitagroi III, Drama Plain, northeastern Greece. (a: after Vasić, Pre-istoriska Vinča I; b: excavation by Renfrew and Gimbutas, 1968.)

Figure 14. Decorated shoes (part of a sculpture), probably leather. 1: Vidra tell near Bucharest. Gumelniţa branch of the Karanovo civilization, ca. 4500-4200 B.C. (After Rosetti 1938.) 2: Ghelăieşti, Moldavia. Cucuteni B culture, ca. 3700-3500 B.C. (After Cucoş 1973.)

Figures 15a & b. Masked heads from Vinča sites showing long hair. a: hair divided into two panels by a hairband. The masks are beaked, i.e., bird-like, and with no human mouth, ca. 5000-4500 B.C. a: Vinča at Belgrade (found at 6.5 m depth). b: Crno Kalačka Bara near Niš, southeastern Yugoslavia. (a: after Vasić, Preistoriska Vinča III; b: Tasić and Tomić 1969.)

Figure 16. Cylindrical seals engraved with symbolic signs: chevrons, zigzags, me-anders, double-snake spirals, and dotted snake-skin design. 1: Sitagroi III, ca.

4500-4300 B.C. 2-5: Maliq IIA, from about the same period. (1: excavation by Renfrew and Gimbutas, 1968; 2-5: after Prendi 1966.)

Figure 17. Examples of vase decoration in panels with different symbols in each. 1: Bükk culture from Bogács-Hintóvölgy, northeastern Hungary; 2: Vinča; 3: Linear Pottery, from Tirpeşti, Moldavia. (1: after Kalicz-Makkay 1977; 2: Winn 1973; 3: Marinescu Bîlcu 1971.)

Figure 18. Signs on figurines showing Bird Goddess features, on bird-shaped vases, and other objects serving the cult of this goddess. Vinča, Tisza, Karanovo, Petreşti, and Cucuteni culture groups.

Figure 19. Beaked (Bird Goddess) figurines marked with Vs, chevrons, an X, and a combination of a V with four lines. 1: Turdaş, early Vinča; 2: Tešetice-Kyjovice, near Znojmo, Moravia; 3: Jablanica, central Yugoslavia. (1: after Roska 1941; 2: *Pregled vyzkumu*, 1971; 3: Winn 1973.)

Figure 20. Symbols and their modifications by lines, curves, dots, and by duplication, inversion, and juxtaposition.

Figure 21. Inscribed terracotta figurine from Tangiru tell in the lower Danube basin, southern Romania. End sixth millennium B.C. Boian IIa phase of the Karanovo civilization. (After Berciu 1961.)

Figures 22a & b. Inscribed spindle whorls with extended inscriptions. a: Fafos at Kosovska Mitrovica, southern Yugoslavia, ca. 5000-4500 B.C. b: Dikilitash, near Phillipi, north of the Aegean Sea, ca. 4500-4300 B.C. (After Winn 1973.)

Figure 23. Shallow vessel from Gradešnica near Vraca, a Vinča site in northwestern Bulgaria, with inscriptions on both sides. a: outer side with signs around the symbolic figure; b: inner side with four lines of signs, ca. 5000 B.C. (After Nikolov 1974.)

Figure 24. Petroglyph. Two lines of inscriptions 3.4 m long on the wall of a cave at Sitovo near Plovdiv, central Bulgaria. Probably Karanovo VI, ca. 4500-4200 B.C.

Figure 25. Kurgan Wave No. 1, ca. 4400-4200 B.C.

Figure 26. Kurgan Wave No. 2, ca. 3400-3200 B.C.

Figure 27. Kurgan Wave No. 3, ca. 3000-2800 B.C.

PLATE CAPTIONS
Main Types of Deities Represented in Figurine Art

Plate 1. Bird Goddess with a duck mask. Note V sign on the chest, triple lines on the arm, and skirt marked with parallel lines. Late Vinča from Supska at Čuprija, central Yugoslavia. H. 15 cm, ca. 4500-4000 B.C.

Plate 2. Squatting figurine decorated with bands of snake-skin design. Probable Snake Goddess. Late Vinča from Vinča site (at 5.1 m depth). H. 7.9 cm, ca. 4500 B.C.

Plate 3. Pregnant variety. Torso with hands above the abdomen. Porodin, southern Yugoslavia. Starčevo culture, early sixth millennium B.C.

Plate 4. "Madonna" from Rastu, western Romania. Early Vinča terracotta, ca. 5300-5000 B.C. H. 12.4 cm.

Plate 5. Probable death aspect ("Taker-of-All"). Nude, triangle-centered with a masked head. Karanovo VI, ca. 4500-4200 B.C. H. 15 cm. Lovets, near Stara Zagora, central Bulgaria. Flat bone. (After Gimbutas 1974.)

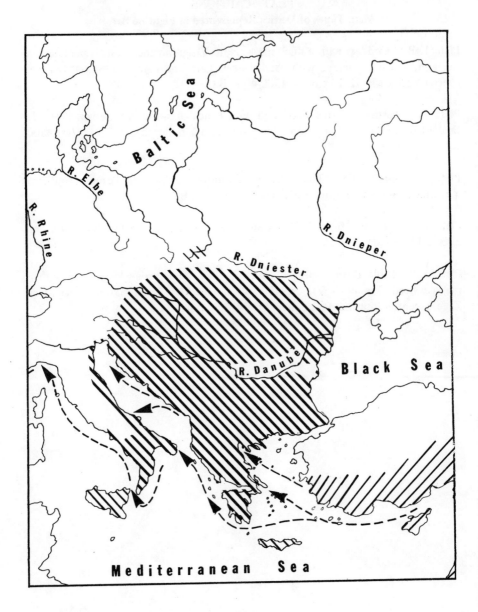

Figure 1

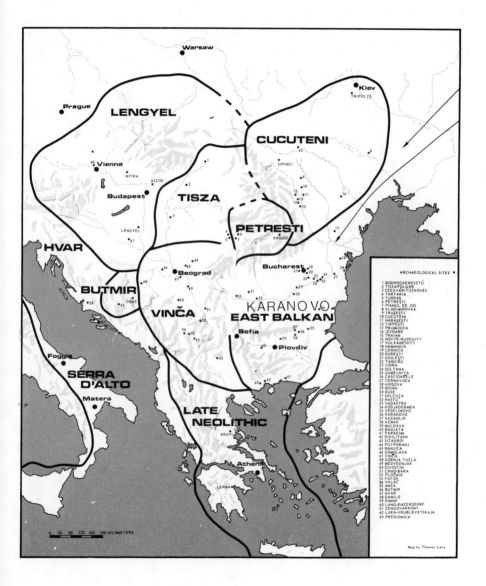

Figure 2

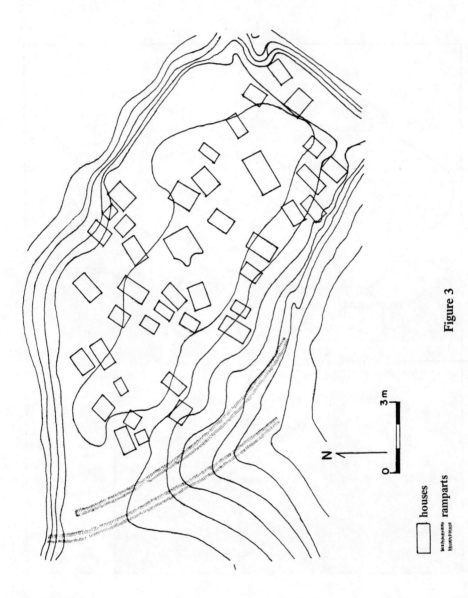

Figure 3

houses

ramparts

3 m

N

0

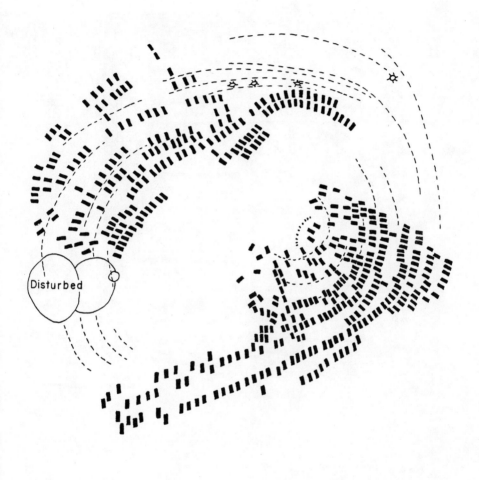

0   500m.

Figure 4

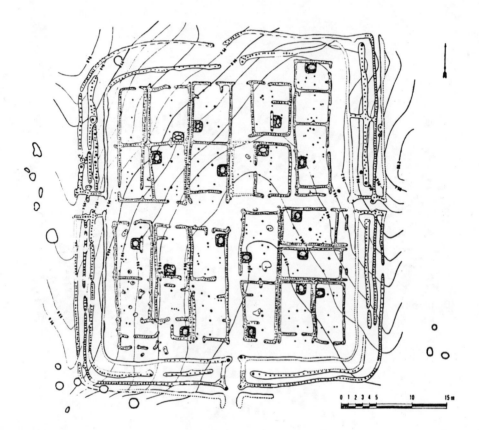

0 1 2 3 4 5   10   15 m

●●● POSTHOLES
▬▬▬ PALISADES
☼ OVENS
⊛ PITS

Figure 5

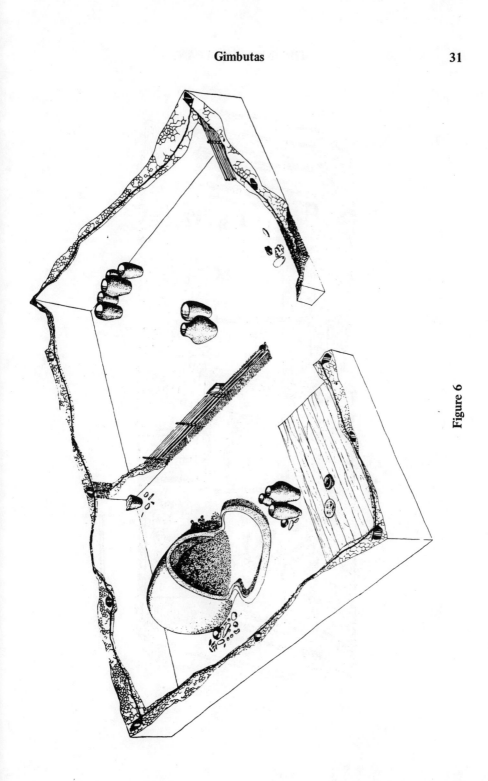

Figure 6

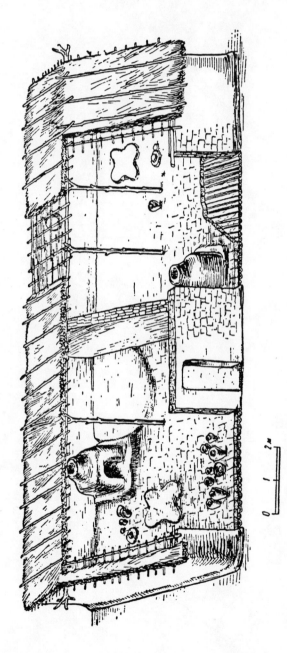

Figure 7

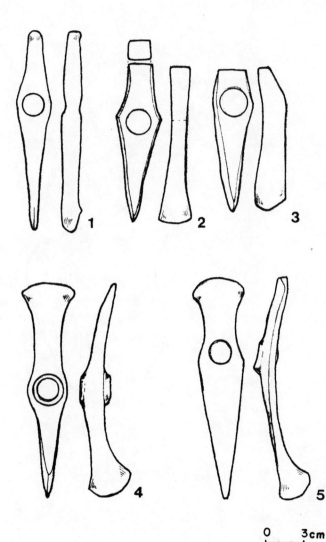

Figure 8

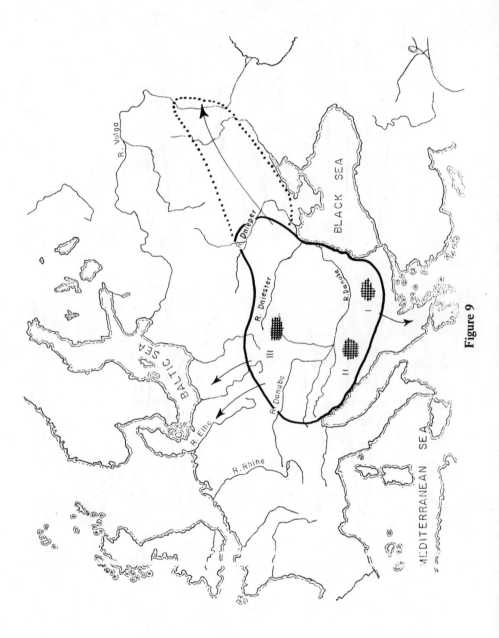

Figure 9

Figure 10

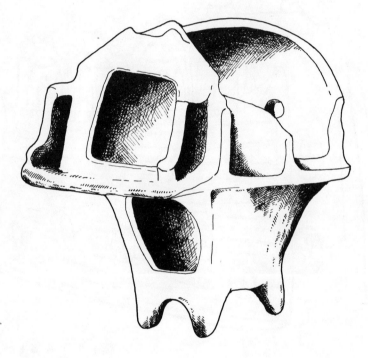

Figure 11

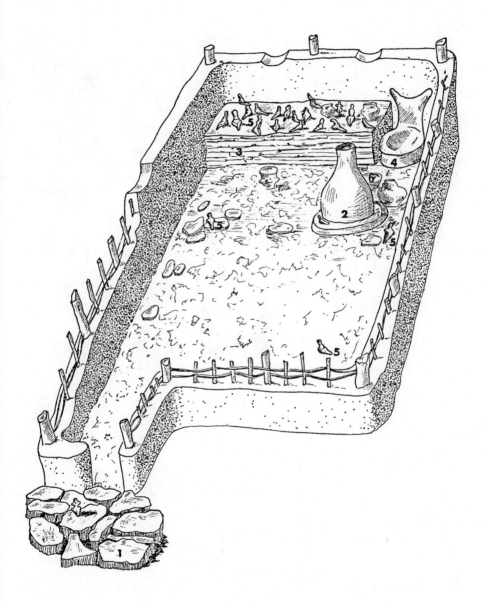

Figure 12

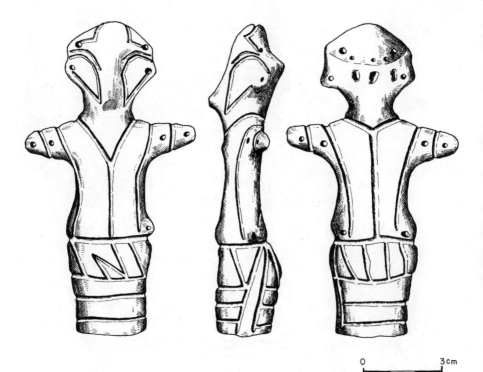

Figure 13a

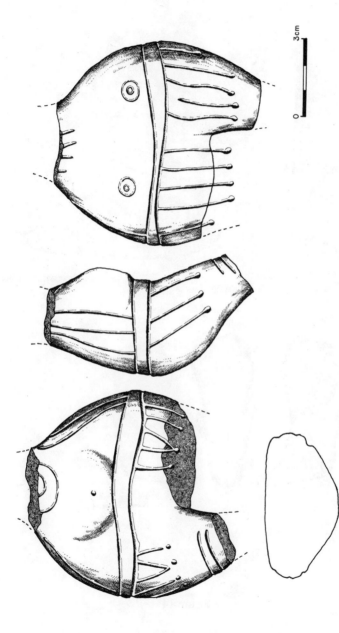

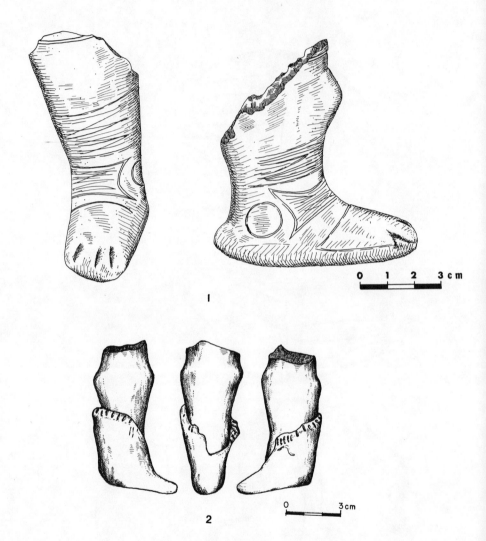

Figure 14

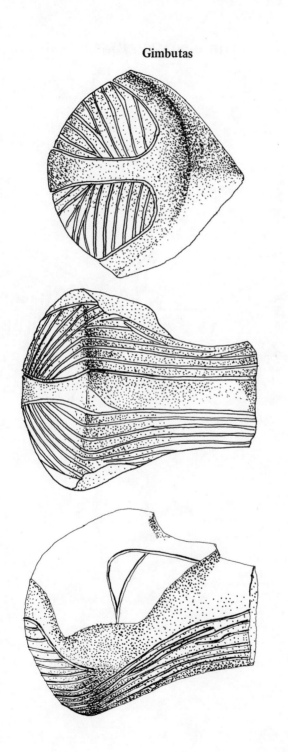

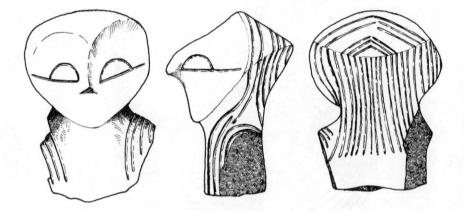

Figure 15b

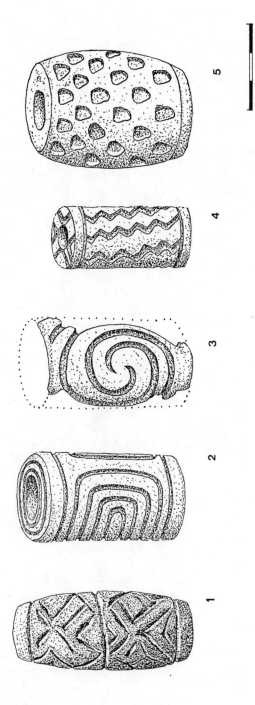

Figure 16

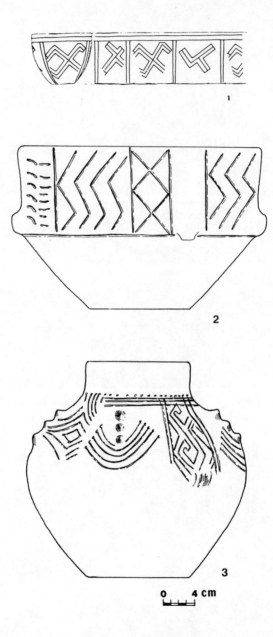

Figure 17

Figure 18

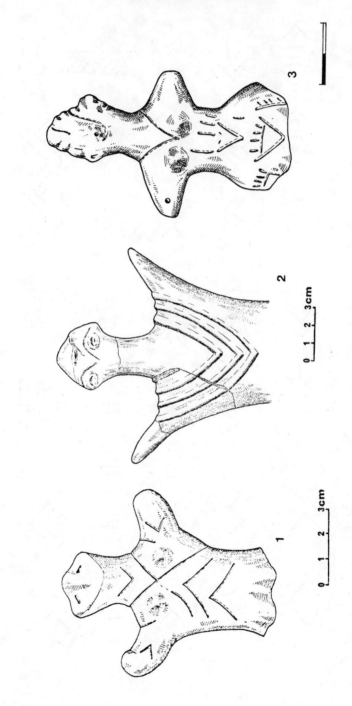

Figure 19

IDEOGRAM | MODIFICATION

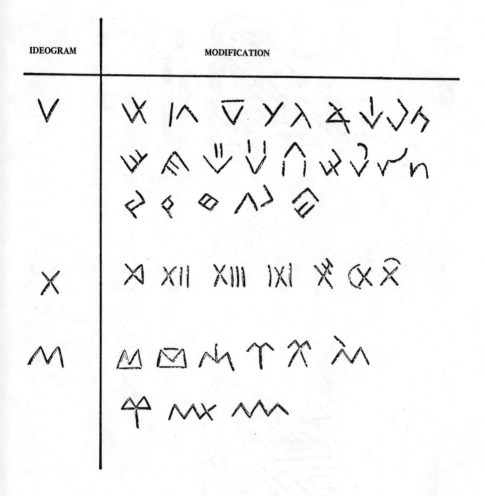

Figure 20

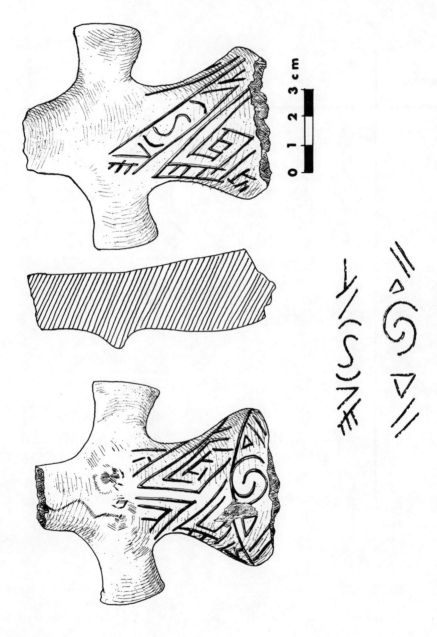

Figure 21

Figure 22a

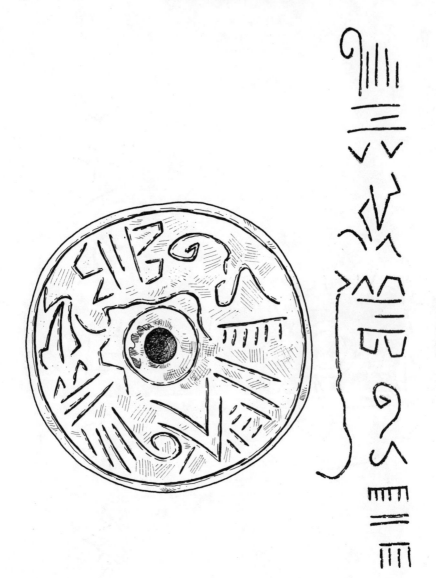

Figure 22b

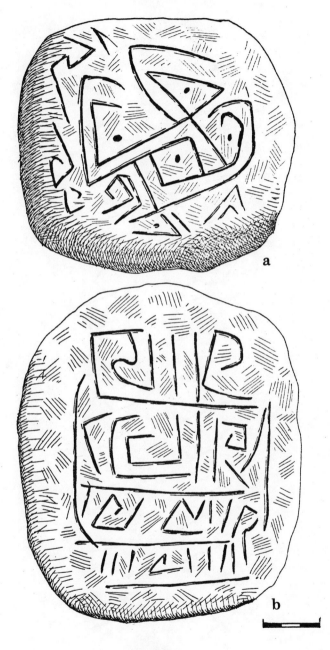

Figure 23

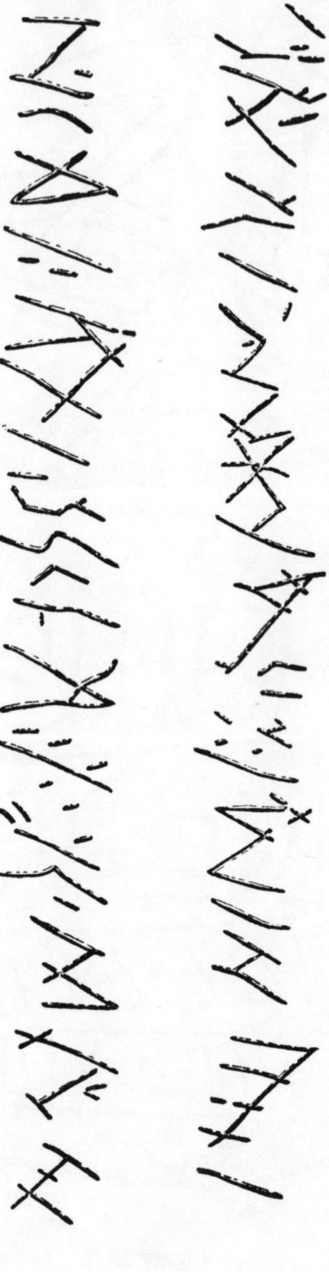

Figure 24

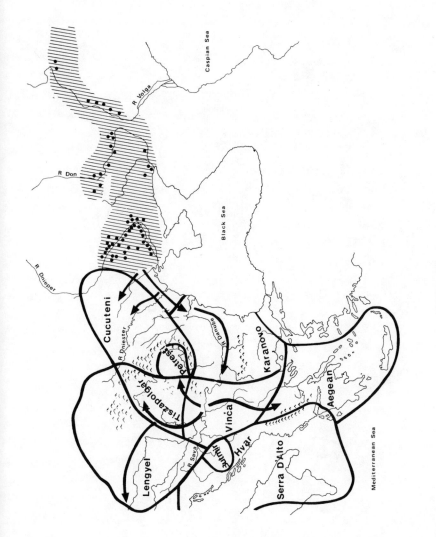

Figure 25

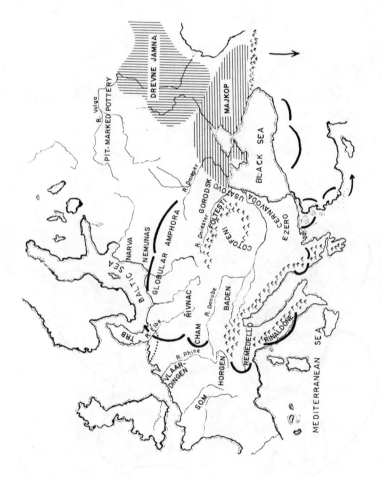

Figure 26

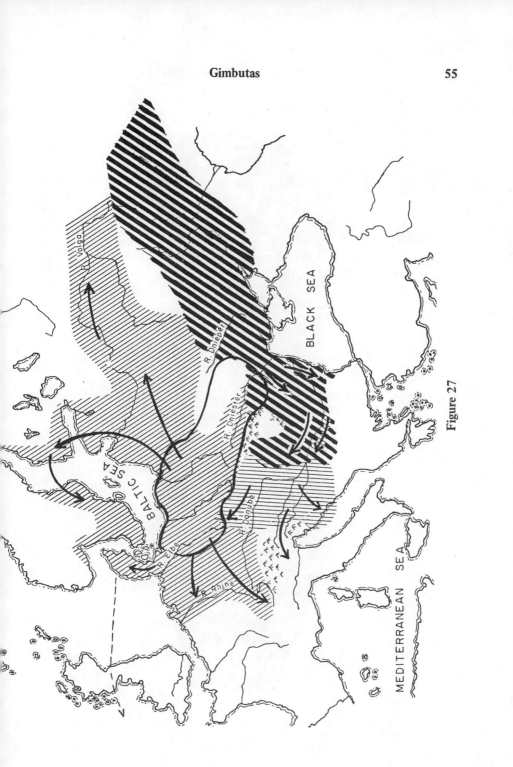

Figure 27

Plate 1

Plate 2

Plate 3

Plate 4

Plate 5

ARCHAEOLOGICAL EVIDENCE FOR THE MIGRATIONS
OF THE INDO-EUROPEANS

Homer L. Thomas
University of Missouri at Columbia

Controversy over the migrations of early Indo-Europeans has been current since the late eighteenth century, when scholars discovered that similarities among Sanskrit, Greek, and Latin indicated that they probably had a common origin. In the course of the last two hundred years, although emphasis and interest have shifted, philologists, linguists, historians, and archaeologists have constantly returned to the now deeply entrenched and intractable problems concerning the dispersal of the Indo-European peoples. Notwithstanding major advances in historical, linguistic, and archaeological studies, there is still little agreement on how to define the Indo-European homeland or how to trace their migrations from their homeland (Mallory 1973). Although this paper offers no general solution, it may suggest approaches that could lead to the unraveling of some problems, the solutions of which might open the way to the resolution of the long-standing Indo-European problem.[1]

In the study of archaeological evidence concerning the early Indo-European migrations, most archaeologists recognize that there are important limitations imposed by historical and linguistic evidence. Historical evidence establishes the chronology of the early Indo-Europeans who settled in southwestern Asia, and in so doing roughly fixes the chronological horizon of related early Indo-European peoples living in Eurasia. In much later ancient and early medieval times, it permits the correlation of archaeologically known cultures with historically known Indo-European peoples. On the other hand, linguistic evidence is more general in character. It allows only a very general characterization of early Indo-European culture, making it difficult to correlate cultures defined by paleo-linguistic reconstruction with cultures known from archaeological excavations. Linguistically, one can establish the existence of a Proto-Indo-European culture at a late Neolithic stage of development. Linguistic reconstructions are equally ambiguous about the character and location of an Indo-European homeland, for one has the choice between a vast geographic area in Eurasia or a more limited region such as southeast Europe, north Europe, or south Russia. Given the ever-changing climate and thus also the environments of the past, it is difficult to define and locate the Indo-European homeland by linguistic reconstruction (Friedrich 1970). The linguistic interrelations among the Indo-European languages should provide an important guide to the many possible synchronic and diachronic correlations among the cultures which have been attributed to the Indo-Europeans. Yet until recently there have been only relatively rigid linguistic classifications to assist the archaeologist in this choice. Now, however, the linguistic advances of the last decade have brought new concepts of the successive relationships that existed among these languages as they developed. These new concepts, together with existing historical evidence for the early Indo-Europeans, may well offer a much more valid basis for correlating archaeologically known cultures with specific early Indo-European-speaking groups of people.[2]

In correlating cultures and peoples, the archaeologist is hedged in by the limitations of his own discipline. Not only are there fluctuating and inconsistent chronologies, but conflicting ideas as to sets of relationships among cultures and divergent explanations of their development. In many ways the choice between such sets of relationships and theories of explanation turns upon decisions made concerning chronology, particularly absolute chronology. Two quite different approaches to absolute chronology have been available to archaeologists during much of the twentieth century. Briefly stated, one of these was the "low chronology," which placed the development of the European Neolithic within the third millennium and restricted cultures that are often associated with the Indo-Europeans to a narrow horizon of three to four hundred years at the end of the third and the beginning of the second millennium (Schuchhardt 1935, Hawkes 1940, Childe 1948). The other involves the "high chronology," which placed the beginning of the European Neolithic as early as the sixth millennium and allowed the whole of the third millennium for the dispersal of the Indo-Europeans (Müller 1905, Montelius 1906, Pittioni 1949).

Although as early as the 1950s radiocarbon dating indicated major changes which broadly supported the "high chronology," there were few attempts to make fundamental revisions during the next decade. Actually, it was only in the late 1960s, following the dendrochronological calibration of carbon-14 dates, that there were major changes in archaeological chronology. For some, such as Renfrew (1973), the calibrated radiocarbon dates made it possible to construct a very high chronology which seemed to create a "fault line" that isolated the cultures of Europe from those of the Aegean area and southwestern Asia. Radiocarbon dating had forced the abandonment of those connections among European, Aegean, and southwest Asiatic cultures that were based upon the "low chronology." The new chronologies, which are based upon calibrated radiocarbon dates, raise serious problems for the interpretation of the migrations of the early Indo-Europeans, because they make it difficult to correlate the development of cultures of Europe with those of the Aegean area and southwestern Asia. This isolation of Europe has resulted in the widespread adoption of theories of culture explanation characterized by an increasing emphasis upon the independence (Renfrew 1973) and continuity (Clarke 1968) of the prehistoric European cultures. With this has come an increasing stress on narrowly regional culture development, which has given support to many widely held theories of the indigenous character of cultures associated with the Indo-Europeans.[3]

In the rush to the "new," it is often forgotten that another set of relations between the prehistoric cultures of Europe and those of the Aegean area and southwestern Asia have supported a "high chronology" since the days of Montelius and Müller. Archaeological advances have of course brought changes in the interpretation of connections which are defined by elements such as pottery and metal types. Their presence in distributions extending from southwestern Asia through the Aegean area to Europe probably reflects trade rather than the spread of culture. This trade was probably accompanied by the spread of techno-complexes such as metallurgy through what Kroeber (1952:344-45) has called "stimulus-diffusion." Contact among cultures was followed by the rapid adoption of elements and complexes which became elaborated along local lines, thus creating the illusion of independence and continuity. These elements and complexes not only serve as a basis for culture explanation, but are also horizon markers that make possible the determination of relationships and the construction of chronologies.

The shifts in chronological outlook that have come about during the last thirty years have not only drastically altered the chronology of cultures thought to be associated with the Indo-Europeans, but have also greatly changed our ideas concerning the development and dispersal of these cultures. Formerly, their dispersal was assigned to a brief episode of migratory expansion limited to a period of two to three hundred years. Today, their dispersal and development are thought to have extended through a period of more than a thousand years. Thus, we now have more than enough time to allow for the infiltration and amalgamation of Indo-European invaders with older peoples. It is also possible to understand the persistence of older cultural elements, the roots of which extended back through the Neolithic and perhaps even into Mesolithic and Paleolithic times.

Many archaeologists, especially the "new archaeologists," who rightly emphasize the role of continuity in the development of these older cultures, insist that complexes usually attributed to the Indo-Europeans were really indigenous creations. While the persistence of pottery shapes and decoration might be understood in these terms, cultures such as that of the Corded Ware peoples brought major shifts in settlement patterns, economic and technological activity, and, above all, burial and religious practices which are difficult to explain in terms of internal development. Culture change of this complexity must have involved the intrusion of new peoples (Ehrich 1963). Here it is assumed that the arrival of the Indo-European peoples was characterized by major breaks in local development involving the displacement, assimilation, or transformation of older cultures. Ideally, to be attributed to an influx of Indo-Europeans, a complex should mark the beginning of a tradition that continued without major breaks into historic times, when there is evidence, other than archaeological, for its association with the Indo-Europeans.

I. THE INDO-EUROPEANS OF SOUTHWEST ASIA AND THE AEGEAN AREA

Until the late 1950s, the arrival of the Indo-European peoples in Iran, Anatolia, and the Aegean area was dated to the early second millennium. During the last two decades, new archaeological discoveries rather than the reinterpreting of older evidence through the use of carbon-14 dates have pushed the time of the arrival of the Indo-Iranians, the Proto-Anatolian forebears of the Luwians, Hittites, and Palaic peoples, and the Mycenaean Greeks back into the third millennium. The coming of the Indo-Iranians, which is dated to the early third millennium by a decisive transformation of culture in northern Iran, defines the beginning of a tradition destined to continue into historic times, when it can be identified as Iranian. Interlocking historical, linguistic, and archaeological evidence indicates that the Proto-Anatolian peoples pushed into Anatolia in the course of the third millennium. In the Aegean area, recent linguistic and archaeological work proves the presence of Greek speakers in Mycenaean times, while archaeological sequences define an associated cultural tradition which goes back to the late third millennium. These shifts in dating are of considerable importance, because now the expansion of the Indo-Europeans into southwestern Asia and the Aegean area did not follow but was contemporary with their dispersal in Europe.

A. The Indo-Iranians of Iran (Chart I, p. 65)

The available historical and linguistic evidence for Indo-Iranians that is earlier than the first millennium comes from outside Iran. It consists of personal names found in Akkadian and Hurrian texts, divine names in Hittite-Mitanni treaties, and technical terms concerning the training of chariot horses in a Hittite treatise written by a Mitanni "Aryan." These indicate that Indo-Europeans must have been known in the Kassite, Hurrian, Mitanni, and Hittite courts about the middle of the second millennium. Scholars have usually assigned these names and terms to Indo-Iranians and taken this to indicate that they were rulers of the small Hurrian states of northern Mesopotamia and Syria. Their presence there has also been taken to indicate that the Indo-Iranians were on the Iranian plateau at this time. Today many would argue that these names and terms are probably Proto-Indic rather

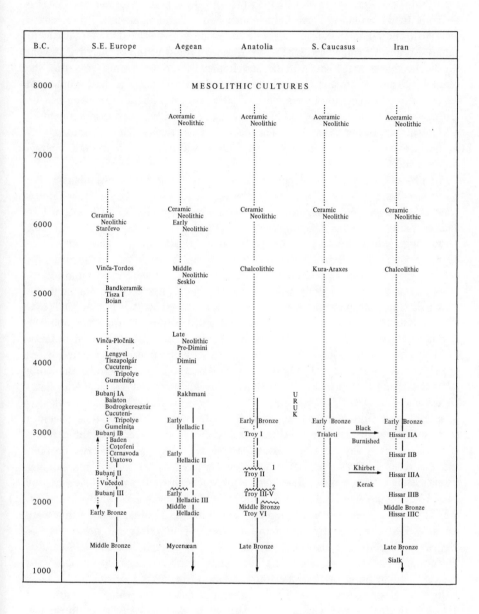

B.C.	S.E. Europe	Aegean	Anatolia	S. Caucasus	Iran
8000		MESOLITHIC CULTURES			
		Aceramic Neolithic	Aceramic Neolithic	Aceramic Neolithic	Aceramic Neolithic
7000					
6000	Ceramic Neolithic Starčevo	Ceramic Neolithic Early Neolithic	Ceramic Neolithic	Ceramic Neolithic	Ceramic Neolithic
5000	Vinča-Tordos Bandkeramik Tisza I Boian	Middle Neolithic Sesklo	Chalcolithic	Kura-Araxes	Chalcolithic
4000	Vinča-Pločnik Lengyel Tiszapolgár Cucuteni-Tripolye Gumelniţa	Late Neolithic Pre-Dimini Dimini			
3000	Bubanj IA Balaton Bodrogkeresztúr Cucuteni-Tripolye Gumelniţa Bubanj IB Baden Coţofeni Cernavoda Usatovo	Rakhmani Early Helladic I Early Helladic II	Early Bronze Troy I Troy II	U R U K Early Bronze Trialeti Black Burnished	Early Bronze Hissar IIA Hissar IIB Khirbet Hissar IIIA
2000	Bubanj II Vučedol Bubanj III Early Bronze	Early Helladic III Middle Helladic	Troy III-V Middle Bronze Troy VI	Kerak	Hissar IIIB Middle Bronze Hissar IIIC
1000	Middle Bronze	Mycenæan	Late Bronze		Late Bronze Sialk

Chart I: A Provisional Archaeological Chronology

than Proto-Indo-Iranian or Indo-Iranian (Thieme 1960). Others point out that it is difficult to determine if Proto-Indo-Iranian had differentiated into Proto-Iranian and Proto-Indic and therefore call these Indo-Europeans either Mitanni Aryans or simply Aryans (Crossland 1971:837-38). Although the question of the development of the languages that became Indic and Iranian is for the linguist to settle, the general indications are that Proto-Indo-Iranian was no longer at the beginning of its development. This must mean that their Proto-Indo-Iranian forebears can no longer be brought in at the time of a supposedly widespread abandonment of settlements following 2000 B.C. The decline of settlement in Iran must surely be due to the southward movement of these "Indo-Iranians" to northern Meso-potamia and Syria.

This makes it possible to associate the arrival of the Proto-Indo-Iranians with a break in culture tradition that is marked by the transformation of the older Painted Ware cultures and the emergence of the Gray Ware culture in northeastern Iran and southern Turkestan (Dyson 1965:220; Masson and Sarianidi 1972:97-111). This change, which is traceable at Tepe Hissar and related sites, has been attributed by some archaeologists to internal development and by others to the intrusion of new peoples. Both groups assume that new peoples who were in part Indo-Euro-pean played a role. One group believes that this took place in the older tradition, which remained strong enough to absorb the newcomers, while the other holds that these newcomers played a major role in the transformation (Dyson 1973:690-91). The date of formation of the Gray Ware culture must still be reckoned in terms of Tepe Hissar. Here, Gray Ware appears along with the traditional Painted Wares in Hissar IIA (usually equated with Early Dynastic I in Mesopotamia, ca. 2900-2750 B.C.), and then displaces the Painted Ware in Hissar IIB (equated with Early Dynastic II-IIIa, ca. 2750-2500 B.C.) (Dyson 1968:310-11). Many archaeologists who think that Gray Ware was an internal development believe that its appearance represented one of the many technological advances associated with the develop-ment of the Early Bronze Age of southwestern Asia. The color, the crisp profiles, and the various details would thus have been inspired by the increasingly popular metal vessels of the times. There is also the question of the role played by the Gray Ware of the almost immediately preceding Uruk civilization of Mesopotamia, the influence of which was felt directly or indirectly in other regions that were penetrated at this time by the Indo-Europeans. The widespread occurrence of gray wares in cultures found not only in Iran and Turkestan but also in Anatolia, Greece, and the Balkans, which have all been attributed to Indo-Europeans, is suggestive of the importance of the still unresolved Gray Ware problem.

In southwestern Asia, Gray Ware marked the onset of a period of turbulence that is indicated by the widespread movement of peoples of older cultures. The force of the movements of presumably related Indo-European peoples through the Caucasus Mountains into Transcaucasia is suggested by the southeastward movement of peoples of the Late Chalcolithic cultures of eastern Anatolia and the related Dura-Araxes culture of Transcaucasia (Dyson 1968:309-11). Their movement into northwestern Iran, which is dated to the beginning of the Early Bronze Age, is marked by the appearance of their Black Burnished Ware at Yanik Tepe (Burney 1964) and Godin Tepe (Young 1974). The possibility that this movement was caused by the pressure of peoples moving southward through the Caucasus is supported by the discovery of a pit grave covered by a kurgan at Uch Tepe in Azerbaijan. This grave, which is dated by calibrated Leningrad carbon-14 dates (LE-300 and LE-305) to the late fourth millennium, has burial and metal objects similar to those of the Maikop culture (Sulimirski 1970:122, 146). On the other hand, it marks the rise of the Trialeti Kurgan culture which became dominant in Transcaucasia in the middle of the third millennium and then continued into the second millennium. Although this movement cannot be related directly to the movement of the Proto-Iranian peoples, its date suggests that it may have been a parallel movement. This indicates that both migrations were probably part of a more general advance of Indo-European peoples into southwestern Asia.

Possibly of even greater importance is the realization that the culture tradition that began with the Gray Ware culture during the third millennium continued through the second and into the first. Dyson (1973:688-90) has pointed to a continuity not only in the development of pottery shapes and techniques but also of metal types from the third to the first millennium. Although evidence for this is limited during the Middle and Late Bronze Ages (second millennium), there are increasing indications that occupation persisted at settlements like Tepe Hissar after the time of the destruction of Hissar IIIB. All of this now suggests that the long-held idea of a hiatus in Iranian development beginning after 2000/1900 B.C. and continuing down to the time of cemetery B at Tepe Sialk (late second millennium) was an illusion. This long continuity of culture development makes it possible to associate the peoples of the Gray Ware tradition with the Indo-Iranians.

If the arrival of the Indo-Iranians in northern Iran can be dated as early as the early third millennium, they must be associated with the Gray Ware tradition. Their gradual expansion on the Iranian plateau would account not only for the pressures behind the Guti invasions of Mesopotamia in the late third millennium, but would also explain the appearance of Indo-Iranians in northern Mesopotamia and Syria during the middle second millennium. This process of expansion and displacement continued through the second millennium and led to the departure of those groups who became the Proto-Indic people of India. Although there is no linguistic evidence for Iranians until Achaemenid times, archaeologists such as Ghirshman (1954:73-89) and Dyson (1973:715) believe that the grave assemblages of cemetery B at Tepe Sialk (late second millennium) define a culture tradition associated with the Iranians.

B. The Hittites of Anatolia (Chart I, p. 65)

Somewhat firmer evidence for early Indo-Europeans comes from Anatolia. Here, the Boghazköy texts attest to the presence of Hittites, Luwians, and Palaic peoples in the middle second millennium, while onomastic evidence from Akkadian tablets of the Assyrian merchant colony at Kültepe places the Hittites in the early second millennium. In order to allow sufficient time for the differentiation of what is now called Proto-Anatolian into Luwian, Hittite, and Palaic, most scholars believe that the arrival of the early Indo-Europeans in Anatolia must be pushed back into the third millennium (Crossland 1971).

Mellaart's investigations indicate that archaeological evidence from Anatolia associated with the coming of these peoples consists of three destruction horizons. The first, which is dated to the time of the fall of Troy I (usually dated 2600 B.C., but more recently as early as 2800 B.C.), affected only northwest Anatolia. The second, which is dated to the time of the fall of Troy II, ca. 2300 B.C., is found not only in northwest, but also in southwest and south central Anatolia. The third, affecting north central Anatolia, belongs to the transition from the third to the second millennium (Mellaart 1971a:363-416; 1971b:681-706). Mellaart has associated the Luwians, who presumably came from the west, with the first two destruction horizons. The third is associated with the Hittites, who are thought to have come from the east. Crossland (1971:842-45) has criticized this view and points out the difficulties in bringing peoples speaking dialects of the same language into Anatolia not only at different times but also from different directions. Whatever may be the resolution of this issue in the future, the combination of historical, linguistic, and archaeological evidence suggests that the Indo-European-speaking ancestors of the Hittities, Luwians, and Palaic peoples were in Anatolia by the beginning of the third millennium.

The first of these horizons parallels in time the appearance of cultures attributed to Indo-European peoples in southeastern Europe and Iran, while the second horizon, which was much more widespread in Anatolia, must date to ca. 2300 B.C., making it contemporary with the destruction horizon marking the end of Early Helladic II, now usually related to the coming of the Indo-European-speaking Greeks. Unfortunately, there is little positive archaeological evidence beyond that for the destruction of settlements and the displacement of cultures associated with all three horizons. There is of course the illusive Gray Ware found in surveys made by French in 1959-60 and 1961 and by Mellaart in 1955 and 1960 in northwestern Anatolia. Initially Mellaart (1958:15-21) dated this Gray Ware by its connections with similar pottery at Troy V-VI and the Minyan Ware of Middle Helladic I in Greece, but the discoveries at Lerna require that it be pushed back from the early second millennium to the late third (Mellaart 1971b:701-2). Although the date of Anatolian Gray Ware will not be known until it is found in stratified context, from the time of its appearance in southeastern Europe and northern

Iran we can speculate that its beginning goes back as early as the first destruction horizon. It is difficult to relate these Anatolian horizons to other movements in the highlands of southwestern Asia. While it is impossible to detect any relationship with the earlier movement of the Black Burnished Ware culture into northwestern Iran, it is possible that the movement associated with the first destruction horizon (2800/2600 B.C.) had some connection with the displacement of peoples from Transcaucasia and eastern Anatolia, which can be traced by the dispersal of Khirbet Kerak pottery through Syria and Palestine during Early Bronze III (Palestine, 2700-2200 B.C.) (Amiran 1952; Todd 1973; Thomas 1978:182). However, this movement could have been caused by a further movement of peoples from Ciscaucasia into Transcaucasia. Whatever the relationships of the three destruction horizons, they occurred in a time of great turbulence in the highlands, but early enough to allow sufficient time for the Proto-Anatolian languages to differentiate and to account for the rapid emergence of the Hittites sometime after the third destruction horizon.

C. The Greeks of the Aegean Area (Chart I, p. 65)

In the Aegean area, the discovery of the Linear B tablets establishes the association of the Greek language with Mycenaean civilization. On the basis of its unbroken tradition, one can argue that the Greek arrival is traceable to the beginning of Mycenaean civilization. Until the late 1950s, the origin of the tradition leading to Mycenaean civilization was considered to be the beginning of the Middle Helladic culture, the formation of which was in part marked by the appearance of Minyan pottery. In the late 1950s, the excavations at Lerna made it clear that Minyan pottery actually appeared in the preceding Early Helladic III period (Caskey 1958). Furthermore, the Lerna excavations, as well as investigations at Tiryns, Asine, and Zygouries, showed that the transition from Early Helladic II to III was marked by destruction attributable to the invasion of new peoples (Caskey 1971:786-88). Since this roughly parallels the second destruction horizon across Anatolia, many archaeologists now assume that the arrival of the Greeks should be dated to the beginning of Early Helladic III, ca. 2300 B.C.

This complex of linguistic and archaeological evidence suggests that the Greeks arrived in Greece later than did other Indo-European speakers in either Iran or Anatolia. Unfortunately, there is no evidence for an earlier presence of Greeks in either Greece or immediately adjoining lands. Furthermore, there are no firm archaeological connections between the Early Helladic III culture of Greece and the late Early Bronze cultures of Anatolia or the Late Neolithic (Copper Age) cultures of southeastern Europe. What scanty evidence there is for relationships consists of the distinctive light-gray Minyan pottery which is so well known for its goblets and bowls with two high-swung handles. There have been many attempts to discover the origins of Minyan ware. Mellaart (1958:15-16) and others have traced it to northwestern Anatolia, but as has been noted above, this hypothesis was pushed aside by the discoveries at Lerna. Beyond the Aegean and Anatolia, Minyan pottery has generalized connections in both fabric and vessel shape in the pottery of cultures such as the Ezero-Cernavoda of the Lower Danubian area, the Coţofeni of Rumania, the Baden of the Middle Danubian area, and the Bubanj of Serbia. The frequent attribution of these cultures or components of these cultures of southeastern Europe as well as the cultures of late Early Bronze Anatolia to the Indo-Europeans raises the possibility that the Greeks were in the general region of southeastern Europe, the Aegean area, and Anatolia much earlier in the third millennium.[4] Furthermore, this is supported by the dating of the beginning of these southeast European cultures to the late fourth millennium as well as the dating of the arrival of the Proto-Anatolians. We shall return to the significance of these relationships after consideration of the southeast European cultures and cultures situated farther east, in the Caucasus and Soviet Central Asia.

II. THE INDO-EUROPEANS OF EUROPE
   Beyond southwestern Asia and the Aegean area, there is only archaeological evidence for the migrations of the early Indo-Europeans. At the end of the Late Neolithic (Copper Age) in southeastern and east central Europe, the Middle Neolithic in south central Europe, and the Early Neolithic in northern and eastern Europe, there is archaeological evidence for a widespread displacement or transformation of older cultures. During the late fourth and the third millennia, these older cultures, whose roots extended back to the earliest Neolithic, and perhaps even to the Mesolithic and Paleolithic, gave way to new cultures with quite different settlement patterns, economies, and technologies, and burial and religious practices. For almost one hundred years, archaeologists have associated these new cultures with incoming Indo-Europeans, because they often marked the beginning of new traditions that continued through the Neolithic, Bronze, and Iron Ages into historic times, when they could be associated with Indo-European peoples.
   Today, it is increasingly realized that continuities of culture traditions may be established in central and northern Europe for the Proto-Celtic and Proto-Germanic people, but are more difficult to establish in southeast Europe for the Thracians and Illyrians, and in eastern Europe for the Balts and Slavs. Our difficulties are further compounded by the increasing awareness of the persistence of elements of the older cultures in the new ones. Although the complexity of the change argues for an intrusion of new peoples, many archaeologists, today as well as in the past, hold that these changes can be understood as internal developments of the older cultures. The idea of Indo-European migrants becomes an illusion. Many European areas are thought to have been Indo-European since the beginning of culture development in early Neolithic or even Mesolithic or Paleolithic times. If this is supported by evidence of cultural distribution for later migrations, it

would imply that the diaspora of Indo-European peoples must have taken place at a time when, as many archaeologists hold, it was not supported by broad cultural distribution or evidence for later migrations.

A. The Indo-Europeans of Southeast Europe (Chart I, p. 65)

The archaeological evidence for an influx of Indo-European migrants into southeast Europe is ambiguous and therefore much disputed. A series of culture changes or transformations can be dated to the late fourth or early third millennium in terms of an archaeological chronology based upon calibrated radiocarbon dates, or to the late third and early second by a "low chronology." There is general agreement, however, that whatever the cause and whichever chronology is used, the late Karanovo culture of Bulgaria, the cultures in the Vinča-Tordos and Vinca-Pločnik tradition in Yugoslavia, the Sălcuţa, Gumelniţa, and Petreşti cultures of Rumania, the Cucuteni-Tripolye cultures of Rumania and the western Ukraine, the Bodrogkeresztur culture of eastern Hungary, and the Lengyel derivative cultures of western Hungary and the lands to the west and north gave way to or were transformed into new cultures in the course of the third millennium.

Many archaeologists such as Gimbutas (1965, 1973, 1978) see this widespread culture change as due to an intrusion of peoples from the steppe. On this basis, the interpretation of culture change would be a straightforward matter if it were just a question of intrusions by steppe peoples followed by the establishment of steppe cultures in southeastern Europe which could be associated with the Indo-European peoples. Excavations during the last two decades, however, have shown that while there was a displacement or submergence of older cultures, the new ones that replaced them retained much of the older tradition, although in greatly modified form. In the western Ukraine, Tripolye gave way to Usatovo-Gorodsk, which seems to be a fusion of older and steppe elements. The pottery retains Tripolye features but has some cord-impressed decoration, while burials were made in both flat graves and kurgans (Brjussow 1957:280-87). Along the Lower Danubian Valley, the Gumelniţa culture was transformed into the Ezero-Cernavoda complex, which had Aegean-Anatolian (metalwork and pottery including Proto-Minyan ware), Coţofeni (pottery including vessels with high-swung handles), Baden (metalwork, burial practices, and pottery with channeled decoration and high-swung handles), Circumpontic (metalwork), and steppe (contracted ocher burials, scepter-heads, and cord-impressed pottery decoration) connections (Berciu 1967:70-75; Georgiev et al. 1979:535-43). On the other hand, to the west in Oltenia and to the north in Transylvania, the older traditions of the Sălcuţa, Pe-treşti, and Cucuteni cultures survived in the Coţofeni culture. But the pottery displays the use of cord-impressed decoration and has vessels with high-swung handles, and there are occasionally both contracted ocher burials and kurgans (Roman 1976). Farther to the west, in the Middle Danubian basin, the Baden culture first appeared in western Hungary and then, in its mature phase, spread eastward to take the place of the Bodrogkeresztur culture. It brought the widespread displacement of older cultures, accompanied by the introduction of new patterns of settlement, a new channeled pottery including some vessels with high-swung handles, the use of the horse and wheeled vehicles, and the keeping of cattle and sheep. The Baden (Channeled Ware, Radial Ware or Pécel) culture is found not only in Hungary but also in Yugoslavia, eastern Austria, Bohemia, Moravia, Slovakia, and southern Poland (E. Neustupný 1973).

There is an increasing cleavage among archaeologists over the origin of these cultures which mark the end of older traditions in southeastern Europe. One finds widespread support for the view that these cultures represent massive transformations of older ones during times of rapid economic and/or climatic-environmental change such as characterized the transition from the Late Neolithic or Copper Age to the Bronze Age. Although the hybrid character of the Usatovo-Gorodsk complex seems clear, archaeologists such as Passek (1962) explain its development within the Tripolye tradition. Emphasis is placed on the local development of the Cernavoda (Georgiev et al. 1979:535-43) and Coţofeni cultures (Roman 1976). Archaeologists have long sought a local origin for the Baden culture within or near the Middle Danubian basin. J. Neustupný (1967:10-11) seeks such an origin, in which the Funnel Beaker culture played a major role.

Many other archaeologists point out that all these cultures have new elements, such as kurgan graves, contracted ocher burials, pottery vessels with high-swung handles, horses and wheeled vehicles, and often a new economy with emphasis on the keeping of cattle and sheep. The appearance of these new elements came at the time of the formation of new culture traditions, which, once established, continued to develop during the subsequent Bronze and Iron Ages, leading many to conclude that they were introduced by Indo-European migrants. The difficulty that arises when one seeks the quarter from which these new elements (and presumably their bearers) came is the realization of the generalized character of their connections in cultures such as the Pit Grave or Kurgan culture of the steppe (Gimbutas 1978) or in the cultures of Late Chalcolithic or Early Bronze Age Anatolia (Kalicz 1963). In the case of the steppe, aside from the use of kurgan burials and a limited but much altered use of cord-impressed decoration, there are few specific connections with the Pit Grave culture.

The widespread transformation of cultures in southeastern Europe, accompanied by the introduction of new culture elements and followed by the establishment of culture traditions that continued without interruption through the Bronze Age into the Iron Age, provides forceful argument in support of the hypothesis that there was an intrusion of new peoples and that these peoples were probably Indo-European migrants. Further support is given by evidence for an expansion from the steppe in the middle of the fourth millennium which was responsible for the southwestward displacement of Gumelniţa, Sălcuţa, and Krivodol elements into southern Serbia, where their fusion led to the formation of the Bubanj IA culture, and the southward displacement of Lower Danubian Valley elements which explain the Crusted Ware of the late phase of the Late Neolithic of Greece (Thomas 1967:39-40; Weinberg 1965:300-301). If all the new elements were traceable to the Pit Grave culture, it could be argued that its expansion into southeastern Europe would account for the arrival of new peoples who played a role in the formation of the new cultures. However, the presence of elements such as scepter heads and vessels with high-swung handles, as well as metal types that are not found in the Pit Grave culture, indicates that the source of the migrants must be sought on the Eurasiatic steppe in other cultures than the Pit Grave culture.

Today, after more than a century of scholarly investigation, the issue of the origin of the Indo-Europeans of southeastern Europe is still difficult to resolve. There are some who think that all the Indo-European peoples originated in southeastern Europe, or southeastern Europe and the adjacent lands of the Aegean and Anatolia, a view first advanced by Professor Benfey as long ago as 1868 and then kept alive in the scholarly tradition until its restatement with modifications in the 1950s by Hencken (1955:48-56) and Palmer (1955). Present-day archaeological evidence shows that the older cultures of the Neolithic could hardly have been Indo-European, thus eliminating southeastern Europe as their homeland (Gimbutas' contribution to this volume). Their arrival in southeastern Europe probably coincides with the time of the new cultures' marking the transition from the Late Neolithic to the Early Bronze Age. The complexity of the change involved in the formation of these new cultures suggests that it involved new peoples—even small groups of new peoples—who gained sufficient regional dominance not only to transform the older cultures but also to impose their language upon the surviving older inhabitants. The extraordinarily complex question as to how this region came to be inhabited in much later times by peoples known as Thracians and Illyrians lies beyond the scope of this paper.

B. The Indo-Europeans of Central and Northern Europe (Chart II, p. 74)

The lands of central and northern Europe have been associated with Indo-European origins since the days of Ludwig Geiger (1871). The archaeological interest in this region as a homeland for the Indo-Europeans followed the discovery of single grave burials in Denmark and of Saxo-Thuringian barrows covering single contracted burials accompanied by cord-impressed pottery and often a battle ax. By the beginning of the twentieth century, the Corded Ware-Battle Ax culture of the North European Plain, which was thought by some to have been centered in Denmark and by others in the Saxo-Thuringian lands of central Germany, came to define a culture horizon that seemed to mark a decisive period in the development of prehistoric Europe. Today, it is still thought by many

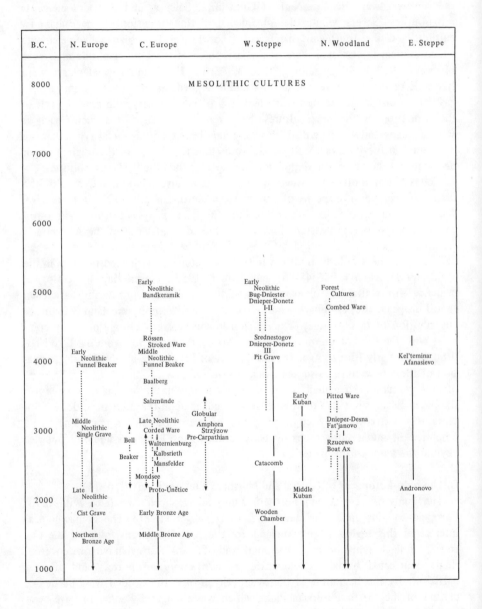

B.C.	N. Europe	C. Europe	W. Steppe	N. Woodland	E. Steppe
8000		MESOLITHIC CULTURES			
7000					
6000					
5000		Early Neolithic Bandkeramik	Early Neolithic Bug-Dniester Dnieper-Donetz I-II	Forest Cultures : Combed Ware	
4000	Early Neolithic Funnel Beaker	Rössen Stroked Ware Middle Neolithic Funnel Beaker	Srednestogov Dnieper-Donetz III Pit Grave		Kel'teminar Afanasievo
		Baalberg			
		Salzmünde		Early Kuban	Pitted Ware
3000	Middle Neolithic Single Grave	Late Neolithic Corded Ware	Globular Amphora Strzýzow Pre-Carpathian	Dnieper-Desna Fat'janovo	
		Bell Walternienburg		Rzucewo Boat Ax	
	Beaker	Kalbsrieth			
		Mansfelder	Catacomb		
		Mondsee			
2000	Late Neolithic	Proto-Únětice		Middle Kuban	Andronovo
	Cist Grave	Early Bronze Age	Wooden Chamber		
	Northern Bronze Age	Middle Bronze Age			
1000					

Chart II: A Provisional Archaeological Chronology

that this horizon marked the end of cultures which started with the oldest Neolithic, if not before, and the beginning of new ones which are traceable through the Bronze and Iron Ages to a time when they can be associated on historical grounds with Indo-European speakers, more especially with Celtic and Germanic peoples.

After World War II, when many of the older archaeological theories of Indo-European origins were abandoned, investigators turned to classifying the abundant finds that had accumulated in the course of almost eighty years of excavation. Energies were now directed to the establishment of an adequate basis for the study of the development of and interrelationships among the numerous regional groups of the Corded Ware-Battle Ax culture found in central and northern Europe. In the middle 1950s, Sturve (1955) proposed a relatively simple division of the Corded Ware culture into two groups, one characterized by burials furnished only with beakers and the other by burials with both beakers and amphorae. It was followed by geographic classifications using this simple scheme but attempting to account for regional differences. In 1958, Fischer proposed a division into Hercynian, Balto-Rhenish, and Pontic Steppe groups. The latest classification was published in 1969 by Klejn, who makes his division in terms of the Amphorae cultures of south central Europe, the Beaker complexes of northern Europe, and the steppe cultures of eastern Europe except for the Yamno (Kurgan or Pit Grave) and Catacomb cultures of the Russian steppe. Within each of these major regional groups, there are local ones, each with its own sequence of development established by barrow stratigraphy, typology, and interrelationships. While we cannot discuss them in detail here, we must note their more general significance and, to some extent, the reorientation of their interpretation since World War II.

The Balto-Rhenish groups of Fischer (1958), or the northern Beaker group of Klejn (1969), include the Dutch, northwest German, northeast German, and Polish Corded Ware groups as well as the Single Grave culture of Denmark. Although all of these possessed much in common in the beginning, they soon differentiated along local lines. Most of the early beakers show elements of form and decoration deriving from the preceding Funnel Beaker culture, which the Corded Ware-Battle Ax culture succeeded in the late fourth millennium B.C. In the Netherlands, an interplay of Corded Ware and Bell Beaker contacts is detectable in the pottery (Waals and Glasbergen 1955; Lanting 1971). Bell Beaker influence was also felt in northwestern Germany, where the initial Corded Beakers also show traits not only of Funnel Beaker pottery but also of the *Tiefstichkeramik* (Sturve 1955). The Corded Wares of northeastern Germany had an early development similar to that of the northwest and led to the formation of distinctive groups in eastern Germany and western Poland (Wetzel 1969). In western Scandinavia, the closely related Single Grave culture soon developed along distinctive regional lines because of its interpenetration with the Middle Neolithic culture so well known for its famous passage graves (Glob 1944). The fusion of these two complexes, perhaps catalyzed by eastern influences associated with the Pitted Ware culture, led to the emergence of the Late Neolithic Cist Grave complex that marks the beginning of a development which continued without interruption through the Bronze and Iron Ages into Roman times, when the area is known to have been Germanic in speech (Becker 1961).

A much more complicated situation characterizes the Hercynian uplands of south central Europe, which extends from the Rhineland through southern and central Germany and Czechoslovakia to southern Poland and southwestern Russia. This was probably due as much to the great cultural diversity of this region during the Middle Neolithic as to its inherent natural diversity. In the classic Saxo-Thuringian region, the place of the discovery of Corded Ware and once regarded as its homeland, a very few finds suggest that the Corded Ware people penetrated into a land dominated by the Salzmünde culture. During what is called the Kalbs-rieth phase, it is clear that these newcomers were forcing those associated with the Walternienburg culture back into the hills. The Corded Ware of this phase displays motifs and shapes taken over from the displaced Salzmünde culture. By the time of its final phase, the Mansfelder, the Corded Ware culture of Saxo-Thuringia, which now dominated the entire area, had a pottery decoration indicating that it had absorbed much of the Walternienburg ceramic tradition (Milden-berger 1961).

The investigations of Sangmeister and Gerhardt (1965) show that the Saxo-Thuringian groups spread down the Main to Hesse and the Middle Rhine, and across Bavaria to Switzerland. Again, the pottery styles reflect an assimilation of local traits, such as the taking over of Altheim elements in Bavaria and of Horgen ones in Switzerland (Strahm 1969). Along the Rhine Valley, there is the further complication of influences associated with the contemporary Bell Beaker complex, which we cannot deal with here (Sangmeister 1976; Harrison 1974).

South and east of Saxo-Thuringia, closely related Corded Ware groups arose in Bohemia and Moravia, where their development is now usually traced according to the theories of development proposed by Buchvaldek (1966). His theories not only take into account relationships with the Rivnáč culture of Bohemia, but also account for a somewhat different course of development than is found in Saxo-Thuringia. The differences found in Bohemia and Moravia are due to interaction with the Baden or Channeled Ware culture of the southern areas of these lands, and the influence of the Bell Beaker complex. The flux of influences that characterized the later stages of Bohemian and Moravian Corded wares became more complex because of the influence of East Alpine centers, which probably played as great a role as the Bell Beaker complex in laying the foundations for the Early Bronze Age.[5]

In southern and southeastern Poland, the Corded Ware people encountered the surviving Globular Amphorae and Funnel Beaker cultures (Machnik 1966). These encounters are reflected in the incorporation of decorative motifs and modification of pottery shapes (Krzak 1976). Further changes in Corded Ware pottery came from the adoption of pottery traits that radiated from the most northeasterly centers of the Baden culture in southern Poland.

The diversity of the Corded Ware groups, which had resulted from the assimilation of the traditions of the older Neolithic, gave way before the consolidation of cultures that was finally achieved in south central Europe in Proto-Únětice (Aunjetitz) times. This consolidation, which paralleled the fusion of intrusive and native elements during the Late Neolithic of northern Europe, was characterized by the development of a widespread uniformity of pottery style and metal types. Undoubtedly, the important Bell Beaker and East Alpine Mondsee-Laibach-Vučedol complexes, as well as the Baden culture, played important catalytic roles in this consolidation which laid the foundations for the Early Bronze Age, but this is hardly the place to deal with the complexities of the Bell Beaker problem, the puzzling influences of the East Alpine centers, or the influence of the Baden culture.

Many would agree that the consolidation of the Corded Ware groups led to the formation of Early Bronze Age ones which in turn define the beginning of those traditions that were destined to continue uninterruptedly through the Middle and Late Bronze Age into the Iron Age, when on historical grounds we can identify the population of southern central Europe as Celtic. The cleavage between the Corded Ware groups of central and southwest Germany and those of Czechoslovakia, Austria, and southern Poland raises the possibility that these regions were initially occupied, respectively, by Proto-Celtic and Proto-Italic peoples. Once established, the Celtic peoples emerged in central and southwestern Germany and spread into France. This is not the place to undertake an analysis of the association of the Celts with the Beaker cultures of the Lower Rhineland and the British Isles. The Italic peoples would have emerged in the lands to the east and remained there, possibly until the end of the Middle Bronze Age, when they departed for Italy.

Still other archaeologists believe that central and northern Europe were Indo-European much earlier, even as far back as Mesolithic times. This view is quite old in the archaeological circles of central and northern Europe. Although most archaeologists today no longer seek to localize the home of the Germanic peoples or the Indo-European homeland, many often insist that the Corded Ware cultures originated in central and northern Europe. Malmer (1962) has sought to demonstrate through the use of quantitative methods that not only Corded Ware beakers but also All-over-Corded Beakers, which can be regarded as Bell Beaker-Corded Ware hybrids, represent a straightforward transformation of pottery in the Funnel Beaker tradition. Although no one mentions the Indo-Europeans, cultures which have long been associated with them become indigenous creations.

C. The Indo-Europeans of Eastern Europe

The concept of a south Russian homeland from which the Indo-Europeans spread into central and northern Europe, into the Balkans and the Aegean area and into southwest Asia has been current since the nineteenth century. Support for this view has long been sought in archaeological evidence from the kurgans (burial mounds or barrows) of south Russia, which have been known since the eighteenth century. Nineteenth-century excavations led to an initial division of the burials into Pre-Scythian and Scythian groups. Finally, just before World War I, Gorodtsov proposed that the Pre-Scythian cultural developmentof south Russia be defined by the succession of pit graves *(yamno)*, catacombs, and wooden chamber tombs *(srubno)* found in kurgans (Childe 1947:149). Not long after World War I, Childe (1926:183-200) proposed that the culture of the "oldest *kurgans*" could be associated with the Indo-Europeans. In subsequent years, the culture associated with these early kurgans came to be designated as the Pit Grave culture. It was only in the late 1950s that the development of this culture was finally divided into four phases or periods (Merpert 1961; Gimbutas 1961). Later Gimbutas (1965), who prefers to call the Pit Grave culture the Kurgan culture, proposed that the first real expansion from the steppe should be dated to the time of the Pit Grave III culture. After the chronology of prehistoric European development was revised on the basis of calibrated carbon-14 dates, Gimbutas (1978) shifted the first major expansion back to the time of the Pit Grave I culture, ca. 4400-4200 B.C., leading to the widespread "kurganization" of the cultures of central Europe that ultimately gave rise to those of the Corded Ware. A second "wave" of steppe peoples, ca. 3400-3200 B.C., penetrated into eastern areas of southeastern Europe, while a third "wave," ca. 3000-2800 B.C., pushed into southeastern Europe and later into Greece, ca. 2300 B.C.

During the 1960s and 1970s, Russian archaeological work made it increasingly evident that the early Indo-European migrations can no longer be interpreted primarily in terms of the Pit Grave culture. With much more known of the cultures of southern Russia, it is clear that initially the Pit Grave culture did not play a dominant role. It penetrated into a land held by the Bug-Dniester and Dnieper-Donetz cultures. During Pit Grave II times, the western steppe was taken over by the Tripolye culture, while the Dnieper-Donetz culture gave way to the Srednestogov culture (Telegin 1969). Even in the time of Pit Grave III, it does not seem to have expanded much beyond the steppe. While the Pit Grave culture did not expand as dramatically to the northwest and southwest as formerly thought, its pottery is similar to that of the Kelteminar and Afanasievo cultures, pointing to connections extending deep into Soviet western Asia (Sulimirski 1970:265; Chard 1974:145-46).

In the northern and western Ukraine, central and northwest Russia, the Baltic States, and Finland, there are Corded Ware cultures, the origins of which have been variously attributed to the expansion of the Pit Grave culture of the south Russian steppe, the intrusion of the Globular Amphorae and Corded Ware cultures of the North European Plain, and the development of older Steppe and Forest traditions. Here, as on the North European Plain, where the Funnel Beaker culture is thought to be the source of the Corded Ware cultures, some think that the Dnieper-Donetz culture played a similar role. Dolukhanov (1979:148-50) points out that although the Funnel Beaker and Dnieper-Donetz cultures have quite different economies and technologies and even different pottery shapes, they date to much the same time and share a similar pottery decoration, which he takes to be "a reflection of some fundamental process." The Pre-Carpathian culture (southeast Poland and western Ukraine) and the Strzyżów culture (eastern Poland and Volhynia) have early pottery that illustrates the problem. They have high necks suggesting Funnel Beaker connections, but body shapes that can be explained in terms of either Dnieper-Donetz or Pit Grave III shapes. In later phases the pottery increasingly displays the influences of the Globular Amphorae culture, which persisted in southern Poland as indicated by the investigations of the Złota culture (Krzak 1976). In their final phases the Sub-Carpathian graves yield a pottery showing the influences of the Late Baden tradition, while that of the Strzyżów culture strongly exhibits influences from the woodlands to the east and the North European Plain to the west (Bérézanskaia 1971). While many would regard these two cultures as geographically transitional between the Pit Grave culture of south Russia and the Corded Ware cultures of the North European Plain, their battle axes, together with extended or contracted flat burials in the one case and kurgans in the other, argue for affinities with the cultures of the North European Plain.

Immediately to the north of the Pit Grave culture, the Dnieper-Desna culture developed in the northern Ukraine, where it is known from both settlements and kurgan burials. Archaeologists such as Bérézanskaia (1971) attribute it to an intrusion of Corded Ware peoples from the west, but its early pottery clearly relates to that of Pit Grave III. On the other hand, pottery vessels with squat bodies and thickened rims which are used as areas for decoration point to connections with the woodlands. Still farther north, there is the Fat'janovo culture of the valleys of the Upper Volga and Oka. The pottery of the early Moscow group still closely resembles that of the Pit Grave III or Dnieper-Desna cultures, but with it there are globular vessels recalling those of the Globular Amphorae culture and battle axes indicating connections to the west. In the subsequent Yaroslav and Chuvash groups, the pottery displays an increasing assimilation of Forest elements in both pottery shapes and decoration. This has led some Russian archaeologists to conclude that the Fat'janovo was a local development of the Forest cultures of Central Russia, with pottery and battle axes pointing to external contact explained in terms of trade (Gimbutas 1965:485-86; Brjussow 1957:101-9). Whatever may be the origin of these two cultures of the northern Ukraine and central Russia, their assemblages have interpretative problems that are typical of northern east Europe, where it is difficult to separate intrusive elements from those of the deeply rooted Forest cultures.

Far to the northwest of the steppe, there is the *Haffküstenkultur* or Rzucewo culture of the coastlands of the Danzig, or Gdańsk, Bay, and beyond still farther to the north is the *Bootaxtkultur* or Boat Ax culture of the eastern Baltic States, Finland, southern and central Sweden, and southern Norway. The *Haffküsten-kultur,* which is known from both settlements and single graves, has a pottery with cord-impressed decoration and globular amphorae that tie it to the North European Plain, but there are elements such as carvings of human figures suggestive of a Northern Forest component (Šturms 1970:162-85). The origins of the Boat Ax culture are equally disputed because its battle axes indicate an origin within Scandinavia, while its pottery has shapes and decoration pointing to a preliminary transformation in the forest lands of the southeast Baltic (Oldeberg 1952:148-213; Šturms 1961).

All these cultures have been associated with the Indo-Europeans, which suggests that they must have been related to one another. Their origin and the explanation of their relationships are often defined in terms of an expansion or expansions of the Pit Grave culture. Encounters with Funnel Beaker and Globular Amphorae elements in central and northern Europe and with Forest elements in northern eastern Europe not only transformed the steppe culture but also accounted for the diversity of its derivative Corded Ware cultures. Some insist that the Globular Amphorae and Corded Ware cultures played an intermediary role between the steppe and the diverse Corded Ware cultures of northern Europe. Others hold that fundamental differences in burial rite and varying use of the battle ax point to indigenous local origins. Yet there are generalized similarities among these cultures that set them off from the older cultures of the areas in which they are found.

III. THE INDO-EUROPEANS OF WESTERN ASIA AND THE CAUCASUS

Many archaeologists maintain that the Pit Grave culture of the south Russian steppe extended eastward beyond the Lower Volga and into Soviet western Asia and southeastward beyond the Don to the Caucasian Mountains. Although there are generalized similarities between the Pit Grave culture and the Kelteminar culture of western Kazakhstan, northwestern Uzbekistan, and western Turkmanistan and the related Afanasievo culture of the Upper Ob-Upper Yenisei region, their development proceeded along somewhat different lines. Although connections between the south Russian steppe and the north Caucasian area were much closer because of their geographic proximity, the latter area had connections not only to the south but also to the east in Soviet western Asia which argue for a reconsideration of its traditional interpretation in terms of the cultural development of the south Russian steppe.

A. The Indo-Europeans of the Eastern Steppe (Chart II, p. 74)

The early Kelteminar culture is largely known from habitation sites found near lakes and streams, while the early Afanasievo culture is defined by its early flat graves which are surrounded by stone circles. These habitations and graves yield pottery vessels that have round or pointed bases and a decoration made by the use of incision and a comb stamp. There are close similarities between Kelteminar and Afanasievo pottery, and both have generalized similarities to the Neolithic pottery of the Urals and the early Pit Grave culture which suggest some sort of ultimate relationship among these cultures (Chard 1974:145-48).

The Kelteminar culture, the development of which is thought to have paralleled that of the Namazga I-V culture of southern Turkmenistan, is now known from four distinct groups of sites: the Akcha Daryan group along the Lower Amu Darya, the Kyzyl-Kum group of the lands between the Amu Darya and Syr-Darya, the Uzboian group of the Kara-Kum, and the Tuzkan group of the Zeravshan River area. Their later pottery is characterized by undecorated vessels with flat bases which have been found with bifacial points and occasionally copper artifacts (Masson and Sarianidi 1972:73-74). The later Afanasievo graves, which are now covered by a kurgan as well as surrounded by a stone circle, yield a pottery suggesting a similar culture development (Mongait 1961:145-46).

During the third millennium the Kelteminar and Afanasievo cultures played a role in the formation of the Andronovo culture, which many scholars would associate with the Indo-Iranians, more specifically with the Iranians and ultimately the Scythians (Jettmar 1972). Their tombs carried on the traditions of the Afanasievo, but the actual graves now consist of stone cists or wooden chambers. Some archaeologists such as Masson and Sarianidi (1972:146-54) link the wooden chamber or timber graves of western Turkmenia with those of the Timber Grave culture of the Lower Volga area and the Ukraine, on the basis not only of grave type, but also of similar burial rites and similar pottery. The Andronovo culture is now known from an extraordinarily large number of local variants scattered through Soviet Central Asia, each with its own distinctive burials but tied to the others by similarities in pottery and other elements of material culture. The Andronovo culture with its many regional variants is of interest not only because the associated peoples are thought to have been Iranians, but also for the possible association of some of the Andronovo groups with the Tocharians.

B. The Indo-Europeans of the North Caucasus

The Early Kuban culture of the North Caucasus area, which is situated immediately to the southeast of the Pit Grave culture of the south Russian steppe, has long been associated with the Indo-Europeans. Most archaeologists assume that these two cultures were closely related but developed along somewhat different lines through the exploitation of local mineral wealth and through trade with the

urban centers of southwestern Asia. Rich tombs such as Maikop and Novosvobodnaya yield metal vessels, tools, weapons, and ornaments which would have been at
home in the Sumerian cities of Mesopotamia and centers such as Tepe Hissar in
Iran and Alaca and Troy II in Anatolia. The globular pottery vessels which are
found not only at Maikop but also at other north as well as south Caucasian sites
are related to northern Mesopotamian and Syrian ones which are datable to Gawran
and Amuq F times (last half of the fourth millennium) (Andrétéva 1977). At
Maikop, they are said to have been made in a gray fabric with Iranian connections
(Childe 1948:151). There are also the wagons found in burials at Tri Brata and
Losinsky in the North Caucasus area, which were adapted from those of the Kura-
Araxes culture of Transcaucasia that derive ultimately from the Uruk culture of
Mesopotamia (3500-3100 B.C.) (Piggott 1968). On the other hand, the tripartite
wooden chamber tomb at Maikop and the stone cist of Novosvobodnaya, notwithstanding the megalithic porthole slab of the latter, point to connections with the
eastern steppe. These connections become more attractive now that calibrated
radiocarbon dates make it possible to place the beginning of the Andronovo culture
in the third millennium (Dolukhanov et al. 1976:199).

When these eastern connections of Maikop and the North Caucasus are taken
together with the connections of southwest Asiatic metalwork and the distribution
of wheeled vehicles extending westward from the Caucasus through the steppe to
Rumania and Hungary, it becomes clear that the North Caucasus provides clues to
the problem of gray ware origins for northern Iran, northwestern Anatolia, and
Greece, as well as the derivation of related elements in southeastern Europe. All
these connections occur at the time of or immediately following that of the Uruk
culture, when gray ware, whatever its origin, could have been carried northward by
trade. It would thus have been adopted by Indo-Europeans pressing southward
through Soviet Central Asia toward Iran as well as through the steppe toward the
Caucasus. This would fit not only with the adoption of the Uruk wheeled vehicle
(Piggott 1968), but also with the taking over in subsequent times of elements of
Mesopotamian metalwork. It would likewise go far to explain the origin of what
Georgiev (1979:541-43) and others have called the Circumpontic metallurgical
zone.

IV. THE PROBLEMS OF THE INDO-EUROPEAN MIGRATIONS

Archaeological evidence does permit the association of some, but not all, early
Indo-Europeans with prehistoric cultural traditions that extend into historic times.
In Iran, the Aegean area, and central and northern Europe, the Indo-European
arrivals are marked by breaks in culture development that are followed by the
establishment of new traditions, such as Gray Ware associated with the Proto-
Indo-Iranians, the Minyan Ware with the Mycenaean Greeks, and the Corded Wares
with Proto-Germanic, Proto-Celtic, and perhaps Proto-Italic peoples. Unfortunately,

in Anatolia the evidence is less definitive, but inferences made from Proto-Indo-Iranian and Mycenaean Greek developments suggest that the Proto-Anatolians arrived equally early and quite possibly shared a common cultural background, perhaps to be defined by a generalized Gray Ware complex. Archaeological evidence indicates that the Corded Ware cultures of the Proto-Germanic, Proto-Celtic, and presumably the Proto-Italic peoples were in place in northern and central Europe by the late fourth and early third millennia. This, together with the same date for the arrival of the Proto-Indo-Iranians, Proto-Anatolians, and Mycenaean Greeks, suggests that a marked differentiation had already taken place in the once common Proto-Indo-European culture by the time that we meet Indo-Europeans in their respective lands. Although archaeological evidence for associating other cultures with Indo-European peoples is tenuous at best or does not exist at all, groupings such as the Ezero-Cernavoda, Coţofeni, and Baden cultures of southeastern Europe, the Corded Ware culture of eastern Europe, the Pit Grave culture of the western steppe, the Early Kuban culture of the north Caucasus area, and the Kelteminar, Afanasievo, and Andronovo cultures of the eastern steppe indicate that Indo-European differentiation had reached an extraordinarily complex stage by the beginning of the third millennium.

There is evidence for the formation of new cultures and similarities among cultures that has been taken to indicate movements explaining the widespread distribution of Indo-European cultures. The earliest of these movements took place in the fifth millennium. This is projected on the basis of the similarity of pottery decoration of the roughly contemporary Funnel Beaker and Dnieper-Donetz cultures, which are thought to have been the source of the Corded Ware cultures. It can be argued that the early Pit Grave, Kelteminar, and Afanasievo cultures, which have not only similar pottery decoration but also pottery shapes, arose at much the same time and became the source of the steppe cultures. It has long been held that a movement out of the steppe in the middle of the third millennium produced the displacement of Lower Danubian elements that led to the formation of the Bubanj IA culture of Serbia and probably accounts for the appearance of crusted ware in the late phase of the Late Neolithic of Greece, ca. 3500 B.C. (Garašanin 1975; Thomas 1977:184-85). This movement can also be explained in terms of the formation of the Volga-Oka Combed and Pitted Ware complex around 3500 B.C., to judge from a cluster of calibrated carbon-14 dates for its Volossovo group (Dolukhanov et al. 1976:195-96). The pressures associated with its formation led to the displacement of older Forest cultures to the southwest, where their Combed Ware turns up in Tripolye C1 sites. The movement of Indo-Europeans into southwestern Asia, the Aegean area, and southeastern Europe as well as the formation of the Corded Ware cultures of central and northern Europe took place at the time of the widespread expansion of the Pit Grave III culture in south Russia. It is tempting to relate these movements to pressures on the steppe, which are marked by the appearance of Kelteminar elements in the Urals region (Sulimirski 1970:104; A. P. Vinogradov et al. 1966:318). The redating of the Catacomb and Andronovo cultures, which has been made possible by calibrated radiocarbon dates, makes possible speculation concerning movements on the steppe which were felt around 2600 B.C. and 2300 B.C. in southwestern Asia and the Aegean area.

The diversity of cultures and movements which can be associated with the early Indo-European peoples has led many archaeologists to maintain that the problem of the migrations of the early Indo-Europeans cannot be solved on the basis of present evidence. Others among them believe that answers have not been found because the dispersal of the Proto-Indo-Europeans took place in the much earlier Mesolithic or even Paleolithic (Bosch-Gimpera 1961). Assuming a linguistic model calling for an inital Proto-Indo-European homeland, the task of the archaeologist becomes one of tracing in terms of cultures how an initial family differentiation of peoples such as the Proto-Germanic took place in the homeland, and then how this was followed by the diaspora of these "Proto" groups leading to the emergence of distinct entities which can be recognized in archaeological, linguistic, and/or historical terms. Although it is not yet possible to define all these "Proto" cultures, the distribution and similarities, admittedly generalized similarities, of cultures found in southeastern Europe, the Aegean, Anatolia, and Iran point to the possible existence of such a culture (Chart I, p. 65). Much the same could be said of the cultures of the eastern and western steppe, as well as the Single Grave and Corded Ware cultures of central and northern Europe (Chart II, p. 74). However, if the search is to succeed, much more must be known of culture development not only in Europe but also in southwestern and western Asia. The search must extend, furthermore, beyond the Neolithic back through the Mesolithic into the Upper Paleolithic. There is the need not only for much more field evidence but also for a widespread application of the best available archaeological methods to demonstrate, where possible, the existence of relevant culture continuities. Although the archaeologist may not be in a position to solve the long-standing Indo-European problem, there is at least the possibility of major archaeological contributions to the question and a widespread awareness of its extraordinary complexity.

NOTES

1. In the preparation of this paper, I am indebted for many useful ideas and suggestions to Robert W. Ehrich. I must also express my thanks for help given by Ralph M. Rowlett and Elsebet S.-J. Rowlett.
2. Discussions with Edgar Polomé and Winfred Lehmann gave the writer some

understanding of the new concepts concerning the development of the Indo-European languages.

3. Unfortunately, the hope of constructing relatively exact absolute chronologies based upon radiocarbon dates vanished during the 1970s. Today, it is evident that exact dating by means of carbon-14 determinations is not possible without local dendrochronological controls. Without them, carbon-14 dates can fall only within a range of one to three hundred years (Pilcher and Baillie 1978; Campbell, Baxter and Alcock 1979). Radiocarbon dates of course will continue to provide an excellent guide to relative culture successions, to the choice between sets of relationships in the building of chronologies, to the approximate dating of cultures and to equations between areas. In this paper, the dating is based upon revisions of my chronology (1966), in which radiocarbon dates have been revised through the use of the calibration curve proposed by R. M. Clark. In his table the radiocarbon dates are given in terms of the 5568 half-life but have been converted against a calibration curve based upon "radiocarbon dates expressed in terms of the revised half-life of 5730 years." See R. M. Clark, "A Calibration Curve for Radiocarbon Dates," *Antiquity* 49 (1975), 251-66.

4. Some archaeologists see a similarity between Minyan and Hissar II pottery shapes which points to even wider connections.

5. It has long been realized that a single region such as Bohemia could be occupied by cultures at the same time as different as the Rivnáč and the Corded Ware cultures because their differing economies made possible the occupation of differing ecological niches. See R. W. Ehrich, "Some Comments on the Rivnáč Complex with Reference to the Site of Homolka," *L'Europe à la fin de l'âge de la pierre,* ed. by J. Böhm and S. J. De Laet, 349-52. Prague: Editions de l'Académie tchécoslovaque des sciences, 1961.

WAS THERE AN INDO-EUROPEAN ART?

S. M. Alexander
University of Texas at Austin

The tomb of Childeric, king of the Franks, A.D. 458-481, discovered at Tournai, displayed a wealth of ornate weapons, buckles, jewelry, and other items common to notable burials for millennia. The king's purple robe was sewn with numerous gold ornaments in the shape of winged insects, and a purse containing 100 gold coins was buried with him (Figure 1a, p. 88). Several items are less usual for the period, however, and are therefore of special interest: the gold ornament in the shape of a bull's head with a rosette on the forehead; the skull of a horse; and the skeleton of a groom who had been buried with the king.

Human and animal sacrifice are not unknown in the Migrations Period in Europe, and horse burial is relatively common. But these customs were evidently of much earlier origin, recalling third millennium B.C. rituals at Alaça Hüyük in Anatolia and Maikop in the North Caucasus. In these burials animal heads and human sacrifice, purses, and gold-appliquéd garments were also found. The association of these burials, according to one theory, is with the early stages of development of the Indo-Europeans. The coincidence of type of grave goods between Merovingian Gaul and early Anatolia raises the questions whether an early Indo-European element survived in various geographical areas until the coming of Christianity, and whether Indo-European art was part of that element.

Stylistically there can have been an Indo-European art only at the period of a hypothetical Indo-European unity, i.e., one people, the original Indo-Europeans, producing an art with a recognizable style. If, however, the Indo-Europeans cannot, at so early a stage in their development, be visualized archaeologically as a single uniform culture (Mallory 1976:261), then similarly, the identification of an early Indo-European artistic style becomes an impossibility. For this reason, and others which will become clear later, I propose, for the purposes of this paper, to limit the definition of the word "art" to iconography, i.e., the representation of subject matter, whether naturalistically or symbolically rendered. Iconography changes

Figure 1a: Winged insect from
Childeric's tomb (after Chifflet
1955); not to scale

Figure 1b: Winged bead from Catacomb
grave at Konstantinovka (after Gimbutas
1956:Figure 50)

Figure 1c: Breast bead from Paleolithic levels at
Dolni Vestonice (after Marshack 1972:Figure 164)

less than style in visual art, and can frequently be traced through a sequence of manifestations to an original source.

Thus, the usual archaeological material (very fully treated in the archaeological literature), such as pottery and tool types, which enables the archaeologist to suggest dates and directions of influence, and which under other circumstances might be considered "art," will not be used as evidence in this paper unless it also possesses a viable iconography.

Gimbutas has identified three or four phases of Indo-European development and migration which form a convenient chronological framework on which to base this inquiry into Indo-European artistic expression (Gimbutas 1970:177-90; 1977: 277). Within this framework, the earliest archaeologically identifiable culture associated with the Indo-Europeans is that of several closely related groups living in south Russia between the Dnepr and the Urals in the fifth millennium B.C. Numerous excavations in the area have revealed a pastoral people (the Yamna or Pit Grave cultures) characterized by their custom of raising mounds over graves (Sulimirski 1970:127ff.). The mounds, or kurgans, have led to the adoption of the name of Kurgan culture for these people.

By the fifth millennium, notable artistic cultures had already come and gone in many places. Paleolithic art had been produced throughout Europe in the later stages of the Ice Age. In Anatolia, "art" is presented by the figurines, wall paintings, and plaster reliefs of Hacilar, Çatal Hüyük, and Beycesultan. Early Jericho has left us sculpture. Eastern Europe had already produced the remarkable monumental sculpture of Lepenski Vir and the painted pottery of the Starčevo levels of Yugoslavia. Pre-Sesklo and Sesklo sites in Greece have yielded pottery, figurines of animals, birds, and human females (Mellink and Filip 1974).

The fifth millennium itself was a productive period in the Balkans, with Vinča sculptures and Karanovo metalwork and pottery. Tepe Yahya in Iran has also produced some interesting fifth millennium sculpture. From Mesopotamia comes the Halaf and Samarra pottery and small sculpture, with related painted pottery and figurines from Can Hasan in Anatolia (Mellaart 1975). By contrast, the early Kurgan culture of south Russia, in the Kurgan 1 phase, has struck its excavators as being consistently poor and undeveloped, yielding a little pottery, a few copper and shell beads, bone ornaments, tools in stone and copper (Mallory 1976; Sulimirski 1970:127). A zoomorphic stone shape, the Kujbyshev scepter, was a chance find assigned to this period (Figure 2, p. 90) (cf. Gimbutas 1977:Figures 4 and 5).

Closely associated and perhaps identical with Kurgan 1 is the culture represented in numerous sites and called after the type site of Serednij Stog 2 in the area of the lower Dnepr-Don. This early Copper Age mixed culture appears to mark the beginning of the westward expansion of the Kurgan people (Kurgan 2 phase) into the Pontic steppe—an infiltration which gradually became dominant over the

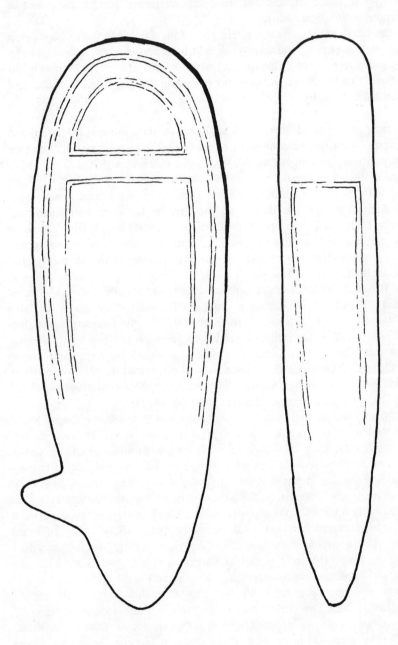

Figure 2: The Kujbyshev "Scepter." Actual size.
(After Gimbutas 1977: Figure 5(1))

indigenous culture without eliminating it (Gimbutas 1970:178-79). The Kurgan graves are again poorly equipped, more than half of them being without offerings at all. The mixed nature of the population is shown by the absence of the characteristic mound over the burials, so that identification relies on other features of the Kurgan groups.

Finds where present include tools (flint knives, scrapers, bone awls), weapons (arrowheads, stone battle-axes), ornaments (copper bracelets, pendants, neck ornaments made of animal teeth, shell, or boar tusk), pottery (pointed base, decorated with furrows and cord-impressed patterns), and a small clay figure of a boar from Dereivka (lower Dnepr), second half of the fifth millennium (Figure 3, p. 92).

There is evidence for a further infiltration of Kurgan 2 cultural traits in the late fifth millennium into the Ukraine, parts of the Balkans, and the north Caucasus. The sites are transitional Neolithic-Early Bronze Age, and bear the Kurgan hallmark of minimal equipment.

A few notable exceptions occur. At Decia Muresului in Transylvania, tumulus graves had stones set up around the skeleton, a custom of venerable ancestry. The finds included flint weapons, copper shaft-hole axes, and, more interesting from our point of view, a stone mace-head with four spherical faces (Figure 4b, p. 93) (Gimbutas 1977:328).

The double grave at Suvorovo in the Danube delta was surrounded by a circle of stones, 13 m in diameter. The woman who accompanied the male occupant of the grave wore a garment to which mother-of-pearl plaques were attached. A stone zoomorphic "scepter," similar to that from Kujbyshev, was also found in this grave (Gimbutas 1977:285). The site of Nal'chik in the northern Caucasus presents the familiar tools (flint and obsidian knives and scrapers), arrowheads, ornaments (bracelets of bone or stone, or boar tusk; beads of shell, stone, or animal teeth), and a highly stylized female figurine (Gimbutas 1956:53; Mongait 1961:104).

These early phases represent the Kurgan 1 and 2 cultures, united under the earliest of the westward movements postulated for the latter half of the fifth millennium B.C. The archaeological record shows a relatively poor culture whose grave goods reveal little about the people. Although we cannot know what was produced by way of objects of perishable materials such as wood, leather, or textile, the impression we get of people uninclined to express themselves in a visual way is probably correct, as it is borne out by the later phases of their activity also.

The few objects singled out above are important for future developments. The mace-head from Decia Muresului, with symmetrically arranged convex surfaces, appears in the third millennium at Alaça Hüyük, dealt with later in this paper, and later again, still with Indo-European connections, in the similarly sphered and decorated stone balls from Scotland, which may date from the Bronze Age. However,

Figure 3: Clay boar figurine from Dereivka
(After Gimbutas 1970:Figure 17)

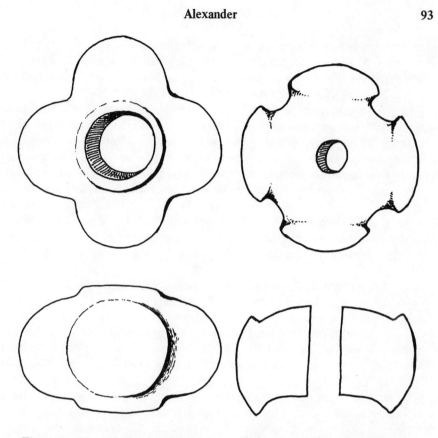

Figure 4a: Mace-head from Mariupol.
Not to scale. (After Gimbutas 1956:
Figure 22e)

Figure 4b: Mace-head from Decia
Muresului. Not to scale. (After
Gimbutas 1977:Figure 20(2))

Figure 4c: Mace-head from Alaça Hüyük. Actual size. Gold.
(After Akurgal, *The Art of the Hittites*, pl. 20)

such mace-heads were not an independent invention of the Kurgan people. They were made during the Neolithic period. Precisely the same four-knobbed type, although different in profile, comes from the Neolithic cemetery of Mariupol on the Sea of Azov (Figure 4a, p. 93) (Gimbutas 1956:48).

The stone zoomorphic "scepters"—it has taken some time for archaeologists to agree that they represent sculptured heads of horses—are among the few items originating in the early Kurgan period which may be identified as art objects. Ranging from approximately 15 cm to 25 cm in length, they are for the most part made of hard stone. The muzzle, quite unlike that of a horse in most of the dozen or so examples known to date, has led to identification as boars, hippopotami, or dogs. They have been found from the west Caspian and Caucasus region to the Balkans, and all are closely related in general shape and size. Their eastern origin, with a westward movement through trade or the migrations of the Kurgan people, has been suggested by various authors (Dumitrescu 1957:89ff.; Berciu 1962: 397-409).

These horse-heads recall the experimentation with flat carved bone horse-heads of the Middle Magdalenian sculptors of late Paleolithic France. The Paleolithic examples are mostly small and highly naturalistic, in contrast to the extreme stylization of the later "scepters." They must also be associated with the contemporary burials of actual horse-heads, as found at Zolotaya Balka (Kherson), Odessa, and Dereivka on the Dnepr, indicating a special cult of the horse (Gimbutas 1977:286).

The same may be postulated for the clay figure of a boar, seen against the frequent occurrence of boar tusk ornaments and armlets, and the placing of boar mandibles in later graves. Comparison might be made with the earlier animal figurines from Mariupol. The custom of burial with boar mandibles goes back to the Neanderthal period at Mugharet-es-Skhul, Mount Carmel (Clark 1967:Figure 22).

The grave at Suvorovo is an early example of the application of expensive materials—here, mother-of-pearl—to decorate or otherwise elaborate the garments of important people, worn perhaps only in the grave. This practice also occurs in the Mariupol cemetery, where boar tusk plaques were sewn on grave garments.

Several rich graves from Stepanakert in the Kura-Araxes valley (Azerbaijan) are considered to be of Kurgan type by the mid-fourth millennium B.C. (Gimbutas 1973:177). The evidence indicates human sacrifice on a large scale—Barrow 119, for example, had thirty-six human skeletons who may have been sacrificial victims. Rich gifts accompanied the dead—bronze and stone weapons, a gold hair ring (Figure 5a, p. 95), and obsidian blades. A stone mace-head was of simple circular form. The ritual of human sacrifice in these graves (if such it is) bears a striking resemblance to that of the much later Royal Cemetery at Ur. Moreover, the gold hair ring from Stepanakert Barrow 125 is precisely the same as type 2 gold "earrings" from the Royal Cemetery (Figure 5b, p. 95), dated to the later third mil-

Figure 5a: Hair ring from Stepanakert. Actual size.
(After Gimbutas 1973:Figure 13(4))

Figure 5b: Earring (?) from Ur. Not to scale.
(After Woolley 1934:Plate 219)

lennium B.C. The resemblance between the finds from Sumer and those from the Caucasus region has frequently been noted. The Caucasus area as the origin of Sumerian metalwork was postulated at the time of the excavation of the Ur material (Frankfort 1928), a viewpoint probably supported by Woolley himself at that time (Woolley 1928:447).

The Kurgan 3 period, second half of the fourth millennium B.C., saw a more impressive influx of eastern ideas and influences into eastern Europe. That this is due to the arrival of a new people rather than the simple diffusion of ideas postulated by some authors (Tringham 1971:205) is suggested by the abandonment of several sites in eastern Europe, the fortification of others, and the nonselective appearance of Kurgan characteristics. The horse and wheeled vehicles make their appearance in Europe at this time (Piggott 1960:285-94; 1965:95).

Not all sites were deserted (Coles and Harding 1979:134). Among those which continued in use was Ezero (Tell Dipsis) in Bulgaria with nine Bronze Age levels representing the same culture. Mace-heads and tools of stone (adzes, axes, sickle blades) and bone (hammers, hoes, needles) and the pottery of the indigenous population continued to be produced. A new type of pot, evidently contributed by the newcomers, had a pointed base and crosshatched decoration with cord ornament. Pottery figurines of animals were found, as well as spindle whorls and models of battle-axes and wheels (Georgiev and Merpert 1966:33-37).

A contemporary culture, the Gorodsk-Usatovo of the western Ukraine, is best represented by the type site of Usatovo on the Black Sea coast. The culture is a mixture of Tripolje and Kurgan elements, transitional from Copper to Bronze Age. The wealthy dead were buried under large tumuli, with central shaft graves quite richly furnished. Lesser graves were shallow pits covered by flat slabs, and rather poorly furnished. Both copper and bronze tools and weapons occur—chisels, awls, knives, daggers, flat axes. Silver was used for hair rings and as plating for daggers. A small percentage of the pottery was black-painted Tripolje ware, the rest being unpainted pottery with impressed decoration. Clay figurines were found in some graves, but are unrecognizable as human forms. One of the most impressive of the tumuli, Usatovo Grave Mound 3, was surrounded by a circle of vertical stone slabs. One slab was roughly incised with a man and animals, the identification of which has proved difficult, and remains inconclusive. A silver-plated bronze dagger lay beside the left hand of the body. Human sacrifice was in evidence; the skeletons wore animal-tooth necklaces, copper diadems, and boar-tooth ornaments (Childe 1925:144-47; Sulimirski 1970:182-84).

The third millennium, or Kurgan 4 phase, is seen as progress of the Kurgan culture within the steppe area, and as intensified emigration from the steppe into eastern and central Europe, the Caucasus, Anatolia, and elsewhere. In the steppe, between the Dnepr and the Lower Volga, the new phase is called the Catacomb culture, made up of tribes having a common basis, with local variations. New customs are in evidence, such as skull deformation, but most authors see the Catacomb culture as a development from earlier phases in the region, the new practices indicating stratification of society rather than an influx of new people (Childe 1925:154-56; Gimbutas 1956:80; Coles and Harding 1979:124-29, etc.).

Some graves were considerably richer than others, but burials without offerings were common. In general the finds are little different from those in earlier Kurgan graves. Much of what appears to be exotic, such as weapon heads of semiprecious stone, carnelian and faience beads, are seen by Sulimirski as imports from elsewhere (Sulimirski 1970:122). Characteristic objects are weapons (heeled battle-axes, mace-heads, battle-axes of semiprecious stone, copper daggers); bone tools; silver hair rings and earrings; beads made of mother-of-pearl, faience, carnelian, bone, copper—including winged shapes (Figure 1b, p. 88); copper rings and bracelets, stone arm rings. Pottery was cord-impressed or with spiral patterns, concentric circles and semicircles, as well as zigzags. Cruciform-footed lamps were characteristic of the Catacomb culture. Fragments of woolen cloth were found, with red and black stripes.

Beyond the steppes in the Caucasus region, Kurgan elements are seen in the well-known graves of Maikop and Novosvobodnaya. The Maikop tumulus, 10.65 m high, was surrounded by a circle of stones. Inside was a wooden funerary structure divided into three separate rooms, communicating with each other by means of round holes cut through the walls. The main skeleton, that of a man, was in the largest compartment, richly equipped. The other two compartments housed a male and female skeleton, respectively. The chief skeleton was covered with gold foil ornaments of bulls, lions, and rings, which had originally been sewn onto a garment or a canopy. Probably the person had worn a headdress decorated with gold rosettes and turquoise, lapis (Childe 1925:151), and carnelian beads, some of them fluted. A canopy had been supported on six gold and silver rods, with ribbons attached to the upper ends. Four of the rods passed through the bodies of solid cast gold and silver oxen, pierced for the purpose (Figure 6a, p. 98). Seventeen gold and silver vessels, and eight clay pots, were placed in the tomb. Two of the silver vessels were engraved with scenes. Weapons of copper and polished stone completed the offerings—axes, adze-axes, blades, knives, chisels, and a sickle-shaped whetstone (Rostovtzeff 1922:19; Frankfort 1956:113; Gimbutas 1956:58; Childe 1925:151; Sulimirski 1970:116).

At Novosvobodnaya, perhaps contemporary (Rostovtzeff) or slightly later than Maikop (Gimbutas), two tumuli were excavated, each about 10 m high. The funerary structures inside were of stone, with stone roofs, called "megalithic cists" by Childe, and compared with the contemporary dolmens of the area by Rostovtzeff

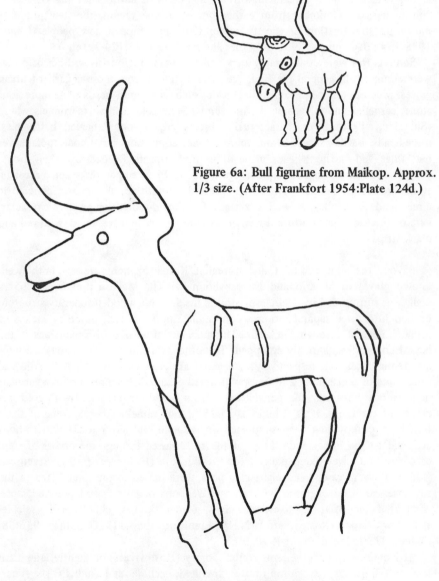

Figure 6a: Bull figurine from Maikop. Approx. 1/3 size. (After Frankfort 1954:Plate 124d.)

Figure 6b: Stag from Alaça Hüyük. Approx. 1/3 size.

(1922:21). One tomb was surrounded by a circle of upright slabs. Each stone structure was divided into two compartments, one for the body and one for the grave furniture. The bodies were covered with red ocher, as were the walls of one room and some of the grave goods. In addition to copper tools and weapons, and a trident ornamented with human figures, the one undisturbed tomb yielded simple gold earrings, plain gold and silver pins, beads, and pendants; and carnelian beads. Related finds come from Staromyshastovskaya in the Kuban valley, to the northwest of Maikop. Here a silver vessel with a lid, comparable in shape to the engraved Maikop examples, contained a silver bull (Rostovtzeff) or goat (Gimbutas) (illustrated Gimbutas 1956:Plate 11), a gold headband with rosettes, a gold lion head from a necklace, gold earrings, and hundreds of gold, silver, and carnelian beads.

Somewhat related to the Caucasus group of tombs are the thirteen early Bronze Age burials at Alaça Hüyük, as well as related finds from Horoztepe and other sites in Anatolia. The similarities with steppe practices which associate them with the Kurgan 4 phase lie in the structure of the tomb and the burial ritual. The tomb pits are rectangular, lined with stone or wood, roofed with timber covered with clay, the whole under a tumulus; head, hoofs, and hides of sacrificed oxen were arranged on the roof of the tomb; inside were hammerhead pins, battle-axes, and wooden funerary carts with solid wheels (Piggott 1962:112).

Important differences from the Kurgan culture are the evident lack of knowledge of the horse in Anatolia (compared with its introduction, perhaps by Kurgan people, into Europe in the Kurgan 3 phase) and the appearance of rich art objects. Finds include iron daggers, bronze spears and battle-axes, mace-heads in stone and metal (Figure 4c, p. 93), gold vessels with chevron designs and concentric circles, small metal female figurines three to four inches high, jewelry (diadems, pins, beads), and above all, the pole tops or standards in the shape of bulls and stags made of copper and overlaid and inlaid with gold and silver or shaped as openwork "sundisks" with rays and swastikas (Figure 6b, p. 98).

Sitagroi in Macedonia may also date from this period. Level 5b produced cord-impressed pottery and a schist battle-ax incised and carved at one end with a feline head (Figure 7, p. 100) (Renfrew 1970:Plates 19b and c; Renfrew 1971).

The above tombs from the Caucasus and Anatolia are by far the richest of all those associated with the Kurgan 4 expansion. The many other sites, enumerated by Gimbutas in various parts of Europe, Iran, Russia, and elsewhere as possibly of Kurgan type, continue the rather poor graves, with a notable lack of "art" objects.

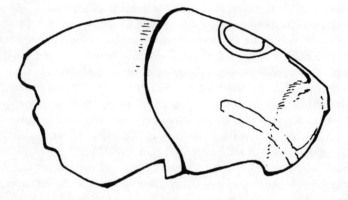

Figure 7: Feline head from Sitagroi. Actual size.
(After Renfrew 1970:Plates 19b and c)

This situation naturally causes one to cast a suspicious eye on the extraordinary tombs from Maikop and Alaça Hüyük. Their wealth of precious metals and variety of objects, and their relationship to the migrating peoples of the Kurgan culture, have engaged the attention of archaeologists for a long time.

Frankfort believed that the engraved silver vessels from Maikop are closely related, both technically and iconographically, to comparable work in Mesopotamia. The silver vase of Entemena from Lagash, for example, dated the early third millennium, is engraved with symbolic animals repeated on four sides. Motifs on the Maikop vessels have parallels in the third millennium steatite bowls from the Diyala region of Mesopotamia. Frankfort, however, considered that the landscape features of mountains, trees, and river shown on the vessels were non-Mesopotamian features, and might have been a local contribution. Thus, he evidently considered them to be of local manufacture under Mesopotamian influence. In connection with these elements, one might recall that the earliest landscape painting so far recorded came from Çatal Hüyük in Central Anatolia (Mellaart 1967: 176). The spotted leopard on one of the Maikop vessels recalls the same animal in painted plaster at Çatal Hüyük.

The bulls supporting the canopy may also be considered as having strong Mesopotamian connections, where small-scale cast bull heads and larger-scale hammered bulls are of frequent occurrence, perhaps more naturalistically rendered than those from Maikop. The profile bull, with one visible horn, on one of the vessels and as one of the gold figurines from the canopy, is likewise a Mesopotamian characteristic.

Beads in gold, lapis, and carnelian are typically Mesopotamian, as are also the fluted shapes. The winged copper beads from Konstantinovka may be related to the Royal Cemetery gold and lapis amulets and pendants described as "flies" by Woolley, but not illustrated (U 10801, 12085, 12127, etc.) (Woolley 1934). Childe considered that the transverse and straight axes from Maikop were directly derived from Sumerian types (Childe 1936).

The gold and silver bulls from Maikop have been compared to the copper bulls of Alaça Hüyük, with their long, curved horns and stylized, elongated muzzles. Both were intended to be supported on or pierced by rods for purposes associated with the funerary ritual. Technically, however, and—in my opinion, stylistically— they are quite different. The application of gold foil to the muzzles and parts of the body of the Alaça Hüyük bulls and stags, and the inlaying of electrum or silver in concentric circles and zigzags on the bodies—the same patterns as on the metal vessels from Alaça Hüyük, and on the Catacomb culture pottery—are unique features of Anatolian work.

The feline head from Sitagroi recalls, both in style and function, the horse-head "scepters" of the Kurgan 2 period. The same stylization and simplicity of form is found in both.

Viewing the above material, which extends over the 1600 years of the proposed Kurgan expansion, as a whole, there is little to suggest a common ancestry such as one would expect if there were an established Kurgan (i.e., Indo-European) tradition of art. It is impossible in any case to come to any firm conclusions on so slight an amount of evidence. The very sparseness of finds of artistic intent from areas of Kurgan domination throws the Maikop culture finds and those from Alaça Hüyük into sharp and ambiguous relief. The Maikop (N. Caucasus) and Alaça Hüyük (Anatolia) objects belong to two entirely different traditions, even though they have a few features in common. The main similarities are the significance afforded the bull (which is widespread all over the ancient world), the use of animal forms in a funerary context, and the manufacture of art objects in metal. The differences are stylistic, iconographic, and technical. Maikop art objects—gold ornaments attached to garments, gold diadem of rosettes and beads, gold and silver bull figurines, engraved metal vessels, earrings made of interlocking rings— are largely associated with Mesopotamia, or a source shared also by the Sumerians, as demonstrated earlier in the discussion of the material.

The Alaça Hüyük work, on the other hand—copper animal figures, sun disks, etc., gold vessels with chevron and concentric circular designs worked in repoussé, female figurines, openwork diadems, gold necklaces, pins, and other ornaments— has few affinities with Mesopotamia or any other known contemporary or earlier work, including Troy. It is to be noted also that the conflagration layer associated with the arrival of a new people spreading destruction in many parts of Asia Minor and the Near East covers the Alaça Hüyük tombs (Mellink 1966:11). Presumably, then, the art objects were already buried by the time the invaders destroyed the sites. The logical conclusion, for want of other evidence, is to consider the Alaça Hüyük finds as native Anatolian work, made before the influx of Kurgan 4 people. It has been noted on p. 91 that Kurgan influence or infiltration had reached the Caucasus with Kurgan 2 movements. It is not difficult, therefore, to visualize a diffusion of Kurgan tomb-building methods and rituals, rather than a Kurgan occupation of parts of Anatolia, to account for their appearance in the more easterly parts of Anatolia by the third millennium. The Kurgan elements visible at Alaça Hüyük need not have been contemporary with the Kurgan 4 expansion.

The evidence of the Kurgan tombs has far wider implications than the fact that the fifth to the third millennia was a period of artistic quiescence.

Some of the rituals, notably the burial of boar mandibles and the forelegs of animals in the grave of the deceased, are survivals from the Mousterian (Neanderthal) period of about 40,000 years ago (boar mandibles from Mount Carmel, forelegs of bison from Corrèze in France). The same is true of the small hillocks or small-scale kurgans over the graves—such as were found at La Ferrassie in Mousterian levels, where the body was placed just below the surface of the mound rather than dug into the earth below it (D. Peyrony, La Ferrassie, *Préhistoire* 3, 1934).

In his discussion of the custom of offering an animal's head, forelegs, and hide, as at Alaça Hüyük, Piggott (1962:110) suggests that "the roots of this tradition may well strike back to the Final Palaeolithic," but does not substantiate his assumption. The Upper Paleolithic engraved bone from Raymonden in the Dordogne shows the detached head and forelegs of a bison, and its skeletal spine, the body presumably having been eaten by the bystanders shown on each side of the spine (illustrated in Marshack 1972:207). One might also cite the roughly modeled clay animal body from Montespan (N. Pyrenees) thought to have been made to support an actual bear pelt and head for use during "hunting magic" ceremonies (Giedion 1962:182).

Numerous other coincidences of custom between Mousterian and Upper Paleolithic practices and those of the Kurgan cultures may be cited, suggesting that the chief role of the Kurgan peoples up to the third millennium B.C. was as preservers of traditions, rather than as innovators in the arts.

As Neanderthal man and Upper Paleolithic man after him have left remains extending from the Atlantic in the west, across the Pontic steppe to the Caspian and beyond, there is nothing impossible in proposing that customs found at La Ferrassie or elsewhere in France should have been practiced also in south Russia. The findspots of the Gravettian female figurines, from France to Siberia, are proof of the widespread appearance of common cultural traits during the Ice Age. From the evidence, it seems feasible that the Paleolithic art of south Russia is an early expression of the people who were later to form the Kurgan culture.

I have intentionally omitted from this study the stelae and motifs on pottery and metal vessels (concentric circles, chevron patterns, etc.). They are so widespread as to preclude a distinct Kurgan association and require research beyond the scope of this paper.

And what of Childeric as the descendant of the Kurgan warriors of the fifth and fourth millennia? The animal and human sacrifices in Childeric's tomb could be survivals of Kurgan practices, but the art has its origins in a later period. I would like to see the "winged beads" of Kurgan graves at Konstantinovka and elsewhere as the predecessors of Childeric's winged insect ornaments. However, even these are not a Kurgan feature; they are widespread in Neolithic Europe, and appear in Natufian levels at Mount Carmel, and are probably derived from the "breast" beads of Paleolithic central Europe (Figure 1c, p. 88) (Marshack 1972:291). Thus, Childeric's insects may be related to the "flies" from Sumer and Egypt, conceivably themselves a variant of the original breast bead.

ASPECTS OF INDO-EUROPEAN POETICS

Calvert Watkins
Harvard University

Indo-European poetics[1] goes back to a passing observation by Adalbert Kuhn, in an article on the nasal presents which appeared in 1863, in Volume 2 of the *Zeitschrift* which still bears his name (Kuhn 1853:467). Kuhn's innovation was a simple one: instead of making an etymological equation of two lexemes from cognate languages, he equated two bipartite NPs: Homeric Greek *kléos áphthiton* and Rig-Vedic Sanskrit *śráva*(s) . . . *ákṣitam,* both meaning 'imperishable fame'. The equation of the individual constituents was and is self-evident; what was new was the conclusion that the whole NP is an inheritance in both languages and represents a formulaic phrase of Indo-European antiquity, a feature of Indo-European poetic language, independently preserved in two traditions widely separated in space and time. Kuhn's claim has stood the test of time. Not only have articles, chapters, and whole books been devoted to the examination and analysis of the formula "imperishable fame," but many other such formulaic phrases of probable or possible Indo-European antiquity have subsequently been adduced by scholars; the terrain remains anything but exhausted, and there is a vast body of texts still to be explored and reexamined.

The middle of the nineteenth century also saw the halting beginnings of a comparative Indo-European metrics, with Westphal in 1860; it remained for Meillet in 1923 to put the equation of Vedic Sanskrit and Greek lyric meters on a firm foundation, and other scholars (myself included) have since with greater or lesser success adduced the evidence of virtually all the other metrical traditions in the Indo-European world (see West 1973). It is even possible to combine metrics and phraseology, and to argue for a genetic relation of the metrical contexts of the formula "imperishable fame" in Greek and Vedic, as suggested by this author in 1969 and investigated in detail by Nagy (1974a). It has been justly cautioned, by Kuryłowicz (1975, 1976), and most recently by Wolfgang Meid (1978), that the hierarchical dependence of metrical form on phonological and phonetic form makes actual reconstruction of metrics an unrealistic goal; in my opinion, we should content ourselves with the observation of certain recurrent similarities which are consistent with the hypothesis of a common prototype, without seeking to define that prototype in too narrow a fashion.

It should be emphasized from the outset that the concept and nature of Indo-European poetic language cannot be separated from that of the society in which it operated. On the diachronic as well as the synchronic plane, we require a holistic model of language as a social fact, of language and culture, language and society, language and pragmatics. Only on this basis can we understand, for example, the vocabulary-designating poetry and poets in the various historical languages. Indo-European tribal society was dominated by the Maussian principle of reciprocity and exchange or potlatch, of the gift entailing the counter-gift. The poet did not function in that society in isolation; he had a patron, and the two were precisely in an exchange or reciprocity relation. The poet gives poems to the patron, who in turn bestows largesse upon the poet. This relation was a moral and ideological necessity; only the poet could confer on the patron what he and his culture valued more highly than life itself: precisely what is expressed by the "imperishable fame" formula. A number of Indo-European lexemes express this reciprocal, circulatory relation by focusing on either facet of a unitary process; the root *dō- (*deh₃-) means 'give' in most languages but 'take' in Hittite; German *nehmen* is 'take' but Greek *nemō* is 'give, apportion'; English 'give' is cognate with Irish *gaibid* 'takes'; and so on. The general notions of the semantics of the root *dap*-group themselves around the idea of gift-giving, and of generosity to the point of destruction of wealth, the *potlatch:* Latin *daps* 'sacred banquet offered to the gods', but *damnum* (from *dapnom*) 'damage entailing liability'. The Irish cognate *dúan* (with identical suffix from *dapnā*) is the supreme gift of the poet; *dúan* is the unmarked word for 'poem' in Irish. Just so in Irish the word for 'poetry' is *dán*, the cognate of Indic *dānam*, Latin *dōnum* 'gift': the title of Marcel Mauss's classic work on the total system of reciprocity is *Essai sur le don.*

The same reciprocity relation as between poet and patron existed between the poet and the gods. We have the same eulogistic model: a good hymn of praise, the gift of the poet to the god, then *obligates* that deity to bestow as counter-gift that which is prayed for: prosperity, fruitfulness, long life. Poetry was not a "frill" in Indo-European society, but a necessity of life, a necessary condition for existence. The spoken word, properly formulated, could produce a physical effect on the world. This is the truth-formulation of India and Iran, the solemn pronouncement of a Truth (Ved. *ṛtá, satyá*), the ruler's *dīkē* in Greece, the ruler's *fír* in Ireland, which assures the prosperity of his tribe.

The study of Indo-European poetics thus presents two aspects: the functional and the formal. The first, with which we have begun, concerns the social function of poetry and the poet: his *purpose.* The question is: what for? The second, formal aspect, to which we will come later, concerns the poet's *technique.* The question is: how? Both must be looked at together, complementarily. For the art of the Indo-European poet is precisely to say something in a new and interesting, but therefore *more effective* way. It is verbal activity, artistically elaborated, but directed toward a more or less immediate, concrete goal.

One of the poetic self-designations of the Indo-European poet was the formulaic kenning 'craftsman of the word': Gk. *epéōn téktones* and related phrases in Indo-Iranian, Germanic, and Celtic. The poet is a professional, as emphasized by Enrico Campanile in his very good, recent *Studies in Indo-European Poetic Culture* (1977); his title is programmatic for the approach I have also advocated. The poet is a professional, and the poet is worthy of his hire. Aeschylus can call an unwanted fear (*Agamemnon* 979) *akéleustos ámisthos aoidá,* an 'uncommissioned, unrewarded song'; see below for Old Irish *cerd cen tothacht.* The Indo-European poet was without doubt the highest paid professional in his society. The *dānastuti*s or 'praises of the gift' of the patron to the poet incorporated in the hymns of the *Rig-Veda*—the same traditional genre recurs in Irish poetry—regularly record such rewards (or fees) as 200 cows, 4 horses, and 2 wagons (e.g., RV 7.18). The poet of the long *dānastuti* in RV 8.46.21-33 calls himself Vaśa, son of Aśva *(Vāśa Aśvyáḥ):* obviously a speaking name (which recurs in RV 1.112.10), literally, 'Desire of Horse'. He evidently got more than his wish; if the reward of 60,000 geldings is a fanciful poetic exaggeration, the reward of 'this great bedizened maiden' *(syā́ yóṣanā mahī́ . . . ádhirukmā)* probably is not.

What was the ideological base for this extraordinarily high valuation accorded the poet by society, which we can observe from India to Ireland? Campanile expresses it (1977:32), after a lengthy survey of the figure and function of the traditional poet in Celtic and Indic society, simply and well: The poet "is the preserver and the professional of the spoken word. It is he who is by definition competent in all the areas where the word is, or is considered, operative." This must be understood as a very concrete, practical notion. Those areas where the traditional spoken word is operative, indeed mandatory, impinge upon virtually the totality of the culture. For a selective yet still wide-ranging picture of that culture, I refer globally to Benveniste (1969), which despite its faults is still perhaps the finest ethnosemantic description of a culture yet written.

It is no accident that the vast majority of our earliest Indo-European texts, those valued and preserved in their own cultures as a testimony of the tradition, are ritual or poetic or both. The new "hardliners" of Indo-European studies must realize, as they often do not, the importance and indeed necessity of poetics, both synchronic and diachronic, as a technique in philological and linguistic analysis. We do not talk about Indo-European poetics because of a tender-minded interest in "lit'rature," but because as historical linguists we want to go beyond basic things like sound-correspondences, and try to understand the underlying semantic and semiotic systems of a reconstructed language and culture, as it can be inferred from the evidence of documented texts.

Consider an illustration from the rather mundane area of etymology, the historical linguist's daily bread. Before examining the data, let me introduce some technical terms and concepts which I take from Roman Jakobson (1971:241-59). All of these may be presented in the classic linguistic model of the intersecting axes, vertical and horizontal:

For Jakobson, in conformity with his view of the twofold character of language, every speech act involves two processes: *selection,* and *combination.* Elements are selected from the vertical, *paradigmatic* axis, and combined on the horizontal, *syntagmatic* axis. The vertical is the axis of *simultaneity;* the horizontal, the axis of *successivity.* Elements on the vertical axis are in a relation of *similarity;* on the horizontal axis they are in a relation of *contiguity.* Finally, and of central importance for poetics: the vertical, paradigmatic axis of similarity relation is the basis of *metaphor* (the figure in "ship of state," "wagon of life," etc.). On the other hand, the horizontal, syntagmatic axis of contiguity relation is the basis of *metonymy* (the figure in "the spear and the distaff," "the pen is mightier than the sword," etc.).

Let us turn to the problem of etymology. Early Irish has a word *cerd,* meaning both 'craft' and 'poetry', both 'craftsman' and 'poet'. Early Welsh has the same word *cerdd,* meaning both 'craft' and 'poetry, poem'. In their synchronic semantics the two meanings of these Celtic words, 'craft' and 'poetry', exhibit a *metaphoric, similarity* relation: poetry is like a craft, and the poet like a craftsman. But now consider an actual utterance on the syntagmatic axis of combination: the Old Irish legal phrase *cerd cen tothacht* (Binchy 1979:1529.33), *cerd gan bunadus tothachta* (CIH 2219.30) 'poet without (a basis of) substance', or *beirid(h) lecerd leth cerda* (CIH 2220.23) 'a *l.* provides half (the legal reward for?) poetic art'.[2] Between the two constituents of the formula, 'poet' and 'substance', we have a contiguity relation, a potential metonymy. And the same contiguity relation, as a real me-

tonymy projected back on the diachronic plane—reconstructed, if you will—
exists semantically between the Celtic words *cerd, cerdd* 'craft, poetry' and their
unique cognate, Greek *kérdos,* which means 'gain, profit'. The etymology is sure;
but it rests on a metonymic figure: *craft is profit.* We can prove the etymology only
by making explicit the poetic nature of the semantic relation between the cognates,
namely, metonymy, and in this particular case also by making explicit the cultural
and pragmatic context in which such a metonymy was meaningful.

The previous etymology rests on a metonymy: consider the case of Irish *saithe,*
Welsh *haed,* meaning 'a swarm (of bees and the like)'. The reconstructible preform
is **satio-,* which can be exactly equated with the base of Latin *satietas,* meaning
'satiety, sufficiency'. The etymology rests on a metaphor: a swarm of bees is like
a satiety of bees. And that metaphor has left its trace in the Homeric formula
melissáōn hadináōn 'bees in abundance, bees galore', where *hadinós* and *satiētas,*
etc., are derivatives of the same root. Again, we can prove the etymology only by
making explicit the poetic nature of the semantic relation between the cognates,
namely, metaphor.

Both etymologies—that involving the contiguity relation of metonymy and that
involving the similarity relation of metaphor—are cases of what we may term
applied diachronic poetics. And the moral is simply that linguistics needs poetics,
just as it needs pragmatics.

In these examples and in those to come, we can observe that the "output" of
the study of Indo-European poetics is the reconstruction not of a poetic text, but
of a tradition. As Campanile puts it, we cannot reconstruct Indo-European poetry,
but we can reconstruct much of the cultural and ideological ambience in which it
operated. Or put another way, as I have done on several occasions (Watkins 1976,
1978), we can reconstruct some of the things the Indo-Europeans talked about,
and some of the ways they talked about them in their traditional poetry, some
7000 years ago.

We pass now to the formal aspect of Indo-European poetics: the nature of the
poet's technique, the character of his poetic language, and of his poetic message.
In discussing these aspects we will of necessity move freely between the diachronic
and the synchronic, and between the genetic and the typological, much as Benveniste did for ethnosemantics in the *Vocabulary of Indo-European Institutions.*
Many characteristics of poetic language are widespread among the languages of
the world; some are universal. But we look for the way these features are articulated; it is the configuration and conjunction of these features, some universal
and some language-particular, which gives the characteristic flavor, the Indo-
European touch, the art of the Indo-European poet. To discuss poetics, even in the
most formal terms, necessitates a certain amount of subjectivity of judgment. I can
only point out that this is no different from many other aspects of philology and
text-based linguistics.

Indo-European poetic language may be thought of, rather grossly, as having a phonological component, where meaning per se and meaningful units are not in play. This includes in the first place metrics and other rhythmic features, which serve to organize, and very importantly, to demarcate the message. Compare the universal principle expressed by Jakobson (1979:241) that the essential mark of verse is that "equivalence is promoted to the constitutive device of the sequence." Indo-European verse was syllable counting: as Jakobson puts it, "If a syllable is treated as a pertinent constituent of a verse-line, then one syllable is equated with any other syllable of the same sequence, whereas speakers do not measure the number of syllables in their ordinary speech." The phonological component of Indo-European verse also includes various sound devices which we can refer to globally as "phonetic figures," such as alliteration and rhyme. Optional in Indo-European itself, alliteration, for example, is raised to the status of a virtually obligatory "constitutive device of the sequence" in some traditions, notably those which develop fixed initial or final stress like Germanic, Italic, and Celtic.

On a higher level this poetics has a morphological component, where grammatical meaning and grammatically meaningful units are or may be in play: this is the realm of what we can refer to globally as the "grammatical figure." Phonetic and grammatical figures share numerous properties. Here, again, "equivalence is promoted to the constitutive device of the sequence," whether that equivalence is of sound, of grammatical form (e.g., a particular suffix), or of grammatical meaning. All are indexical in function; they serve primarily to point to the message itself.

Such figures could be illustrated by the hundreds and thousands from archaic Indo-European texts. Their appeal is an enduring one, and they are continuously re-created. Paradoxically, perhaps, we may take as a prototypical Indo-European sequence or poetic formula the English cliché:

Last but not least

Here metrics, the mirror-image choriambic foot ($\stackrel{\prime}{-}\!\cdots\!\stackrel{\prime}{-}$), is combined with both the phonetic figure of alliteration and the grammatical figure of the superlatives: the whole in four syllables. Small wonder that this cliché, as modern stylistics would view it, is embarrassingly and enduringly popular; it appeals to a far older aesthetic, for it is cast in an Indo-European mold.

The principle that "equivalence is promoted to the constitutive device of the sequence" operates on higher levels, both of language and of the sequence of speech. Consider the stylistic device known as ring-composition, which is an extraordinarily widespread organizing device in the archaic Indo-European-speaking world, and not terribly common outside of it. Ring-composition is the beginning and the ending of a discourse or complex utterance higher than the sentence level, with the same or equivalent word, phrase, or even sound. Ring-composition is a signal of demarcation: a series of sentences is thereby symbolically transformed into a finite set, a closed text or text segment. The same function that is served in English by the indexical sign *amen* in the language of prayer, or the common formula "It is finished" in mythological narrative in many native languages of North America, is served in Indo-European by repetition, an equivalence-identity token.

Ring-composition is of enormous importance in oral literature for isolating unities within a larger discourse, as in the case of Greek epic. Like most poetic features, it is by no means confined to verse; in Vedic prose, for example, it may function virtually as punctuation, as an index of topical paragraph boundaries.

We may take some illustrations from Greek, outside of Homeric epic, where it has been most studied. Hesiod in the *Works and Days* (202ff.) says, "Now I will tell a fable for princes . . ." The fable begins:

hõd' írēx proséeipen aēdóna
'thus the hawk said to the nightingale'

and ends:

hòs éphat ōkupétēs írēx, tanusípteros órnis
'thus said the swiftly-flying hawk, the long-winged bird'

Here, the discourse is framed by the phonetic identities, *hõd'* and *hòs,* and the phrases with reversed word order, 'hawk said' and 'said hawk', the last simply expanded by the multiplication of epithets.

The second stasimon of Aeschylus's *Agamemnon,* which is an admonitory instruction for princes like the Hesiodic passage, and which is interlaced with Indo-European thematic elements and poetic figures, likewise contains a short beast fable. The strophe begins (717-19) with the verb:

éthrepsen de léontos ĩnin dómois . . . / . . . anḗr
'there reared a lion's cub in his house . . . a man'

and the antistrophe ends (735-36) with the same verb:

ek theoũ d'hiereús tis Á/tas dómois prosethréphthē
'by divine will a priest of Destruction for the house had been reared'

Note here that we have not only repetition of the verb in first and last position, but also a complete syntactic mirror image: the order of the first is Verb-Object-Subject; of the last, Subject-Passive Verb, transformationally equivalent to Subject-

Object-Verb. The real underlying subject of the last sentence is the 'god' of *ek theoũ*, in antithesis to the 'man' *(anḗr)* of the first. In the Aeschylean example, ring-composition is combined with the typical Indo-European syntactic figure of sentence-initial verb at the beginning of folktales and fables, in *cataphoric* function ('referring forward' as opposed to *anaphoric*, 'referring back'), as Wolfgang Dressler (1969) termed it in his important study of this text-syntactic rule of Indo-European word order. One need only compare the numerous Indo-European texts beginning 'There was a king . . .', Skt. *āsīd rājā*, OIr. *boí rí*, Lith. *bùvo karãlius*, Russ. *žil-byl korol'/car'*, Gk. *ẽske tis Kapheùs wanássōn*. Examples of ring-composition could be multiplied from many early Indo-European traditions. In Ireland, it had become a fixed requirement of many types of versification to end a poem with its first word. The Irish technical term is *dúnad*, literally, 'closing', and the image is that of closing a ring-fort, a circular rampart or enclosure, Irish *dún:* it is an image which could have been created millennia ago.

We have considered so far in our formal analysis only those features of Indo-European poetics in which lexical meaning is not pertinent; in which what *is* pertinent is equivalence. Above and beyond this level, Indo-European poetic language can be thought of, again somewhat grossly, as having a syntactic component and a semantic component. To the extent that these differ in kind from those of ordinary language, we will refer to the syntactic component as *formulaics*, and to the semantic component as *thematics*. Formulaics is in traditional oral literature the domain of the formula or repeated formulaic expression, a more or less "ready-made surface structure," to use Kiparsky's term (1976).

Modern concepts of traditional formulaic oral literature emphasize the notion of performer-audience interaction. In practice what this means is that the poet-performer has in his repertoire a large stock of formulas and formulaic expressions, noun phrases and verb phrases with highly conventionalized co-occurrence restrictions both endocentrically and exocentrically, which the poet-performer can presume to be shared by his audience. Formulaic poetry by its nature continually evokes associative chains, along the axes of successivity and simultaneity, of combination and selection. The poetic act of communication is at once a distillation and a complication of the rules governing speech acts of natural language.

I have elsewhere defined the formula in traditional oral literature as "the verbal and grammatical device for encoding and transmitting a given theme or interaction of themes, with the repetition or potential repetition assuring the long-term preservation of the surface structure, the wording." That is to say that *theme* is the deep structure of formula. Consider the by now familiar Indo-European formula 'imperishable fame' *kléos áphthiton*. We have a noun + adjective NP, which can even be reconstructed in its surface phonetic form; but at the same time we have other adjectives which can formulaically qualify 'fame', like 'great', 'lofty', 'broad', and other nouns which are formulaically qualified by 'imperishable', like 'seeds', 'vines'. In the network of all of these we can discern, very precisely, the nature of the *theme* of fame in Indo-European ideology.

In a certain sense—and this is critical for all early Indo-European literature—we can look upon such formulas as different realizations, different performances, if you will, of the same text. This text, synchronically, may be viewed as a sort of thematic "deep structure"; diachronically, it may be looked on as a "proto-text," defined primarily by the specification of a set of semantic—that is, thematic—features, and secondarily (though this aspect is a particularly favorable one for comparative purposes), by the actual verbal expression of these semantic and thematic features.

I mentioned at the outset that Indo-European poetics has from the beginning been concerned with formulaic phraseology. Yet the narrowly restricted search for possible cognate verbal formulas has led most researchers—the great exception is Emile Benveniste, as well as Campanile—to neglect their semantics. More broadly, what is neglected in the study of formulas—and this applies not only to linguists but to students of oral literature as well—is the function of these formulas as expressions of an underlying semiotic system. These poetic formulas in archaic societies are not repeated and remembered just because they delight the ear; they are *signals,* in poetic elaboration and as verbal art, of the relations of things: of the traditional conceptualizations, the perception of man and the universe, and the values and aspirations of the society (see Watkins 1979).

Once again, we must emphasize the social function of poetry and the poet-performer who has the privilege and the responsibility of being both custodian and transmitter of the ideology of that society as a total semiotic system. Campanile has articulated this functional aspect well in his discussion of the metaphoric Indo-European stylistic figure of formula known as the *kenning* (type 'horse of the sea' = 'ship', 'descendant of the waters' = 'fire'), though Campanile did not recognize that it applies equally to the totality of formulaic discourse. In Campanile's words, "the function of the kenning is to underline, from time to time, what reality or what obligation is concealed behind a name. It is a continuous bringing to light—that is, to the consciousness of the listeners [I add, by the poet-performer] of the proposition of a world which is articulated not in its actual factual relations, but which proceeds immutably in the furrow of a venerable tradition, of which the poet is custodian" (1979:113).

To grasp concretely this functional aspect of the poet as custodian of the tradition, which he articulates through the vehicle of the formula, let us let the Indo-European poet speak for himself.

Campanile assumes that secret or cryptic kennings are secondary developments of "descriptive" kennings, which are, or at any rate once were, readily intelligible metaphors. But this is to ignore the evidence from both India and Ireland that "knowledge of the secret names establishes the poet in his prerogative," as I had phrased it a dozen or so years ago (1967). Early Irish poetic metalanguage knows three oppositions:

gnáthberla : *senbérla*	ordinary language : old language
bérla Féine : *bérla na filed*	professional language : poetic language
bérla tóbaithe : *bérla fortchide*	fashioned language : hidden language

The most highly marked discourse in Irish is that which is at once archaic, poetic, and obscure. In the *Rig-Veda* (7.87.4), we find in a highly revealing self-reference by the poet:

Varuṇa said to me, the wise one:
"The cow bears thrice seven names.
He who knows the track should tell them like secrets,
if he wishes to serve as inspired poet to the later generation."

The Vedic poet is calling to mind the same set of oppositions between ordinary and poetic language as the Irish tradition. The poet is "old" to the later generation *(yugáya úparāya)*, with a clear didactic function of transmitting the tradition. The opposition between the simply *professional* and the specifically *poetic* appears in the figure of the poet who is *médhira* 'wise' before Varuṇa speaks to him, and becomes *vípra* 'inspired' after the intervention of the deity. And finally, this *archaic poetic* language is likewise *obscure*. The names of the cow are secret *(gúhyā)*, the 'word' *(padám)* is a secret word, hidden, a track to be found only by those who know through learning: RV 4.5.8cd *padám ná gór ápagūlham vividván* 'having found the hidden word like the track of the cow', /*agnír máhyam préd u vocan manīṣ́ám* 'Agni made known to me the understanding'.

For all that the poet attributes his knowledge to divine inspiration, he knows in practice that it had to be acquired by decades of laborious study. We know this as historical fact in early Ireland; observe that the same Vedic hymn continues (4.5.6):

idám me agne . . . gurúm bhǻram ná mánma . . . dadhātha
'you have placed on me, O Agni, this wisdom like a heavy burden'

For all that it confers privileged status, the poet's knowledge is a heavy responsibility to bear.

The similarity between the Irish and the Indic traditions suggests that we have to deal here with a genuine inheritance from an Indo-European poetic doctrine, an ideology of the nature of poetic language and its relation to ordinary language.

It is clear that this tradition placed an emphasis on secret linguistic knowledge, shared by poets—the full Middle Irish expression is *berla fortchide na filed triasa n-agallit cach dīb a chele* 'hidden language of the Poets through which each of them addresses his fellow'—and secret linguistic knowledge divulged to ordinary listeners on the proper occasion: *gúhyā ná vocad* 'he should tell them like secrets'.

A very profitable area to be explored in Indo-European studies and one very largely a task for the future is the verbal expression of the poet's view of himself, and of his craft. Studies of this in early Greek and Irish literature have been made and are being made, but primarily on the level of vocabulary alone; what remains outstanding is a systematic investigation of their formulaics. For Vedic, I call attention only to the following.

The collective plural of *mánma* 'wisdom, insight' designates 'poetry' itself in Vedic (RV 7.61.2ab):

> *prá vāṃ sá mitrāvaruṇāv ṛtā́vā*
> *vípro mánmāni dīrghaśrúd iyarti*
> 'for you, Mitra and Varuṇa, the inspired poet who possesses Truth
> sends forth his poetry, audibly from afar'

Note the epithet *ṛtā́van* 'possessing Truth', here as commonly in line-final position. The word occurs 77 times in the *Rig-Veda*. It is said to be an epithet of both gods and men (Grassmann, Lüders); in fact, it is a divine epithet 70 times, and of the remaining 7 times, 3 refer generically to mankind *(jána)* when performing the proper worship, but 4 specifically to the poet *(kaví, vípra)*. The poet has a special relation, a "pipeline," if you will, to Truth *(ṛtá)*, cosmic order. In an invective against rival poets in a competition or learned disputation, the composer of RV 4.5 quoted earlier says ironically (verse 5):

> *papā́saḥ sánto anṛtā́ asatyā́*
> *idáṃ padám ajanatā gabhīrám*
> 'Being evil, not possessing Truth, untrue,
> They brought forth this "deep" secret word'

By contrast, note the following, which has the earmarks of a proverb (1.152.2b):

> *satyó mántraḥ kaviśastá ṛ́ghāvān*
> 'true is the powerful formula pronounced by the poet'

The poetic formula *(mántra)* is *satyá*, veridical; it will come true. And in the verse-final epithet *ṛ́ghāvān* we have a formulaic phonetic *echo* of *ṛtā́vā* 'possessing Truth' in the same final position in RV 7.61.2 above. Clearly, there is a poetic ideology in play here.

Note finally the metrical form of the two Vedic lines cited (RV 7.61.2b and 1.152.2b); they are eleven-syllable *triṣṭubh*s but share the rare and archaic "paroemiac" closing: *dīrghaśrúd iyarti, kaviśastá ṛgháván,* which is identical to the closing cadence of the Homeric hexameter. With the paradigmatic Indo-European formula, compare only:

> *kléos áphthiton éstai*
> 'my fame will be imperishable'

The domain of formulas and formulaic composition in Indo-European includes the whole universe of discourse; a humble example not in the literature is 'to piss standing up': Ved. *mekṣyāmy ūrdhvás* (AV 7.102), Gk. *orthòs omeíkhein* (Hesiod, *Works and Days* 727), which is probably the formulaic expression of an Indo-European taboo. No attempt to catalog these will be made here. Rather I prefer to single out for discussion only certain types of formulaic bipartite NP figures—those which exhibit characteristic Indo-European stylistic properties, over and above the ordinary grammatical relations of such formulas as 'imperishable fame' or 'to piss standing up'.

If we examine these Indo-European bipartite noun-phrase formulaic figures as a group from a more formal point of view, certain interesting properties emerge. These can be best understood and described in the terminology developed by Roman Jakobson in his classic paper *Shifters* (1971:130-47).

We may distinguish *simple* figures and *complex* figures. Simple figures may be termed *designators;* designators in turn may be either *quantifiers* or *qualifiers.*

Indo-European quantifier formulas have the structure Argument plus negated Argument, as in:

> 'gods spoken and unspoken' (Hitt. $D^{MEŠ}$ *tarantes* $D^{MEŠ}$ *UL tar.*)
> 'diseases seen and unseen' (Lat. *morbos uisos inuisosque*)
> 'men girt and ungirt' (Umb. *nerf śihitu anśihitu*)

or the equivalent, Argument plus counter-Argument:

> 'gods above and below' (Gk. *tõn ánō te kai kátō*)
> 'be you god or goddess' (Lat. *si deus, si dea es*)

Quantifier formulas are exocentric, and their function is to designate the totality of the notion: 'gods spoken and unspoken, above and below, god or goddess' are alike equivalent to 'all gods'.

The ultimate indefinite is commonly expressed by a "magic square" of two bipartite quantifier formulas in Russian folktales, of a village:

'not far, not near,   *ne daleko, ne blizko,*
not high, not low'   *ne vysoko, ne nizko*

or of a journey:

'long or short,   *dolgo li, korotko li,*
near or far'   *blizko li, daleko li*

Indo-European qualifier formulas have two structures, litotic and nonlitotic. The litotic has the structure Argument plus negated counter-Argument, *Aussage plus negierte Gegenaussage,* in the words of its formulator, Helmut Humbach (1959):

'girt and not ungirt' (Av. *aißiiãsta nõiț anaißiiãsta*)
'true and not false' (OPers. *hašiyam naiy duruxtam*)
'Achaean women, not men' (Gk. *Akhaiïdes oukét' Akhaioí*)

The nonlitotic figure has the structure Argument plus synonymous Argument:

'safe and sound' (Lat. *sane sarteque*)
'whole and roofed' (Lat. *sarcta tecta*)
'with prayers and incantations' (Gk. *litaīs epaoidaīs*)

Qualifier formulas are endocentric, and their function is to intensify the Argument. Both litotic 'safe and undisturbed' and nonlitotic 'safe and sound' are equivalent to 'very safe', though the two are not necessarily stylistic equivalents.

Observe that all these *designators* are also at the same time grammatical figures; each pair has an identical morphological sign. Note also that to express 'A and B', Indo-European had three possibilities: asyndeton, *AB;* enclitic conjunction after the second constituent, *ABk^we;* and enclitic conjunction after both constituents, *Ak^we Bk^we.* Each produces a characteristic rhythm, symmetrical or asymmetrical, and the possibilities for variation are fully exploited by the Indo-European poet.

To these simple figures, or *designators,* we may oppose the complex figures, or *connectors.* Both have the ordinary symbolic function of linguistic signs, but the connectors have as well an *indexical* function: they point to, or refer to, another entity.

The connector formulas in Indo-European are of two types. The first we have seen already; it is the *kenning,* the bipartite figure of two nouns in a noncopulative grammatical relation (A of B), which together refer to another notion: 'descendant of the waters' refers to 'fire'. The ancient Indo-European collocation for 'master', **déms pótis,* is doubtless in origin a frozen kenning, a "dead metaphor."

The second connector figure is the merism: a bipartite noun phrase consisting of two nouns in a copulative relation (A and B), two nouns which share most of their semantic features, and together serve to designate globally a higher taxon. I take the term merism from Hoffner (1974:63), where it is applied to Hittite *ḫalkiš ZÍZ-tar* 'barley (and) spelt', used as a global indication of all cereals. The well-known Indo-European formula of Avestan *pasu vīra* and Umbrian *ueiro pequo* 'men (and) livestock' is a merism, indicating globally all mobile, self-moving wealth; we know that 'men' here means 'slaves'.

The kenning, as long recognized, is a metaphorical figure, based on a relation of similarity. The merism, on the other hand, is a metonymic figure, based on a relation of contiguity.

The connector formulas are both endocentric, in that they are self-contained, and exocentric, in that they refer indexically to an external notion. The "Argument" of the kenning and the merism, the metaphor and the metonym alike, is precisely that indexical reference.

And it is here that we can observe one of the most important functions of the Indo-European poet, as noted by Campanile and confirmed by the self-reference of the Vedic poet cited: to transmit to later generations the knowledge, the total ideology of which he is the custodian. The vehicle for this transmission is precisely the formula, and in particular the indexical formula. Both the metaphorical bipartite kenning, which indexes a notion by semantic and symbolic similarity, and the metonymic bipartite merism, which indexes a notion by semantic and symbolic contiguity, serve as traditional poetic definitions, traditional poetic explications of that notion.

It is clear that the expansion of the bipartite kenning to a multipartite indexical figure results in a form of *myth*. We have indeed a certain number of such Indo-European myths, such as that linking the notions of wind, mountains, trees, a verb of violent action, and the presence of wild and domestic animals, which mythologizes the sexual act of fecundation. Typical is *Sappho* 47 L.P., "Eros has shaken my mind like the wind on the mountain, falling on the oaks." To the dossier given in Watkins (1975) we can add AV 2.30:

> *yáthedám bhűmyā[m] ádhi*
> *tṛṇám vắto mathāyati*
> *evắ mathnāmi te mánaḥ*
> 'As the wind here churns the grass on the earth, so do I churn thy mind'

The first two lines evoke the myth or complex metaphor of the sexual act; allusively they set the mood for the immediate objective to which the charm is directed: "To secure the love of a woman," as William Dwight Whitney rather charitably puts it.

If the expansion of metaphor, of the bipartite kenning of a multipartite connected entity, is a form of myth, then some bipartite kennings may themselves
be elliptical, allusive reductions of more complex myths. This is clearly the case
of the Indo-Iranian epithet seen in Vedic *vṛtra-hán-* 'slaying Vṛtra' and Avestan
vərəϑra-γna-. It may also be the case of Vedic *apā́m nápāt* 'descendant of the
waters', and its congeners in Iranian, Germanic, and elsewhere.

The expansion of the bipartite merism results simply in an indexical list. Such
lists abound in early Indo-European literatures, from India through Anatolia and
the classical world to Ireland. They may be arranged according to very concrete
contiguity relations like the lists of body parts in the "twelve members" of Hittite
rituals (Gurney 1979) or "the twelve doors of the soul" in the archaic Old Irish
"Judgements of Dian Cécht" (Binchy 1965), or in the curses and evil spells *(mala
carmina, defixiones)* of Greek and Latin. But they may also be linked by indexical
phonetic figures, such as the sequential alliterative pairs—phonetic merisms—in an
Oscan curse: *aginss urinss ulleís fakinss fangvam biass biitam aftiim anamúm aitatum
amirikum* 'his actions (and) speech, deeds (and) tongue, strength (and) life, power
(and) soul, life-span (and) livelihood'. The linguistic reality of the alliterative pair
as a poetic unity is here proved by the position of the enclitic pronoun *ulleís* 'his'
(contrary to Vetter 1953:29), which follows the first merism 'actions (and) speech',
not the first stressed word, by Wackernagel's law.

What seem at first sight to be simple lists often turn out to be artistically elaborated merisms, where phonetic figures and features of arrangement are all deployed.
The notion of solid agricultural produce, as a higher taxon, may be expressed by
the merism of the subcategories *legumes* and *cereals*. And each of these may in turn
be represented by a merism of subcategories of each. Consider the traditional
English round:

> *Oats, peas, beans and barley grow*

I am not being facetious when I claim that this is an ideal illustration of the Indo-
European poet's formulaic verbal art. Consider the order of the elements, which is
anything but random. The two cereals *oats* and *barley* are distracted, transposed to
frame the two legumes *peas* and *beans*. The latter are linked by the indexical labial
stop and identical vowel /pi-/, /bi-/. *Beans* must follow *peas* in order to alliterate
with *barley*. *Barley* as the only disyllable comes last, in accord with Behagel's law
of increasing members, the *Gesetz der wachsenden Glieder*. And *oats* must come
first, to form a perfect phonetic ring-composition; the whole utterance begins and
ends with the vowel /o/: *oats, grow*.

This particular utterance now functions only to amuse children; its surface
linguistic expression is of no great antiquity, though doubtless of many generations,
perhaps some centuries older than the present day. But in its essential semantics,

formulaics, and poetics it could perfectly well have been periodically re-created on the same model, over the course of the past seven thousand years. We could have before our eyes the transformation of the central merism of an Indo-European agricultural prayer, harvest song, or the like.

The transposition of a ritual utterance to the contemporary function of a child's pastime has parallels. All and only the Indo-European elements of the myth symbolizing the sexual act of fecundation survive in the verbal behavior, the playing song of a late nineteenth-century North Russian children's game, and the name of the game itself, *ërga,* continues intact as an Indo-European lexeme for the sexual act (Watkins 1975).

That my adducing *oats, peas, beans and barley grow* is not altogether fanciful appears from the consideration of some far earlier Indo-European traditions. We began the discussion of the merism with the Hittite formula:

ḫalkiš ZÍZ-*tar* 'barley and spelt'

This particular Hittite formulaic merism is in fact an Indo-European inheritance, in its principal semantic features and their functional deployment. Compare the recurrent Homeric Greek formula, always verse-initial:

puroì kaì krithaí 'wheat and barley'

The formula is expanded to a full hexameter line, by the splitting of wheat into another merism, and the addition of a traditional epithet to the final member (again, Behagel's *Gesetz der wachsenden Glieder*) in:

puroì te zeiaí te, id' euruphuès krî leukón
'wheat and emmer, and broad-growing white barley'

The hiatus at the caesura indicates that we have actually a juncture of two formulas, each occupying a hemistich. The precise botanical nature of *zeiaí* is not certain; but it is certain that it is a derivative of the Indo-European lexeme for 'barley', **įeuo-.* The same lexeme is found in the same second position in the merism, in Old Hittite:

šeppit euwann-a 'wheat and barley'

and in the *Atharva-Veda,* with substitution of a wholly new grain in the first member:

vrīhír yávaś ca 'rice and barley'

It is not unlikely that the stem *$ieu̯o$- can be reconstructed in this position in the merism for the Proto-Indo-European formula itself. But that is of lesser importance than the semantic and thematic structure of the formula:

GRAIN (sp.) AND BARLEY

where the word order is iconic, the "nobler," more highly marked cereal precedes. The formula is an indexical figure, functioning to designate globally the higher taxon.

Cognate formulas, like cognate cultural institutions, may but need not be accompanied by cognate linguistic expression. Lexical substitution and cultural change in the course of millennia may leave only the semantic features of the original expression present. Put very simply, we have the preservation of the *signifié* (and its associated cultural nexus), but a renewal of the *signifiant*. But this must not mask the fundamental fact of the preservation of an inherited unitary formulaic and thematic "deep structure." In the Hittite, Greek, and Vedic examples above, and I submit, in the expansion in English *oats, peas, beans and barley grow*, we have six versions, six "performances" in the language of oral literature, of the same Indo-European merism, of the same Indo-European text.

This paper could have been titled "On the Track of Indo-European Poetry." The first law of comparative linguistics is: you've got to know what to compare. Hopefully, I have given some idea of what it is we are looking for, some idea of where and how to look for it, and above all, some idea of why it is worth looking for.

Our task as comparatists is that much more challenging, that much more exciting, if our goal is to find, in the words of the Indo-European poet, "the hidden track of the cow."

NOTES

1. An earlier (substantively identical) version of this paper was given as the Collitz Lecture at the Linguistics Institute of the Linguistic Society of America in Salzburg, Austria, on August 2, 1979.

2. I owe the latter example and a full discussion of all of them to D. A. Binchy who would, however, render *tothacht* here rather as 'qualification'.

AREAL TYPOLOGY AND THE EARLY INDO-EUROPEAN CONSONANT SYSTEM

Paul J. Hopper
State University of New York at Binghamton

What contribution, if any, can the science of linguistics make to our knowledge of the early Indo-Europeans? This question has usually been answered in two ways. The first is the obvious sense that a common (proto-)language is taken as a defining attribute of "the Indo-Europeans," without which other kinds of reconstruction would never have been undertaken on a large scale and in a unified way. The language of the Indo-Europeans is in fact known in more detail than any other of their cultural possessions, the kind of detail indeed which is in principle denied to us when it comes to other forms such as religious and legal practices. Yet the social and cultural historian can scarcely be satisfied by the resolution of controversies over the reconstructed grammar and phonology of Proto-Indo-European (PIE), or even of poetic forms in isolation of their cultural context. Linguistic structure is notoriously independent of cultural forms, and so far as we can be sure, any full grammatical system is compatible with any arbitrary sociocultural matrix.

A far more promising source of enlightenment from linguistics, then, is in the area of lexical reconstruction: the establishment of morphemes with a consistent phonemic shape and a textually circumscribed range of uses (meanings). A sufficient number of such morphemes has been reconstructed with wide enough agreement to identify the nature of certain artifacts, cultural and social organization, and topography/ecology of the proto-homeland. Frequently, the interpretation and substance of these reconstructions has been modified in the course of research by advances in the understanding of the phenomena themselves. For example, Friedrich and others (Friedrich 1966) have reevaluated the reconstructed set of kinship terms stemming essentially from Delbrück (1889) by placing these terms into the context of the typology of kinship systems developed by social anthropologists independently of Indo-Europeanists.

Apart from lexical reconstruction, it must be said that linguistics by its nature is not equipped to yield direct inferences about aspects of a proto-society and proto-culture. On the contrary, serious scholars have long abandoned the assumption that linguistic structure can be correlated *via* superordinate concepts such as "primitive," "passive," etc., with supposed corresponding characteristics of societies. If nonlexical data are to be brought to bear on the questions of the culture and early history of the Indo-Europeans, this must occur through the study of linguistic diffusion as inferred from the comparison of PIE with presumably adjacent language groups. Such inferences must by their nature be broad even when their accuracy is agreed upon, and any dating which emerges is more likely to be relative than absolute. In the present paper, I examine a subset of the PIE phonological inventory as established by a controlled reconstruction and compare this subset with inventories of Semitic and Caucasian languages which may be presumed to have been spoken in northwest Africa and southwest Asia at a time contemporaneous with PIE. No absolute dating is proposed for the connections discussed, but the fourth millennium seems more probable than the third.

1. Methodology

Considering once again the work of Paul Friedrich in the reconstruction of PIE kinship terminology, it must be stressed that the substance of this work in one sense is not radically different from the results of Delbrück, given the fact that some seventy years of scholarship separates the two. Essentially, the same set of terms is found in both works, with Friedrich's work showing the obvious effects of the laryngeal theory and adding a few kin terms not known to Delbrück. The distinction between the two monographs can be characterized as one of "paradigm" in the Kuhnian sense. Friedrich does more than simply "use" the results of social anthropology (the inclusion of insights offered by other disciplines has always been a normal procedure of Indo-Europeanists). Rather, the Indo-Europeans are viewed as a sociocultural entity unlikely to diverge dramatically from other such entities known to science, and therefore susceptible of both internal (philological) and external (typological) reconstruction. This initial assumption makes for a sharp distinction between Neogrammarian methodology and that of a modern anthropological linguist like Friedrich. For the first, social anthropology is a neighboring field which can "contribute" insights which can then be "incorporated" into the picture assembled through linguistic reconstruction. For the second, the starting assumption of the reconstruction is the awareness of a limited set of possible kinship systems as described and elaborated by anthropologists. To the Indo-Europeanist this may seem to be a distinction without a difference: the same set of phenomena is arrived at, and the psychological and strategic approaches of the scholars are irrelevant. In the long term, however, the differing implications of the two sets of assumptions are so important as to amount to a paradigmatic gulf. Friedrich's goal is to reconstruct a system. This is not the same as reconstructing a list and subsequently seeing whether or not the terms constitute a system, the "philological" method. For Friedrich, each term reconstructed must contribute to the overall identification of the system, and must occupy a node in the system; the system as a whole must furthermore be congruent with, even derive from, the set of such possible systems known in the present state of research. Thus viewed, the articulation of this system in a coherent theory of social relationships becomes a central goal of the process of reconstruction.

Applied to the grammatical and phonological levels of the proto-language, the same methodological considerations require that the task of reconstruction should take as given the results of linguistic typology and use these results as a set of matrices into which the internally reconstructed facts can be fitted with a high degree of probability. This method has important theoretical and substantive advantages, notably:

1. It offers the linguist a degree of control over the internal (philological) reconstruction.

Thus, it might happen that internal reconstruction yields several competing possibilities, only one of which is congruent with external comparison. I believe this to be the case with the PIE obstruents. Also:

2. It offers the possibility of projecting new information known to be compatible with these matrices but hitherto either unnoticed or passed off as trivial.

Turning again to Friedrich's monograph, we find a nice illustration of this latter point. Having reconstructed an essentially Omaha patrilineal kinship type for PIE, Friedrich writes of the need to find more evidence for "certain key nodes in the terminological system," in order to answer such questions as "Can a case be made for [the wife's father and wife's brother's son] having been grouped with the wife's brother?" (Friedrich 1963:30). Such a question is obviously not a random one, but is virtually compulsory because of its diagnostic value in filling out the matrix of kin terms known or suspected in advance to have existed. It is not, however, a question which would have occurred to a scholar working in the "philological" paradigm.

2. A Revised View of the PIE Consonant System

It is usual to date the beginnings of Indo-European comparative linguistics from the "discovery" of Sanskrit by August Schlegel. The primacy of Sanskrit as a *Schlüsselsprache* in the Indo-European family has endured to the present day, and has essentially survived the Neogrammarians, who were able to demonstrate the derivative nature of its vowel system; the laryngeal theory, which added to the reconstructed phoneme inventory a number of consonantal phonemes lost in most of the dialects; and the discovery of several more documented branches of the family whose phonological systems differed profoundly from that of Indic. Continuing in the recent work of Szemerényi (1967; 1972), a Sanskrit-based reconstruction of the PIE consonant system has survived and flourished to the present day; according to this view, the proto-language had four or five phonemic points of articulation, and four glottal features:

	Voiceless		Voiced	
	plain	aspirated	plain	aspirated
labial	p	ph	b	bh
dental	t	th	d	dh
palatal	k	kh	g	gh
velar	q	qh	G	Gh
labiovelar	q^o	$q^o h$	G^o	$G^o h$

To the above obstruents, most Indo-Europeanists would now add one or several laryngeals, including /h/; for Szemerényi, the single laryngeal /h/ is adequate on both comparative and typological grounds, and is simply added as a further reconstructable entity. For other twentieth-century linguists, however, the laryngeal theory began to undermine the proto-language status of an entire class of obstruents, the voiceless aspirates.

Direct evidence for a class of voiceless aspirates had always been sparse. Yet the sounds existed in Sanskrit, and a few cognates could be found. Furthermore, pattern congruity of the reconstructed system appeared to demand it, since voiced stops came in plain and aspirated pairs with good sets of cognates. Yet indications accumulated that distinctive aspiration in the voiceless stops was a secondary phenomenon which could not be attributed to the proto-language. The arguments against reconstructing these sounds in the period of near homogeneity of PIE involve showing that Indo-Aryan forms containing a voiceless aspirate are largely to be analyzed as stop + laryngeal clusters; thus, Hoenigswald (1965:93-94):

1. The voiceless aspirates cluster more like double consonant clusters than like unit consonants. For instance groups like *phl-, khn-* do not exist . . .
2. . . . *kh* is not palatalized before IE *e, i, y* . . .
3. . . . such extra-Indo-Aryan etymologies which have been advanced with any promise involve mostly root-final position for the voiceless aspirates . . .
4. . . . the list of *-th* final roots contains a number of *CCath* combinations . . .

5. Roots of the type *math-* 'stir', *srath-* 'loosen' are *seṭ* and have a present of the ninth class *(mathnāti).*
6. In Iranian the nominative and genitive of the word for 'path' are Av. *pantå, pathō.*

Eliminating the voiceless aspirates had the advantage of accounting for the anomalous distribution of this class throughout Indo-European. It also had a further effect which became increasingly troubling as Indo-Europeanists became more aware of linguistic realities outside the parochial bounds of their own field. The problem was well known in the 1950s, but was stated perhaps most explicitly by Jakobson (1957:528):[1]

> To my knowledge no language adds to the pair /t/ $\sim$ /d/ a voiced aspirate /dh/ without having its voiceless counterpart /th/, whie /t/ $\sim$ /d/ $\sim$ /th/ frequently occur without the comparatively rare /dh/. Therefore theories operating with the three phonemes /t/ $\sim$ /d/ $\sim$ /dh/ in PIE must reconsider the question of their phonemic essence.

This universal, as stated by Jakobson, had important consequences for Indo-Europeanists, who now had to adopt an anti-universalist stance in the face of Jakobson's admonition that "a conflict between the reconstructed state of a language and the general laws which typology discovers makes the reconstruction questionable" (1957:528), or revert to some variant of the Neogrammarian system, voiceless aspirates and all. Those who, like Szemerényi, chose the latter alternative have usually done so with the reasoning that we are reconstructing a shallow depth of PIE rather than more remote pre-stages. As Vaillant (1950:12) put it in another context: "La grammaire comparée n'a d'ailleurs pas comme tâche unique, ni principale, de remonter au plus profond dans le passé." Yet even this shallow depth must be uniform, or as nearly uniform as possible, otherwise there will still be nonidentical cognate forms to resolve, and I think it is true to say that most scholars have been reluctant to accept a consistent stage preceding even the grosser dialectal divergences in which a distinct set of voiceless aspirates contrasted with plain voiceless stops.

The alternative, then, was an anti-universalist position. Yet a number of trends in linguistics from the Prague School on had conspired to focus attention on what Jakobson called "the general laws which typology discovers." Once linguistic science had matured to the point where its practitioners were seriously grappling with the notions of likely or possible human language as a central objective, historical linguistics could not ignore the new paradigm without becoming fatally isolated.

2.1. Of the various attempts to come to terms with Jakobson's objections to the

traditional system of reconstructed PIE consonants, I shall here expound only the
one elaborated originally by myself (Hopper 1973) and the Soviet scholars Gamkrelidze and Ivanov (1972; 1973). The essence of the substitution in the traditional
system which we made was as follows: The voiced aspirates constituted the only
voiced obstruents; the "plain voiced" series (known as *mediae*) were glottalized,
i.e., were articulated with glottal closure or constriction; and the voiceless stops
had aspirated and nonaspirated variants. Using the dental series T to illustrate
the correspondence with the traditional system, we may illustrate this in tabular
form:

TRADITIONAL SYSTEM:	/t/	/th/	/d/	/dh/
REVISED SYSTEM:	/t/		/t'/	/d/

The positing of glottalization in place of voicing in the mediae (the *d*-series in the
traditional system) has the primary function of obviating the typological objections
to having two types of voiced sound but only one type of unvoiced sound in the
same system. The voiceless member in the revised system was apparently aspirated
in some positions, in onomatopoeia, and in certain expressive words. The voiced
aspirate of the traditional system is represented here as a plain voiced stop; in my
paper of 1973 I suggested that the phonetic realization of this series was with
Ladefoged's feature of "murmur," but in fact the aspiration feature of the "voiced
aspirates" could well have been a secondary development in a restricted area of
Indo-European which included Indo-Iranian and Greek. Ladefoged has now, it
seems, withdrawn the feature "murmur" and is willing to replace it with "aspiration" for sounds of this type. The phonological features in the standard framework for PIE stops would then look as follows (Hopper 1973:157-58):

	/t/	/t'/	/d/
voiced	−	−	+
checked	−	+	(−)

Systems of this kind are commonly attested, being found in numerous African,
Amerindian, and Caucasian languages, so that such a system has the advantage of
being externally validated.

There are, however, other possibilities for reconstructing PIE consonants which
are equally valid in external terms and equally congruent with the internal data,
e.g., Emonds' suggestion of a system along the lines of /th/ ∿ /t/ ∿ /dh/, with a
lax (unaspirated) stop in place of the revised system's glottalic and an aspirated
stop in the "t" (etc.) series. The evidence that the second series (the "t'" series)
was specifically glottalic is, however, compelling.

2.2. Absence of PIE *b*. It has long been known that a labial in the media series is either lacking or significantly rare in reconstructed forms. The importance of this fact was recognized by H. Pedersen (1950), who, aware that a lacuna of this kind in a labial series was almost certainly evidence for voicelessness, suggested that an earlier stage of PIE had had unvoiced stops in place of the later mediae, and that the reconstructed stage of PIE was the result of a series of prehistoric sound shifts in the course of which the voiced and the voiceless stops had switched places. We may note that historically the voiced labial stops of the dialects have a variety of sources that are sometimes, as in the case of Latin, quite complex (e.g., *fūnebris* from **fūnes-ris, hibernus* from **heimrinos, bellum* from **duellum, lubet* from **lubh-*, etc.), as if the language has evolved a "conspiracy" for introducing more instances of synchronic /b/ once this sound was no longer glottalized.

Typological studies make it necessary to reconstruct not merely voicelessness but glottalization in the PIE labial media.[2] The work of Gamkrelidze (1975) shows that the segmental features of voice, aspiration, and glottalization are arranged in a hierarchy which is dependent to a large extent on place of articulation, such that if these features are present in any combination, a lacuna, if any, can be predicted to occur in the order:

1. Glottalized labial.
2. Voiceless aspirated labial.
3. Voiceless unaspirated labial.
4. Voiced labial.

Let us now assume that the PIE consonant system was of the traditionally assumed type, with the labials:

$$p \qquad ph \qquad (b) \qquad bh$$

and the lacuna in the voiced position. Such a distribution contradicts the universal hierarchy, which predicts that if /b/ is absent, then both /p/ and /ph/ will also be absent. The removal of /ph/ from the scene does nothing to salvage this situation, of course. Redistributing the features in the way undertaken by Emonds (1972) and Pedersen (1950) so that the mediae were voiceless but unaspirated and the voiceless stops aspirated likewise does not improve the picture, since the hierarchy now predicts a lacuna in the voiceless aspirate series. The assumption of glottalization is the *only* way of explaining the absence of a labial media in PIE.

2.3. The Root Structure Constraints. PIE roots which contained occlusives *(C)* in initial and second consonant position, i.e., *CVC*- roots, did not tolerate every combination of these occlusives. In the traditionally assumed system of consonants, the constraints involved seem almost bizarre:

A. The first and second stops may not both be plain voiced stops (mediae).

B. A voiced aspirate may not co-occur with a voiceless stop.

We may represent the two consonants as D and $G;$ the permitted and prohibited root types using the traditional system are then:

Permitted	Prohibited
tek	**deg*
dek	**dhek*
dhegh	
dheg	

Phonological explanations (e.g., Chomsky and Halle 1968:386-87) have failed to show how: 1) the plain voiced stops can behave as a natural class in contrast to the voiced aspirates and the voiceless stops taken together; and 2) the voicing assimilation evidently operating between voiced aspirates and voiceless stops (*dhegh* but **dhek*) is able to ignore the plain voiced stops. Thus, Chomsky and Halle, using the traditional system for PIE, are obliged to introduce no fewer than four variables into the constraint; their statement, of course, also assumes that the two constraints A and B are collapsible into a single constraint.

2.4. Absence of Mediae in Inflectional Affixes. A further morphophonemic oddity about the mediae had been noted by Meillet (1936:84). These sounds were evidently the most highly marked set of consonants, as was clear from the defective representation (no labial), the constraint against their co-occurrence in roots (constraint A), and the fact of their rarity in inflectional affixes. The other major classes of phonemes (nasals, glides, vowels, laryngeals, voiced aspirates, voiceless stops) are all represented in suffixes, but unambiguous examples of mediae are difficult to find. We have in fact only the **-d* of the neuter pronoun and the **ōd* of the ablative singular, and in both of these the media is in word-final position, where the possibility of some kind of neutralization is significant (cf. Hopper 1977a:44 for further discussion). That the subset of phonemes admitted in inflectional affixes tends universally to be the typologically unmarked set has often been noted. The absence of specifically glottalized sounds in inflection is characteristic of a number of languages, for example, Georgian and the Salish group (Montler 1980). The high degree of marking of glottalized sounds is shown by text counts carried out by Greenberg (1976): glottalized phonemes are relatively much less frequent than nonglottalized sounds in languages with this feature, and when plain and aspirated sounds are included in the count, glottalized sounds are the least frequent of all. It has now been shown that in the PIE lexicon the least frequent of the root-initial obstruents are the mediae (i.e., the glottalics), which are outnumbered in a ratio of 2:1 by voiced aspirates, and 3:1 by voiceless stops

(Jucquois 1966). These ratios are unexpected if the mediae are voiced stops, since then the voiced aspirates should be the most marked and hence the least frequent set.[3]

2.5. Point of Articulation Skewing. Inconsistencies in the representation of the stops at different places of articulation also point to the positing of glottalization as the source feature of the mediae. The most striking example of this skewing, the rarity or absence of the labial media, has already been noted. But the statistics compiled by Jucquois (1966) show that in the labiovelar series, presumably the most retracted set of stops, the ratios are reversed: here the mediae are the most prominently represented, and the voiced aspirates are the least numerous:

	Voiceless	Voiced Aspirate	Media
Labial	143	129	0
Labiovelar	18	12	37

The phonetic explanation for this distribution is ultimately the same as for the absence of the labial: a supraglottal airstream (the type used in the performance of a glottalized or ejective stop) requires considerable ejective force in the front region of the oral cavity, especially the labial area, but relatively little energy in the back (velar and postvelar) area. Consequently, glottalized sounds are inconvenient in the labial area but are highly convenient in the velar and postvelar areas. On the other hand, for voicing the reverse is true: here the longer buccal cavity is advantageous, and voicing is more convenient in the labial area but much less convenient in the velar/postvelar regions. Jucquois' statistics are therefore consistent with both glottalization in the mediae and voicing only in the voiced aspirates (but in no other set of occlusives).

2.6. Summary. In this section of the paper I have outlined some of the evidence taken from "external" reconstruction for the glottalic paradigm. At present it must be said that although this theory has won the support of a number of scholars, primarily younger ones, and has resulted in some interesting explanations of phonetic changes in the dialects (some of which will be discussed below), this line of research has not in general been discussed by the more established generation of Indo-Europeanists in the West. Such discussions will, we must hope, soon be forthcoming, and it is interesting to speculate on the strategies which those Indo-Europeanists who have not accepted the glottalic theory will use to confront it. Will they attempt to show that the data used in the formation of the theory are wrong (root structure constraints, distribution of *b*, morphophonemics of PIE mediae, point of articulation skewing)? That the data are correct but irrelevant? Or compatible with some other typological facts? Will they maintain that the theory is plausible but applicable to "pre-Indo-European" and can be complacently ignored by "Indo-Europeanists"? Will they cast aspersions on the method of external reconstruction itself, in the hope that none of the internal evidence for the theory can be sustained? Perhaps, on the other hand, those who work in the traditional paradigm will find it less troublesome to ignore the radical revisions which have been presented during the past decade in the hope that these innovations will die of neglect (which is not likely to happen) or that, being accepted by a widening circle of scholars, the changes proposed will have no significant consequences for our view of Proto-Indo-European (an even remoter possibility).

3. Some Recent Applications of the Glottalic Theory

3.1. I have considered up to now the immediate evidence for the substitution of glottalized stops for the PIE plain voiced stops of traditional reconstructions, and thus the reasons for wishing to consider this as a working hypothesis. We may compare this hypothesis with the laryngeal theory, in that while convincing prima facie evidence has been presented (in the case of the laryngeal theory an elegant account of certain ablaut alternations), *applications* of the theory which would make it indispensible to morphology have been slow in appearing. In this section, I shall refer to some work along these lines which has begun to appear.

The drift from glottalized or ejective stops to ordinary voiced stops which took place over most of the Indo-European-speaking area is from a typological point of view a somewhat unusual one. As Greenberg (1970) has noted, it is far more common for this type of stop to become a simple unvoiced stop, i.e., to lose its glottalic feature without "gaining" a voice feature. Yet such a change is not unknown, and is well documented in at least two cases. One of these is described for the Northwest Caucasian language, Kabardian. In this language (Kuipers 1960: 11), glottalized stops are often realized with laryngealized voice *(Knarrstimme)*. That this special type of voicing can develop into plain voicing is shown by the treatment of these sounds in certain dialects of Abaza (northwest Caucasian). The first forms below are from the standard dialect of this language; the second set shows the corresponding forms in the Anatolian dialect (the latter being, significantly, an émigré dialect):

1. Standard Abaza
   a. /s - c′^{yw}a - p′/ 'I sit, I am sitting'
   b. /s - ʕ^w - y - t′/ 'I write, I am writing'
2. Anatolian Abaza
   a. /s - c′^{yw}a - b/
   b. /s - ʕ^w - y - d/

(The above data are from Colarusso 1979.)

A second example of this kind of change is found in the "emphatic" consonants of Arabic. That these consonants are derived originally from glottalized sounds is widely accepted (cf. Martinet 1952), and in the South Semitic languages they remain as ejectives. The voiceless emphatics /t̩/ and /q/, together with the glottal stop /ʔ/, were classified by the early Arab phoneticians not with the voiceless sounds but with the voiced ones (Blanc 1967:128). In some Arabic dialects, /t̩/ and /q/ have developed voiced allophones, with *qaf* merging with /g/. Although the mechanism of this change is not clear, there is some evidence that a change from glottalized to voiced sound is a possible trajectory. In my paper of 1973 I have suggested that such a change involved in Indo-European the reanalysis of a laryngealized sound as a voiced one.

The voicing of the PIE glottalized stops brought about in some dialects a merger of these stops with the inherited voiced stops ("voiced aspirates"). Therefore, it would be of the greatest interest to find that a phonetic effect attributable to glottalization was preserved before voiced stops in one of these dialects just when that voiced stop reflected a PIE media but not when the voiced stop reflected a PIE voiced aspirate. A case of this kind has been described by Winter (1976), and the appropriate conclusion was drawn by Kortlandt in a postscript to Winter's article. The alternation involved here is one of short and long vowels in Baltic and Slavic. The Balto-Slavic reflexes of short vowels in main syllables were generally short vowels. Occasionally, however, an unexplained lengthening occurs. To take a sampling of the data cited by Winter, we have reflexes of the expected short vowels in such words as:

Lith. *debesìs* 'cloud', Latv. *debess,* OCS *nebo* 'sky': Gk. *néphos* 'cloud'.
Lith. *mēdis* 'tree, woods', Latv. *mežs* 'woods', Russ. *meža* 'border': Skt. *mádh-yas* 'intermediate'.
Lith. *medùs,* Latv. *medus* 'honey', OCS *medŭ* 'honey': Skt. *mádhu* 'honey'.
Lith. *dāgas* 'summer heat', OPruss. *dagis* 'summer': Goth. *dags* 'day'.
Lith. *vèžti* 'transport', Latv. *vezums* 'cart', OCS *vesti, vezǫ* 'transport': Skt. *váhati* 'transports, leads'.
Lith. *sāpnas, sāpnis,* Latv. *sapnis* 'dream', OCS *sŭnŭ* 'sleep': Skt. *svápnas* 'sleep, dream'.
Lith. *vētušas, vēčas,* Latv. *vęcs* 'old', OCS *vetŭxŭ* 'old': Latin *vetus* 'old'.
Lith. *pēkus,* OPruss. *peckus* 'livestock': Latin *pecŭ* 'livestock'.

On the other hand, another set of forms with the vowel of the main syllable followed by an obstruent shows evidence of lengthening of the vowel:

Lith. *ėsti, ėmi, ėdu,* Latv. *ęst, ęmu, ędu* 'eat': Skt. *ádmi,* Latin *edo* 'I eat'.
Lith. *sėsti, sėdu,* Latv. *sêst* 'sit down', OCS *sĕsti* 'sit down': Gk. *hézomai* 'sit down'.

Lith. *bḗgti,* Latv. *bêgt* 'run', OCS *bĕžati, bĕžǫ* 'flee': Gk. *phébomai* 'I am in flight'.

Lith. *ožkà* 'goat', Latv. *âzis* 'billy-goat', OCS *jazĭno* 'skin, leather': Skt. *ajás* 'billy-goat'.

On the basis of these and other data amounting to over 40 roots, Winter (1976: 439) concludes that:

> In Baltic and Slavic languages, the PIE sequence of short vowel plus voiced stop was reflected by lengthened vowel plus voiced stop, while short vowel plus aspirate developed into short vowel plus voiced stop.

The mechanism of this change is conjectured by Winter (1976:445) to be a type of lengthening attributable to *distinctive* voicing. Presumably, then, the absence of lengthening before the "aspirates" is due to the fact that these sounds were "phonetically" but not "phonemically" voiced. Such a supposition is hardly realistic. Assimilatory changes of this kind always take place at the phonetic level and are, at most, sensitive to such major class features as [obstruent], etc. Therefore, to realistically maintain that lengthening took place before voiced stops, Winter would have to assume, against clear evidence, that the aspirates were voiceless, at least at the time of the Balto-Slavic lengthening. The counter-hypothesis of Kortlandt, that the lengthening was caused by glottalization in the unaspirated voiced stops, is much more attractive, and also supports the theory that voicing in the mediae proceeded by way of laryngealization of original ejective stops.

3.2. The revision of the PIE obstruent system has suggested reformulations of two well-known phonological processes in Indo-European: Bartholomae's Law and Verner's Law. Miller (1977) proposes that Bartholomae's Law, whereby in Sanskrit a sequence of voiceless and voiced aspirate stops was realized as two voiced stops, the second being aspirated (e.g., /t/ + /bh/ becomes /dbh/), should be viewed in the context of voicing agreement across vowels within the root. Such an assimilation would only be possible, Miller suggests, if the Sanskrit plain voiced stops had originally been voiceless, since otherwise it cannot be explained why the assimilation was not brought about by these sounds also (e.g., *yug+ta-* becomes *yukta-*, not **yugda-*). Miller (1977:36) concludes that in Indo-European "there was a phonetic constraint that made two obstruents in a sequence or across a root agree in voicing," and that the most probable source for the simple voiced stops was a glottalic series.

3.3. Normier (1977), in a wide-ranging and at times rambling article entitled "Indogermanischer Konsonantismus, germanische 'Lautverschiebung,' und Vernersches Gesetz," sets out to show how the revised PIE consonant system can account for a number of phonological phenomena in the dialects. The most interesting aspects of Normier's paper are: 1) his proposals about allophones of the various stop types; and 2) his reformulation of Verner's Law through a radical proposal about the nature of the pre-Germanic accentual system. Normier assumes (following Gamkrelidze and Ivanov 1973) that the basic allophones of the nonglottalized stops were aspirates, i.e., a system /th/, /dh/, /t'/. He goes on to propose positional allophones in which the aspiration was lost: for example, the voiceless stops became unaspirated before voiceless stops and in word-final position. Normier thus arrives at the same account of the neuter singular pronominal suffix *-t' as was proposed in Hopper (1974) and discussed above.

3.4. The long-standing crux of Sanskrit *pibati* 'drinks' is another phonological problem which can be considered from the point of view of the glottalic theory (cf. Hopper 1977:50, where the point is obscured by a typographical error; also Hopper 1978:70). This form can be resolved as a zero-grade form of a root PIE *peʔ-*, that is, as *pʔ*, the cluster of /p/ and glottal stop then being reanalyzed as a single glottalized segment and subsequently undergoing voicing along with the other glottalized stops.

3.5. The problem of Lachmann's Law in Latin has received much discussion in recent years, in a controversy over whether the rule is a phonological or a morphological one. This law involves the lengthening in past participles and supines of the vowel in words like *regō rēctum,* as opposed to *faciō factum.* Kortlandt has now suggested that the lengthening before original mediae is due to the glottalic articulation of these sounds, much as in the Balto-Slavic data presented by Winter (Kortlandt 1978). The same difficulties remain as with earlier phonological solutions, however; in forms like *emo ēmptum* there is no possibility of a glottalized sound to account for the lengthening.

4. Typological and Areal Implications of the Revised Consonant System

In this section I shall turn from the question of the validation of the hypothesis of glottalized consonants in PIE and discuss some of the implications of this hypothesis for the typological and, importantly, areal position of the early Indo-European languages.

The following assumptions about the sound system of the proto-language are in accord with the reconstructions of the grammar and lexicon:

1. There were stops of voiceless, voiced, and glottalic types.
2. There were several "laryngeals."
3. There were at least two "guttural" series, and probably three.
4. Of these "gutturals," one series was labialized and another was fronted (palatal or palatalized).
5. A third tectal series probably consisted of uvular (postvelar) sounds. (The term "tectal" will be used to replace the less accurate term "guttural" in this exposition.)

Obstruent systems having these characteristics are found in the Caucasus (Northeast and Northwest branches; the South or Kartwelian family lacks labialized tectals), and have parallels in Semitic. Because of the typological affinities among the several families (Caucasian—actually three unrelated families—Indo-European, and Semitic), these resemblances deserve special attention. I rely to a great extent on a recent unpublished paper by John Colarusso entitled "Typological Parallels between Proto-Indo-European and Northwest Caucasian Languages" (1979) for the Caucasian parallels. It will be convenient to refer to individual similarities as "isoglosses," although of course it should be noted that the term "isogloss" presupposes an areal or genetic relationship in its normal use.

4.1. Caucasian. As a primary isogloss between PIE and the Caucasian languages, we must count the presence of a triple series of consonants: voiceless, voiced, and glottalized. The voiced stops which are common in the Caucasian languages are considered to be fully voiced by Colarusso, who states categorically that: "Voiced aspirates are absent from the Caucasus with the exception of Eastern Armenian dialects" (1979:§3.1); Colarusso uses this assertion to suggest that Eastern Armenian inherited its voiced aspirated stops from PIE. However, the voiced stops of Georgian may be partially voiced (personal communication from T. V. Gamkrelidze). The question of the precise variety of voicing which we should reconstruct for the PIE voiced aspirates thus remains an open one.

Of the voiceless stops, Gamkrelidze and Ivanov reconstruct aspiration, and this supposition is supported by Colarusso on grounds of internal Indo-European developments as well as of typology. Aspiration does indeed appear to be called for on typological grounds, and explains a number of Indo-European phenomena also. It does, however, cause difficulties in explaining the developments in Greek, where there appears to be no way of avoiding a transitional phase in which one of the "improbable" systems exists, either /t/ $\sim$ /dh/ $\sim$ /d/ (as assumed by Kortlandt 1978:108) or /t/ $\sim$ /dh/ $\sim$ /t'/ (with devoicing of /dh/ and voicing of /t'/, as assumed by Hopper 1973:153). It must be stressed, at the same time, that the justification of the revised obstruent system is not based on the notion of minimal complexity in the diachronic trajectories between PIE and the dialects, but on its explanatory value for facts about the distribution of phonemes in PIE and in the individual dialects. Bearing this in mind, we may conclude that the PIE voiceless stops were phonetically aspirated in some positions and in onomatopoeia, and that the parallel in source features between PIE and Caucasian languages is complete.

A second isogloss discussed by Colarusso is the absence of initial /r/, a feature of PIE noted by Lehmann (1951). The Circassian and Ubykh families have eliminated initial /r/, although it can be reconstructed in Proto-Northwest Caucasian. Colarusso shows that the geographical distribution of initial /r/ is arranged on a gradient, with the Circassian languages revealing the most complete elimination, Ubykh showing some retention of r-, and Abkhaz-Abaza having complete retention.

The developments show Proto-Northwest Caucasian *r- becoming d- normally, but becoming λ- in Circassian when preceded by a prefix, and probably becoming l- in initial position in Ubykh, but retained as r- when preceded by a prefix.

> This is a north-to-south gradient, with the most thorough-going elimination of Proto-NW Caucasian *r- in the north among the Circassians. This is noteworthy, for if the PIE homeland was to the north of the Caucasus, then it may have been contiguous to the Circassian speaking area.
>
> (Colarusso 1979:§4.2)

Colarusso concludes that the extent of Northwest Caucasian *r- reflects the differential degree of penetration of the isogloss emanating from PIE.

There is wide agreement that PIE possessed a series of tectal stops characterized by labialization. This feature provides a third point of similarity with the Northwest Caucasian languages, and again sets PIE off against the South or Kartwelian group. Another tectal series was evidently palatalized, as is suggested by the satem development. In his description of Kabardian, Kuipers (1960:15) points out the extreme realization of the secondary features of palatalization and labialization in the back stops of that language, with, for example, k^y being often realized as [č] and k^o having a labial constriction which results in some speakers in an audible whistling effect. Phonetic details such as these recall the satem effect, and also the development of labiovelars into labials in a number of dialects. After attempting to reconcile the reconstructable PIE system of tectals with that of the Northwest Caucasian systems, Colarusso concludes that "the NWC languages are much richer in the palatal, velar, and uvular areas than is any recoverable stage of PIE and as a consequence can provide little typological guidance for the analysis of PIE gutturals" (1979:§5.2). In a general way, however, we may say that the presence of a distinction of palatality and labialization in the tectals is broadly characteristic of both Northwest Caucasian and Indo-European, and is an isogloss in the sense that no such contrasts are attributable to Proto-Uralic or Proto-Kartwelian. Uvular stops are increasingly being suggested for PIE (Schmitt-Brandt 1970; Hopper 1977b; Normier 1977), and this class of sounds is also universal in the Caucasus, although by no means restricted to this geographical area.

One further phonological parallel must be referred to when PIE is compared to the languages of Southwest Asia. This concerns the laryngeals and their phonetic nature. As with the various kinds of tectals, the problem here is again one of an excessive number of choices with rather little real evidence available for eliminating the various possibilities. Taking as an example the tectal and pharyngeal fricatives of one Northwest Caucasian language, the Apsuy dialect of Abkhaz, we find the following contrasts (Colarusso 1979:§14.3):

   i. voiceless velars (plain, palatal, and labialized)
   ii. voiceless uvulars (plain, palatalized, and labialized)
   iii. voiced velars (plain, palatal, and labialized)
   iv. voiced uvulars (plain, palatal, and labialized)
   v. voiceless pharyngealized uvulars (plain and rounded)
   vi. voiceless pharyngeals (plain and rounded)
   vii. voiced pharyngeals (plain and rounded)

Most of these sounds could plausibly be offered as candidates for PIE laryngeals; and to them should also be added the glottal stop (plain and rounded), and /h/, both of which are common in languages having glottalized stops. Colarusso gives an extensive argument from both philological and phonetic data to justify a *pre*-IE system of laryngeals of the following kind:

$$
\begin{array}{ccc}
 & x & \gamma \\
 & x^{o} & \gamma^{o} \\
 & \d{h} & \d{c} \\
\text{ʔ} \quad \text{ʔ}^{o} & h &
\end{array}
$$

It should be emphasized that this system is not intended to represent Proto-Indo-European, but rather the kind of system from which the putative PIE system might have evolved given reasonable inferences from observed phonetic processes. Such a system is well within the range of systems found in the present-day Caucasus.

   The present-day Caucasian languages occupy an area in the extreme northwest of the Caucasus area. There is some evidence, however, of an earlier and much wider spread to the north and west. Contact with early Indo-Europeans seems very probable on the basis of linguistic evidence. The phonological similarities between Indo-European and the Northwest Caucasian languages seem to become more extensive the further back one goes, and yet to post-date the Northwest Caucasian proto-language itself (Colarusso 1979:§8.4). In terms of internal Indo-European chronology, contact between Indo-Europeans and Northwest Caucasians would have had to precede "decemization," the development of the glottalized series into voiced stops; it would also have had to occur at an early stage in the history of the laryngeal consonants. If we accept the view of PIE which has been defended in the present paper, i.e., with a series of glottalized stops and multiple contrasts in the tectal types, we must also face some strange anomalies which must be resolved. These anomalies involve the absence of further consonantal contrasts in the alveolar and palatal areas. Typologically, we would expect to find such sounds as affricates (*č* and *ǰ*, *c* and *dᶻ*) and perhaps alveopalatal fricatives like *š*, *ž*. Languages with multiple contrasts in the velar and uvular areas invariably possess a comparable degree of crowding in the frontal areas. Indo-Europeanists have traditionally been cautious about adding to the inventory of proto-phonemes (the proposal to eliminate the voiceless aspirate type reflects another aspect of this reluctance). Yet external comparison makes the existence of frontal affricates and fricatives likely, and compels us to seek evidence for them. In more recent times, the correspondence between certain instances of Hittite *z* and the *s* of other dialects suggested to Benveniste (1954) that an earlier affricate had merged with *s* on a large scale in later dialects. Other linguists have seen in the differential treatment of PIE **y* in Greek (e.g., *zugon* but *hēpar*) an indication that **y* reflected a merger of original **y* and another phoneme, perhaps *ǰ*. It must be emphasized that external reconstruction will not alone lead us to posit specific proto-phonemes or even broad classes of phonemes, except in a purely vacuous way; instead, the method yields guidelines for areas of search and forces us to take proposals for additional phonemes more seriously, i.e., to regard such a search as a legitimate occupation.

The parallels in phonological structure between PIE and the Northwest Caucasian languages are striking. At the same time the similarities between PIE and Semitic also deserve attention. It is true that most of the Indo-European and Semitic isoglosses are also shared with the Northwest Caucasian languages, and are, therefore, insofar as they are unlikely to represent typological rather than areal facts, to be attributed to the whole IE-Semitic-Caucasian *Sprachbund*. One such bond that is important is the triple stop system discussed at length here: there can be little question that the "emphatics" of Semitic languages are to be traced back to earlier glottalized (ejective) stops (Cantineau 1951-52:91-92).

The features by which PIE differed from Proto-Semitic are also striking: the reconstruction of the Proto-Semitic obstruent system proposed by Bergsträsser (1928:4) shows: 1) no distinctive labialization in any of the tectals; and 2) an exceedingly rich set of fricatives (but no affricates). Apart from the similarities in source features, then, the Proto-Semitic obstruent system looks very "un-Indo-European." There is some evidence, however, that the extreme crowding of fricatives in the alveopalatal region is a secondary development. Bomhard (1977) has made use of this putative transformation to propose an earlier period of actual identity between the PIE and Proto-Semitic consonant systems, supported by about 150 hypothesized cognates. The attempt to demonstrate a genetic tie between Indo-European and Semitic is, of course, a very old idea, but Bomhard's is the first attempt which makes use of the glottalic paradigm and therefore the first to propose a systematic link between the PIE mediae and the Semitic emphatics.

One obvious isogloss between PIE and Proto-Semitic is the lacuna in the labial glottalized slot. A glottalized /p'/ is found in both the Kartwelian and Northwest Caucasian groups, so that this feature is not shared by all three of the Semitic-IE-Caucasian *Sprachbund*, but is common only to Semitic and PIE. On the other hand, it has been noted (§2.2 above) that such a lacuna is not at all uncommon typologically. There may then be no areal significance to this fact.

5. Conclusions

At the outset of this paper I posed the question whether the history of the early Indo-Europeans could be elucidated by linguistic evidence. I have presented in the body of the paper a view of the nature of the PIE obstruent system in which typological parallels are observable with certain ancient and modern languages of Southwest Asia. There appear to be lexical as well as structural (phonological) links with these languages, as Bomhard's work with Semitic-IE correspondences, and Colarusso's work on Northwest Caucasian-IE lexical ties (which has, however, not been available to me at first hand) suggest. To these may be added Gamkrelidze's work on South Caucasian and Indo-European (Gamkrelidze 1966). Taken together, these parallels point to an early period of residence to the south as well as the north of the Caucasus. Archaeological (Gimbutas [this volume]), ethnological (Friedrich 1966), paleobotanical (Friedrich 1970), and other evidence are all consistent with a proto-homeland in the temperate plain north of the Caucasus, and the linguistic evidence which I have adduced in this paper is also most compatible with this region. The traits common to Indo-European and Semitic, and Indo-European and Kartwelian, are consequently difficult to evaluate: before settling in the steppe region to the northwest of the Caucasus range, did the Proto-Indo-Europeans reside to the south of the Caucasus, or is the trans-Caucasian residence to be seen as post-dating the dispersal of the Indo-Europeans from an original homeland to the north?

Limitations in the use of linguistic evidence of the kind presented in this paper are also apparent when one considers that we know nothing about the languages spoken in the north and west of Europe in pre-Indo-European times, so that we cannot be sure that a Southwest Asian homeland is the only one compatible with the linguistic evidence. However, the phonological system which has been discussed here is radically different from those of other languages presumably spoken in this region in the fourth millennium, such as Uralic, Altaic, and Dravidian, so far as we can reconstruct them. To take one example, the proto-Uralic phonological system (Hajdu 1972:36) probably had the stops $*p$, $*t$, $*c$, $*k$; three sibilants; four nasals; and $*w$, $*y$, $*l$, $*l'$, and $*r$. Such a system is totally different from that of PIE, and, by contrast, the similarities which have been described here among Northwest Caucasian, Semitic, and PIE appear to be closer and less conjectural.

NOTES

1. I have given this quote in full because of the careless use which is sometimes made of it. Jakobson does not state that "voiced aspirates imply voiceless aspirates," as Normier asserts (1977:173), but that voiced aspirates in contrast with

plain voiced and voiceless stops imply voiceless aspirates. It is perfectly possible to have a plain unaspirated voiceless stop in contrast with a voiced aspirate, and I have encountered some Malay dialects with this characteristic.

2. It is the typological method which has led to the positing of glottalized stops in place of plain voiced stops in the PIE mediae, and not, as Kortlandt suggests, the discovery of Winter's "law" and Kortlandt's interpretation of it. Thus, Martinet's mention of such a possibility in his "Remarques sur le consonantisme sémitique" (1952) is provoked immediately by his work on Semitic; the idea first occurred to me in the late 1960s as a result of studying Georgian and Kabardian with Kuipers in 1967; Gamkrelidze is a native speaker of Georgian who has long been occupied with linguistic typology. The important element is the recognition of a triple stop system for PIE and the simultaneous confrontation with languages possessing triple stop systems. Kortlandt's paper of 1978 has unfortunately ignored a great deal of other work done in the 1970s in which his "conclusions" are anticipated.

3. Highly marked phonemes frequently participate in expressive constructions, and it is remarkable that Swadesh, in his posthumously published book (1970), draws attention to the use of glottalization in Amerindian languages to signify sudden, momentaneous, repeated, or vibratory/oscillatory phenomena. Swadesh (1970:150) adds a curious note about Indo-European:

> In the Indo-European family, the combined evidence of component languages makes it possible to discern an old pattern of consonantal alternation. The voiced nonaspirates [i.e., the plain voiced stops, or mediae] have the role played by glottalized ones in American Indian languages. They express what is done quickly or lightly, or is of small size.

FROM PHONETIC FACTS TO SYNTACTIC PARADIGMS:
The Noun in Early PIE

Winfred P. Lehmann
University of Texas at Austin

Proposing to reconstruct Proto-Indo-European syntax of the fourth and third millennia may not be without its hazards. Until a short time ago the syntactic reconstruction posited for the parent language scarcely went beyond the second millennium. Linguists relied heavily on Greek and Sanskrit data, not least the prose, much of which dates from the second part of the first millennium B.C. The Hittite texts were scarcely consulted; Spargo's widely-read translation of Holger Pedersen's survey of nineteenth-century linguistics still wonders in 1931 whether Hittite is Indo-European (1931:165-66). Yet continued study has not only brought about recognition of a further branch of Indo-European, Anatolian, whose best attested language is Hittite, but also, as a result of further study, chronological layers within Hittite have been recognized. The earliest of the Hittite materials are dated by one of the foremost Hittite scholars, Erich Neu, around 2000 B.C., the time which may have applied for the conclusions provided by Delbrück in his authoritative syntax of the Indo-European languages (Delbrück 1893-1900; Neu 1976:241). When we compare the Linear B texts of 1450 B.C., we can start our syntactic reconstruction now from a threshold around the first part of the second millennium B.C., approximately a thousand years before the starting point of earlier scholars.

Here the matter of nominal inflection will be examined, with the aim of proposing a more likely account for Proto-Indo-European than that given in our handbooks. In effect, these reproduce the paradigms for Vedic Sanskrit, which has eight cases, three numbers, and three genders. For a century now we have had Lanman's thorough "statistical account of noun-inflection in the Veda" (*JAOS* 10:325-601). Yet little has been done with the "rank growth of forms which die out later," nor even with "all that is doubtful and questionable" (*JAOS* 10:326-27). The Vedic data must be reviewed in association with the findings from the other early materials mentioned above. In these we have evidence to revise the traditional treatment of nouns in Proto-Indo-European and also to reconstruct an earlier stage of the language, as early as the fourth millennium.

These combined materials are analyzed with increasingly productive methods. Some of these methods have been the focus of searching scrutiny, as in the meeting on historical syntax arranged by the Chicago Linguistic Society several years ago. It may be useful to review them and their application, not least in a conference shared with archaeologists, for much of the great advance in archaeology that has contributed importantly to Indo-European studies has come from the introduction of new methods. The archaeologists of the nineteenth century, e.g., Kossinna, had available sites and artifacts like those since explored so fruitfully (Menghin 1936: 56-67). Many of the subsequent gains have resulted from improved techniques of exploring these sites, as in stratigraphy, and from improved interpretation of the resulting data. Linguistics has made similar gains, such as those I review briefly.

The gains in linguistic study have come in great part from our improved understanding of language, and our consequent capability to deal more intensively with its various components. I note first the treatment of the functional-semantic components as illuminated by Elizabeth Closs Traugott (1981). She recognizes three such components: propositional, textual, and expressive. The propositional component comprises "the resources of the language for making it possible to talk about something, [including] events and their participants." The textual component comprises "resources of the language for creating a cohesive text [including] anaphora, ... temporal and logical connectives," and so on. The expressive component comprises "systemic and deontic modals, ... deference markers," etc. Semantic and grammatical shifts take place according to definite patterns among these components, as illustrated by numerous examples: thus, our indefinite article *a, an,* as well as the anaphoric *one,* as in *which one will you take?,* arose from the numeral *one.* As this example illustrates, textual markers often develop from propositional material. And the adversative conjunction *while* arose from the temporal conjunction *while,* which in turn arose from the noun meaning 'space of time'. Again, propositional matter is the source.

From her observation of such examples, Traugott has set up two hypotheses, the first of which is: "If a meaning-shift during the process of grammaticalization occurs within a component, it is more likely to involve 'less personal' → 'more personal' than vice versa." As one of her examples, *while* has shifted from nonpersonal to time reference to adversative references involving participants. Among examples from Ancient Greek, the affirmative particles of Homer *mén* and *dé,* roughly, 'indeed' "later acquire respectively ... an adversative and an inferential force" (Denniston [1950] 1966:xliii). This hypothesis may illuminate meaning-shifts in the instrumental, dative, ablative, and locative of late PIE.

Traugott's second hypothesis also concerns us in the exploration below: "If a meaning-shift in the process of grammaticalization occurs that involves shifts from one functional-semantic component to another, then the shift is more likely to be from propositional to textual to expressive than vice versa." Among her examples are locatives like OE *butan* 'on the outside', coming to be used as a locative adverb and thereupon a conjunction, New English *but*. Examples from Denniston ([1950] 1966:xxxvii) include Ancient Greek *álla* 'other things' coming to mean 'but', as well as Eng. *well, come, why*. Moreover, examining the development of modals like New English *can* and *may*, and that of deference markers like Japanese *boku* 'servant' to the first person marker 'I', we can extend this hypothesis to cover the third component: expressive markers also arise from propositional elements.

These two hypotheses, proposed on the basis of a recognition of several functional-semantic components in language, can be used on the one hand to account for developments in a given language, as Traugott has done. On the other hand, we can apply them for internal reconstruction, when we do not have the earlier texts, as in Proto-Indo-European. Observing linguistic forms rather than linguistic categories, Traugott's proposal must be particularly welcome to historical linguists who emphasize the surface data of language, as in suggesting that syntax needs phonology.

To one such linguist we owe another method which has yielded insights into earlier syntax. At the Chicago conference of 1976 Eric Hamp proposed and illustrated the "principle of 'derring-do' " (1976:348). Based on Spenser's well-known misinterpretation of a Chaucerian collocation, Hamp sets out to demonstrate "one important requirement for any thesis of syntactic change, i.e., a specification of the conditions under which the phonetic output of one [old] syntax could be mistaken by (speakers and) hearers for that of another [new] syntax" (1976: 348). The principle is illustrated by three innovations, one being the introduction of the Proto-Indo-European locative in *-i*. I refer to this innovation further below.

In welcoming Hamp's proposal I would like to comment on several matters. The first concerns the importance of recognizing the presence of a syntactic category already in the language when derring-do applies. Hamp assumes a locative category in Indo-European when the *-i-* locative is introduced; similarly, in his second example he assumes the presence of a dative singular as well as a nominative plural in Proto-British when its speakers came to use nominative plurals with singular nouns in appositive constructions. Although the thrust of his essay is directed at the importance of phonology in syntactic study, the role of syntactic categories is far more crucial in his examples. If syntactic categories had not been on hand, the phonological markers would not have been subjected to syntactic change. It is good to have Hamp's demonstration that syntax needs categories as well as phonetics.

Several other matters are worth noting in regard to Hamp's principle. First, the previous role of the phonological markers may have had little to do with their new syntactic role. For example, the nominative plural ending in Proto-British did not fill the role of a dative singular, let alone a nominative singular; the shift might be termed awkward, almost comparable to those in folk etymology. A classic example is the -*er*- plural marker of German. A reflex of the Indo-European -*e/os*- nominal suffix, which survived in the plural, underwent a shift in syntactic force as notable as the plural marker cited from Proto-British by Hamp (Gürtler 1912).

The second matter for our attention is the tenuous, even chance, evidence for recognizing that such syntactic change has taken place in a prehistoric period. The evidence for explaining the origin of the -*er*- plural marker is taken from only one noun, the word *calf*. In this way the explanation parallels that for *derring-do* itself, which Spenser, fortunately for subsequent commentators, adopted from the popular Chaucer rather than from a poet whose works have not been preserved in writing. If Spenser had taken it from an oral poet whose works had not survived, we would not be able to provide an explanation for the word *derring-do*.

The principle of derring-do calls to our attention another contribution to historical linguistic methodology: the insistence on minute analysis and description of data before these are used for historical purposes. Such attention to historical data must be credited to Calvert Watkins and colleagues. I will only recall (without further scrutiny) some of the techniques he has applied. On the one hand, in examining poetic materials Watkins suggested a crucial difference between the material in the early part of a line and that in the cadence, proposing that the cadence material was more archaic; on this suggestion see, however, Cardona (1975). As another procedure, Watkins advocated basing inferences on proverbs, suggesting that these tended to maintain archaic patterns. In a further procedure he suggested exploitation of those materials which might be assumed for the stages of culture found at the time of the early Indo-European subgroups. Historical linguists may well be expected to have taken heed of these techniques as they were presented. Accordingly, I review in greater detail the procedures outlined by Nagy.

This review comments on the procedures which must be observed in making use of the linguistic data of the Greek poet Hesiod, and indeed of formulaic verse in general. Such data, which make up a major share of our early Indo-European materials—the *Veda*s, the Homeric poems, *Beowulf,* and so on—provide complex problems to the interpreter because the so-called formulae may be frozen expressions from a variety of dialects, of a variety of periods, and even remodeled toward excessive archaism to suggest authenticity. The possibilities are so manifold that one is tempted to turn to simpler pursuits than historical linguistics.

On the other hand, historical linguistics can rely on increasingly meticulous textual scholars like those in Otten's group, who provide us with more than one hundred and fifty pages of explanation for three scant pages of Old Hittite (Neu

1974). With much gratitude we admit reliance on devoted scholars like Wilhelm Schulze, Friedrich Klaeber, and Karl Hoffmann for other crucial texts. The standards for the interpretation of materials are then being tightened. Besides relying on the textual observations of such scholars, we hope that they will maintain watchful eyes on comparative linguists indulging in excessive generalizations and on editors who publish essays with unacceptable canons of judgment and knowledge.

The tightened standards, as well as the methods and principles cited, provide grounds for suggesting that we can indeed proceed beyond the conclusions reached by previous Indo-Europeanists like Karl Brugmann, Berthold Delbrück, Jacob Wackernagel, and Antoine Meillet, among many others whose deep knowledge was matched by resources they were accorded for their scholarly activities. Although Indo-Europeanists today lack such resources, subsequent scholarship has provided some assistance for improving the presentation of PIE grammar.

For new insights into Proto-Indo-European, it would be helpful to have further handbooks on the dialects, such as the Wackernagel volume on the Old Indic verb, Neu's projected grammar of Old Hittite, and Markey's grammar of Proto-Germanic. Yet even before appearance of these and other current undertakings, we can make inferences about the inflections of the Indo-European noun which led to a different projection from that in our standard handbooks. The Hittite nominal paradigm provides leads concerning the forms themselves and the categories. (See Table 1, p. 145.)

When we review the categories, we observe that gender is poorly represented in Hittite. To be sure, grammars posit a neuter class of nouns as opposed to an animate one. But the neuter class is distinguished only by the absence of the nominative endings in -s. The nominative/accusative plural endings, when distinct, mark collectives. A realistic analysis would lead to a paradigm which allows nouns a gap in a case marked for the agent but does not assume a gender category.

Number and case categories also are defectively represented. The plural contains at most three cases: nominative, accusative, and genitive. Even for these, the markers were not distinct from those in the singular. The genitive plural -an, considered cognate with the distinctive genitive plural marker of the other dialects, is used as singular, while the genitive singular ending is frequent in plurals. Moreover, singular forms rather than plurals are found with numerals. The dative, locative, ablative, and instrumental plurals either have endings taken from other cases or are equivalent to those in the singular. When we examine the probable origin of the nominative and accusative plural forms, we find scarcely more evidence for a number category than we do for a gender category.

The evidence for case inflections is better examined after we recall some characteristics of inflection in other dialects, such as Vedic. But even at this point we may observe that Hittite has a further case ending in -a, which early Hittite scholars lumped under the dative. This case is now known as the directive.

TABLE 1

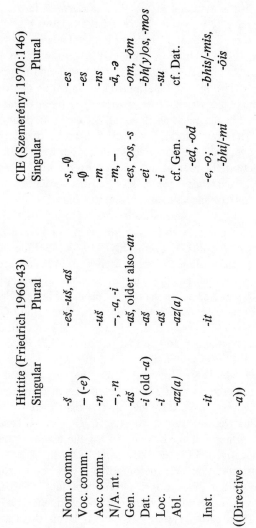

	Hittite (Friedrich 1960:43) Singular	Plural	CIE (Szemerényi 1970:146) Singular	Plural
Nom. comm.	-š	-eš, -uš, -aš	-s, -∅	-es
Voc. comm.	-(e)	-uš	-∅	-es
Acc. comm.	-n	-uš	-m	-ns
N/A. nt.	-, -n	-, -a, -i	-m, –	-ā, -ə
Gen.	-aš	-aš, older also -an	-es, -os, -s	-om, -ōm
Dat.	-i (old -a)	-aš	-ei	-bh(y)os, -mos
Loc.	-i	-aš	-i	-su
Abl.	-az(a)	-az(a)	cf. Gen. -ed, -od	cf. Dat.
Inst.	-it	-it	-e, -o; -bhi/-mi	-bhis/-mis, -ōis
((Directive	-a))			

If, applying observations based on phonetic facts, we compare the Vedic inflection, we find similar skewing in plural cases (see Table 2, p. 147). This skewing is known to every second-semester student of Sanskrit, and even to general linguists who have examined handbooks such as Whitney's *Sanskrit Grammar* (1896:38). Some of the endings in the dual and in the plural observe different phonetic rules from those applied internally in words. These are the locative plural in -*su* and the endings beginning with *bh:* the dual instrumental/dative/ablative -*bhyām*, the plural dative/ablative -*bhyas,* and the plural instrumental in -*bhis,* which is more common in Vedic than -*ais.* For these endings the rules of external sandhi apply rather than those for internal sandhi, as may be determined by comparing the forms of *áṅgirās* with those of an *a*-stem like *devás.* That is to say, in these forms the rules for phonetic combination are the same as those of nominal compounds rather than nominal inflections. The four plural cases which have no distinctive endings in Hittite accordingly give evidence for a loose bond between noun and ending. Rather than by inflection these cases are marked by the kind of nexus found in agglutination. Phonetic evidence then points to differentiation between these four cases and the nominative, accusative, and genitive plural.

Earlier Indo-Europeanists devoted considerable attention to these case forms, as may be determined from references like those in Wackernagel's *Altindische Grammatik* (1930:1-8 et passim) or Szemerényi (1970:143-76; cf. Table 1). One concern is the origin of the endings, whether derived from earlier particles or from affixes. Another concern was directed at the development of declension in general, whether from fewer to more cases, or the reverse—as in the later dialects. Lanman's count of all nominal forms in the *Rigveda* supports assumption of change in the inflectional pattern. Of 93,277 case forms, only 124 are ablative plurals—65 masculine, 44 feminine, and 15 neuter; 363 are dative plurals—329 masculine, 28 feminine, 6 neuter. Even the locative plural with 1,546 occurrences and the genitive plural with 1,595 are relatively infrequent. Only the instrumental plural of the oblique cases is well represented with 3,360 occurrences as compared with 16,333 for the nominative, accusative, vocative plural. The figures are comparable in the dual. Only the nominative, accusative, vocative dual with 4,016 occurrences is well represented; the others fall far behind: 53 for the instrumental, 116 for the genitive, 123 for the locative, 25 for the dative, and 15 for the ablative.

Such evidence illustrates that even before Hittite was known the grounds for reconstruction of an earlier declensional system like that of Classical Sanskrit were weak. Szemerényi's inflection provides a list of pertinent data in the dialects, not reconstructions of an earlier system; he himself labels them as "common to the dialects." If we attempt to determine the earlier system, even on the basis of Vedic alone, it seems clear that some case-forms—those exhibiting external sandhi— are late, in view of their phonetic patterning and their low frequency. But until Hittite became known, cogent evidence for the reconstruction of an earlier nominal

TABLE 2

		Vedic Sanskrit		'you'	Hittite 'you'
		as-stem	*a*-stem	'you'	'you'
Sg.	N	*áṅgirās*	*devás*	*tvám*	*zik*
	A	*áṅgirasam*	*devám*	*tvā́m*	*tuk*
	I	*áṅgirasā*	*devéna*	*tváyā*	
	D	*áṅgirase*	*devā́ya*	*túbhyam*	*tuk*
	Ab	*áṅgirasas*	*devā́t*	*tvát*	*tuēdaz*
	G	*áṅgirasas*	*devásya*	*táva*	*tuēl*
	L	*áṅgirasi*	*devé*	*tváyi*	*tuk*
	V	*áṅgiras*	*déva*		
Du.	N V	*áṅgirasāu*	*devaú/devā́*	*yuvám* (V)	
	A			*yuvā́m* (V)	
	I D	*áṅgirobhyām*	*devā́bhyām*	*yuvā́bhyām*	
	Ab			*yuvát* (RV 1)	
	G L	*áṅgirasos*	*deváyos*	*yuváyos* [*yuvós* (V)]	
Pl.	N V	*áṅgirasas*	*devā́s*	*yūyám*	*šumḗš*
	A		*devā́n*	*yuṣmā́n*	*šumā́š*
	I	*áṅgirobhis*	*devaís (-ebhis)*	*yuṣmā́bhis*	
	D	*áṅgirobhyas*	*devébhyas*	*yuṣmábhyam*	*šumā́š*
	Ab			*yuṣmát*	*šumḗdaz*
	G	*áṅgirasām*	*devā́nām*	*yuṣmā́kam*	*šumḗl*
	L	*áṅgiraḥsu*	*devéṣu*	*yuṣmā́su* [*yuṣmé* (V)]	*šumā́š*

system was difficult to assemble. The Hittite data suggest that nominal forms were distinguished at an earlier period essentially in one number and one gender rather than in the three long posited for both number and gender: singular, dual, pural, and masculine, feminine, neuter. Moreover, these insights lead us to re-examine other evidence in the early dialect which might be relics of the earlier system.

Among such evidence is the Vedic pattern in sequences of two congruent nouns, only one of which had an ending. One such pattern consists of examples of the infrequent plural forms. Among these are ten occurrences of the instrumental -*bhir ūtí* rather than -*bhir ūtíbhiḥ*. I cite one of these from a Strophic Hymn, *Rigveda* 1.158.1:

> *prá-yát—sasráthe—ákavāhir—ūtí*
> ptc-when—you-two-have-rushed-ahead—not-sparing (Inst Pl)—helps [Inst Pl]
> 'when you two have rushed ahead with your excellent assistance'

All ten occurrences of this pattern stand in the cadence of their metrical line, as does this one; by one of Watkins' philological principles, the pattern should therefore be archaic. If archaic, the construction may be accounted for by pursuing long-standing explanation of the -*bh*- endings as originally indefinite for function and number (Wackernagel 1930:13). Interpreted in accordance with subsequent views, such constructions represent affixation of agglutinative elements which we would call postpositions. As the example above illustrates, the postposition may have been used only once in such patterns; items in agreement with the marked nominal are found with a bare stem.

Vedic yields other evidence for such an assumption of bare stems accompanied by suffixed markers. Among this evidence is a pattern which Haudry discusses at the conclusion of his recent book on the uses of cases in Vedic. The pattern may be illustrated by *Rigveda* 1.53.7:

> *yudhā́—yúdham—úpa—gha—id—eṣi—dhṛṣnuyā́*
> combat—combat—ptc—ptc—ptc—you-go—courageously

Following Renou, Haudry translates the line: " 'battle after battle you advance courageously' " (1978:461). After scrutinizing previous scholarship, he parses the first two items as consisting of the stem followed by a connective *ā́* tying the first stem to the second, which in this instance maintains the ending. In further comments at the very conclusion of his book, Haudry (1978:462) accounts as follows for "the use of the bare stem in syntactic patterns as a form without endings: . . . In an ancient state of Indo-European traditionally designated as pre-inflexional, it seems that certain postpositions, the ancestors of case endings, could only apply once in a nominal syntactic pattern or in a group of coordinated syntactic patterns, like prepositions of non-inflected languages." That is, the pattern concerned is somewhat like English prepositional phrases consisting of two nouns, such as "with sword and spear." Haudry cites other traces of this ancient state, such as Greek infinitives without endings. While he does not pursue this analysis further, we may take it as support for the assumption of an earlier nominal system in which affixes were loosely attached to nominal themes. The noun at this point was not inflected. Postposed particles could be affixed to indicate its syntactic relationships.

Evidence for loosely postposed elements is found also in other dialects. The Greek element *-phi* is quite parallel in use, and also in phonology, to the Sanskrit *bh*-elements. Like the Sanskrit *bh*-endings, it has instrumental and ablative value, less commonly, locative. Moreover, in Nestor's often cited exhortation to Agamemnon it has dative value, *Iliad* 2.363:

hōs—phrḗtrē—phrḗtrēphin—arégēi,—phûla—dé—phúlois
that—clan—to-clan—may-aid—tribe—to—tribes
'so that clan may give aid to clan, tribe to tribe'

This exhortation reflects an ancient practice of warfare, where troops are aligned in accordance with earlier social groups. By another of Watkins' principles the linguistic usage as well as the custom is archaic.

Evidence in Homer then supports the assumption of an earlier nominal system in which postpositional elements were loosely attached to stems. Moreover, the singular as well as plural use of *-phi* suggests an earlier system like that of Hittite, in which number was not strongly distinguished, if at all.

Homeric language includes further such postposed particles which appear to form incipient cases. One is *-then* 'from', used for a point from which motion takes place, and also the original point in time or the agent of an action; it is comparable to the ablative, and like this was used with pronouns in comparison, as in *Iliad* 1.114:

epeì—oú—hethén—esti—khereiōn
since—not—from-her—she-is—inferior
'since she is not inferior to her'

Like *-phi, -then* has a broad range of uses, some even genitival. Another such postposed element in Homer is *-si,* as on place-names like *Athḗnēsi.* A further postposed element, *-ōs,* has ablative force. Such patterns in Greek supplement the data found in Hittite and Vedic in favor of an earlier system of loosely postposed endings.

The Greek ending *-ōs* is found on adverbs, much as are several such endings in Germanic. Gothic has adverbs of manner in *-ba,* which is related to the Sanskrit and Greek *-bh-* endings, e.g., *bairhtaba* 'brightly'. Gothic also has adverbs in *-ō,* which Germanic linguists derive from the ending found in ablatives of other dialects, e.g., *aftarō* 'behind'. Another ending is *-a,* as on *inna* 'within', which is derived from an instrumental. Germanic then provides additional information on a nominal system with a large number of postpositional elements rather than the neat declensions of late Sanskrit, Greek, and Latin.

If we set out to determine this earlier system on the basis of the situation in the earliest attested dialects—Hittite, Vedic, Homeric Greek—supplemented by data from other dialects, we can at most construct a nominal system with a relatively well-established set of forms in the singular. Apart from these singular forms we can at best reconstruct nominatives and accusatives in the dual and plural, and a genitive in the plural. Before discussing these dual and plural forms, we examine the singular oblique forms in an attempt to propose the nominal pattern of an earlier period than around 2500 B.C., at which time the system might well have developed to a system like Szemerényi's (see Table 1).

This system of around 2500 B.C. may be analyzed in accordance with established procedures, including those cited above. Beginning this analysis with the ablative, the least frequent form, we may attempt to determine the origin of its distinctive ending. This is *-ōd/-ēd,* found only in thematic stems. These endings are at the same time adverbial. Sanskrit includes adverbs with this formation, e.g., *paścād* 'from behind'; Greek and Germanic, which do not contain an ablative case, include such adverbial forms as Greek *oikō* 'from the house', Gothic *sundrō* 'asunder', which provide evidence for the *-ōd* ending. From the occurrence of these forms to mark ablatives only in the *-o-*stems, we conclude that in this use they were relatively late. In this late declension a derivational marker came to be associated with the new inflection in some dialects to yield a further case form. Greek provides clues for the earlier use of this marker.

In Greek *-d-* is used as suffix on patronymics, as in *Tantalídēs* 'male descendant of Tantalos', *Tantalís* 'female descendant of Tantalos'. These show the same relationship as does the adverbial suffix, that is, 'one having Tantalos as origin'. Common nouns with the affix are *huidoûs* 'grandson', *hûide* 'granddaughter' (see Brugmann 2.466-72, 603-4). If we concern ourselves only with these uses of the *-d-*suffix here, we may examine its possible semantic development in accordance with Traugott's hypotheses. As proposed in the first hypothesis, the suffix was extended from a less personal force to a more personal in the patronymics, and also in the ablatives, which were commonly used for the standard in comparison. In this way we may account for an additional form in the *-o-*stems. Remarkably, this is the use of the hapax dual ablative *yuvát* in *Rigveda* 1.109.1:

nā́nyā–yuvát–prámatir–asti–máhyaṃ
no-other–from-you-two–assurance–is–for-me
'There is no other assurance for me than you two'

The *d*-affix may have been introduced in pronominal inflection with reference to personal referents, and in this way a new case form, the ablative, was introduced.

Examining another case with few attestations in the *Rigveda,* the locative, we may recall Hamp's account. By his view, its origin is to be sought in an Indo-European anaphoric element *i* (1976:348-49). Hamp finds evidence for this element in Latin *inde* versus *unde* [**i-(i)m-dhe* : **ku-m-dhe*]. This ending would then have a different kind of source from that of the ablative; rather than a derivational element, the origin would be in a particle. The particle would have meant something like 'here; at this point, time'. Hamp's proposal would then be an instance of Traugott's second hypothesis, in that a lexical element is taken over for the propositional sphere. We must observe that this change is to be placed in an earlier stage of Proto-Indo-European; for the locative ending *-i* is found also in the older nominal inflections, such as the consonant stems. In agreement with Hamp, we observe that the agglutinative process for specifying the nominal paradigm was in effect even before the *o*-stems became productive. Yet as noted above, even at this time the locative category was already established in the Indo-European noun.

The earlier form of the locative had no ending. Such a situation may well seem remarkable. Yet it can be accounted for by an early syntactic pattern of Indo-European, which may be best known from the Latin *mihi est* construction: lit., 'to me/at me is' = 'I have'. This pattern is found in the citation above from *Rigveda* 1.109.1. Both the initial position of the word for the possessor and its locative force may be understood from Clark's essay in the syntax volume in *Universals of Human Language* (1978:87). Examining constructions in several languages, she points out the relationship between indicating "the location of an object, either in some physical sphere (1 and 2) or in someone's possession (3 and 4)." Her examples from English are as follows:

1. There is a book on the table.
2. The book is on the table.
3. Tom has a book.
4. The book is Tom's.

The *mihi est* construction is like (3).

Assuming this also for an earlier period we may propose that initial position was adequate to identify the location of the possessor. The locative or possessor nominal would not then have required a special suffix. Hence the endingless locatives! But this contention came to be insufficiently marked, for reasons which we might expand on. The most important reason may well have been the incipient shift from OV to VO structure, so that as in *Rigveda* 1.109.1 the possessor would no longer stand initially in the clause. A distinctive marker was then introduced, the suffix *-i*. This came to indicate both the personal location, i.e., the dative, and the physical location, i.e., the locative (Lehmann 1981b).

Neu (1980) provides a complete account of the "endingless locative" in Hittite accompanied by a thorough review of the scholarship; the endingless locative gave rise to the new inflections in Hittite: the locative pronoun *-i* and the directive in *-a*. Thus Hittite provides at the same time evidence for an "old morphological pattern of a very early developmental phase of Indo-European" (Neu 1980:54) and for the expansion of the declensional system. Specific markers were introduced for cases of the singular, the dative as well as the locative. Subsequently, the two cases were differentiated, as has long been known.

Three of the oblique case forms in the singular may be accounted for in this way. The fourth, that is, the instrumental, is relatively late, marked by some kind of suffixed element. In Hittite it has a *-t* element, with preceding *-i-;* the ending is often extended with *-a*. Its origin is unclear; Sturtevant's derivation from the same source as the ablative is unlikely. The markers in the other dialects differ from short and long *e* and *o* to *-phi* and *-mi,* showing some of the rank growth noted by Lanman.

Evidence for the marking of cases by affixation is found not only in these four cases, nor only in Anatolian. Another geographically restricted ending is the genitive singular of *o*-stems in *-syo*. I have long held that this was formed by adding the PIE *-yo* marker to the *-s* which was maintained as the nominative ending (see now Lehmann 1981a). Others have published a similar analysis of this ending (among them are Schmidt and Szemerényi 1970:169). We differ in details. Yet the essential point here is evidence of another instance of the agglutinative process in the development of the PIE nominal paradigm.

The forms of Hittite suggest that the Anatolian languages split off from the Indo-European group at the time the locative was developing a specific marker. For in Hittite, the dative and locative are not yet distinguished. Moreover, Hittite has a further case form, the directive, for the location at which an action was designated. Hittite phonology is too murky to permit relating the characteristic Hittite ending to forms in other dialects, in spite of tentative explanations. What is important is the presence of a further case, not found in any of the other Indo-European dialects. Its formation parallels that of the forms in the Hittite verbal inflection, especially in the middle. Similar processes may be observed in the pronouns, as Benveniste (1962:66-77) has shown in some detail. In the middle, successive particles were suffixed, leading to a sequence of suffixes like those in languages such as Japanese.

Even at this stage of Hittite we must assume thematic inflection. The ablative ending is added to the vowel of this inflection, and it plus the -z came to be the marker in other inflections such as the consonant and resonant stems. Hittite in this way differs from the other Indo-European languages with ablative case. These have the -d suffix only in the vocalic stems; elsewhere the genitive also has ablative function. The difference reflects a stage in which noun stems with various final elements might add postpositional elements.

At a later stage, nominal declension came to be fixed; postpositional elements might be maintained in archaic usage, such as -phi in Homer, or with adverbial forms. Case endings, on the other hand, followed specific patterns within their specific declension, whether thematic, resonant, or obstruent. This patterning is in accordance with the well-known systematization of the Indo-European paradigm—its *Systemzwang*. That systematization led to the fixing of specific endings in the plural and dual, as well as in the singular as illustrated by well-established nominal patterns like those in Sanskrit and other dialects of the first millennium B.C. Fairbanks (1977) provides further evidence for the transitional systems and the gradual development of the system known from Vedic Sanskrit. The systematization of the various adverbial endings also fostered adoption of forms for nouns and adjectives from the pronominal declension, of which there is considerable testimony in the dialects. Moreover, it contributed to a characteristic of the Indo-European system of declension which Oertel long ago noted; in contrast with many languages the Indo-European endings have composite meaning—a single ending like -os marks number and gender as well as case.

The sources of five of the eight singular case markers of late Proto-Indo-European have thus been identified in a kind of agglutination. The others will be briefly noted below. In our analysis here we start out from an early stage of Proto-Indo-European, during the fourth and third millennia, a nominal system somewhat like that of Old Turkish. This consists of forms with case-like postpositional endings (von Gabain 1974:86). Moreover, the endings need appear only once in a phrase, as in the Rigvedic patterns cited above. In early Proto-Indo-European, nouns were affixed with markers to indicate some functions. Several of these markers came to be fixed: -s, -h, -m. The first indicated an individual; the second, a mass, or a collective; the third, a target or nonactive object. This system, as I noted in 1958, may still be recognized in some nouns, not by their declension but rather by their derivational relationships. For example, Sanskrit *himás*, with -s ending, indicates an individual cold event, 'frost'. With the collective ending -h it is maintained in Sanskrit as *hímā* 'winter, a mass of frost'. With -m ending it survives in *himam* 'snow', a phenomenon of the cold period. The stem itself is attested in the *Rigveda* only in the instrumental, with -ā, meaning 'cold' as opposed to the heat of the sun. In the fourth millennium and earlier, such forms were not the bases of separate paradigms; at that time individual elements arranged in sentences with even greater grammatical autonomy than Meillet proposes for individual words in the Proto-

Indo-European he treats. Subsequently, as the various dialects were becoming more autonomous, further affixes came to be fixed on nouns, pronouns, and adjectives. As indicated in articles cited above (Lehmann 1958; Fairbanks 1977), these processes led to the paradigms attested in the various dialects.

With the help of phonetic facts, we have thus identified the nominal system of the earlier period of Proto-Indo-European. This system is similar to that of many OV languages, agreeing then with other syntactic characteristics of Proto-Indo-European which are now widely recognized.

In conclusion, we may turn briefly to the purpose of reconstruction such as that pursued here; for it is also dismissed as glottogonic speculation, scarcely more than the idle product of a fertile imagination. One might scarcely provide a better justification than de Saussure's: for the linguist, "the sole means of reconstructing is by comparison, and the only aim of comparison is a reconstruction. Our procedure is sterile unless we view the relations of several forms from a perspective of time and succeed in reestablishing a single form . . . The aim of reconstruction is, then, not to restore a form for its own sake—this would be rather ridiculous to say the least—but to crystallize and condense a set of conclusions that seem logically to follow from the results obtained at each moment; in short, its aim is to record the progress of our science" (de Saussure 1959:218-19). In addition to the purpose stated by de Saussure, linguists must also practice reconstruction with the aim of recognizing parallels with other languages in the appropriate period; our progress, especially in other families, is so meager that little such work of lasting value has yet been done. Moreover, by reconstructing earlier strata in the prehistory of a language like Proto-Indo-European, linguists can open the way to comparison with the results of archaeological work.

In discussions with archaeologists, an Indo-Europeanist is invariably asked for linguistic details which might assist archaeologists to a closer analysis of their finds. So far we have given them little help; we have produced little linguistic stratigraphy. One important example, however, is Specht's collocation of terms for wagon construction with the thematic declension (1947:99-103). The terminology is not inflected in accordance with consonant nor with resonant inflections, but as thematic stems. Assuming as we have here that the thematic declension was developing in the early part of the third millennium, we can relate this syntactic fact to the lexicon applying for such techniques of transportation. Thereupon, we would like the archaeologists to provide evidence on their part, carbon-14 dating, for example, of the dates for remains of such wagons. Archaeologists have proposed several waves of Indo-Europeans invading Europe. Did the earliest use wagons? If so, we may date the development of thematic inflections even earlier than the third millennium.

One could cite other linguistic evidence for stratigraphy which might be checked by archaeologists. Is there for example any change in burial practice which might correspond to the change of the Germanic kinship terminology around the beginning of the first millennium B.C. (Lehmann 1968)? Further examples may be provided if these lead to fruitful conclusions. What is needed is cooperation. We hope that this conference will lead to such cooperation. There is no shortage of problems, nor even of data to explore, both by current scholars and by students entering the field of Indo-European studies. Those students who are linguists will be able to contribute to the far fuller picture of early Indo-European culture, including language, which we now have thanks largely to brilliant work in archaeology of the last several decades.

INDO-EUROPEAN CULTURE,
With Special Attention to Religion

Edgar C. Polomé
University of Texas at Austin

Pastoralism was the basis of the economy of the Indo-European invaders of Europe. Their first wave and its aftermath, from the middle of the fifth millennium B.C. until about 3700 B.C., appears to have played a decisive role in the way of life of the territories extending from Rumania to the Low Countries (Gimbutas 1977). They were essentially cattle breeders, but they also domesticated sheep, goats, pigs, and dogs. Their technique must have been sufficiently sophisticated to practice castration and, presumably, to use the oxen as draft animals. Though cattle breeding continued to prevail through the centuries, e.g., in the Linear Pottery cultures, there was some fluctuation in the relative importance of the various species involved in animal husbandry, e.g., the flocks of smaller ruminants decreased, while the herds of swine increased in number (Murray 1973:178-79).

While the cultures of Indo-European origin favored cattle over any other domestic animal, other cultures of the fourth and third millennia B.C. concentrated on the swine (for example, the coastal culture of southern Sweden about 2400-2200 B.C.), or on ovicaprid breeding (for example, the Dimini culture in Greece)—but prevalence of the smaller ruminants also occurs in some Indo-European cultures like the Baden culture in Hungary (end of the fourth millennium B.C.), though the bovine continues to play a prominent part in their ritual practices as is shown by some carefully buried skeletons. It is interesting to note that such changes are unparalleled by the change in the size of cattle; as Bökönyi (1974:117-18) pointed out, at the end of the Copper Age and the beginning of the Bronze Age, the size of cattle had diminished so markedly that "perhaps with the Baden culture, a great number of dwarf cattle had reached Central Europe."

By the end of the Neolithic period, cattle no longer served exclusively to provide meat—very little was obtained by hunting game, as appears from the scanty remains of bones of wild animals. Now, the cows were milked (from the rear, like goats).

These facts shed a particular light on the Indo-European lexicon covering animal names: the 'bovine' shows a common term *g^wou-, attested in Indo-Iranian, Greek, Latin, Germanic, and Celtic, and represented in Slavic *govędo 'head of cattle'; similarly, there is a generic word for 'sheep', *owi-, represented by cognates in Old Indic, Greek, Latin, Old Irish, Baltic, and Slavic, and meaning 'ewe' in Germanic, and a number of languages show old correspondences for 'lamb'. In both cases, technical terms associated with animal husbandry are also found: 'to milk' represented by a verbal theme, *(H)melg̃-, shared by Greek, Latin, Germanic, Celtic, and Slavic, and 'wool', found already in the Hittite (ḫulana-) and preserved in Indo-Iranian, Greek, Latin, Celtic, Germanic, Balto-Slavic. Furthermore, there is a generic term for the porcine, *sū-, but it must originally have designated the wild pig, as it still does in Indo-Iranian. Another term has equal claim to IE origin, *porko-, which must have meant 'young pig', and denoted the domestic variety. It is also found in the oriental part of the Indo-European area, proving that domestication was originally practiced everywhere, but abandoned at an early date in India and Iran (Benveniste 1973:23-31). Therefore, it is all the more astonishing that no generic word for 'goat' is to be found. The goat is the earliest ruminant to have been domesticated. It spread in Europe before the coming of the Indo-Europeans. Two types prevail: the scimitar-horned goats and the twisted-horn goats, but none of the limited lexical correspondences point to any of their features: Gk. aíks, Arm. aic, Av. izaēna (adj.) 'of [goat's] skin' is derived from a root indicating its movement, just as Goth. gaits 'goat' : Latin haedus 'kid', usually compared with Lith. žaidžiu, žaisti 'play' < originally 'jump, gambol', and Skt. aja- : Lith. ažys, possibly from the root *ag̃- 'drive'; OHG ziga (Ger. Ziege) : Gk. díza [: aíks, Lákōnes] (Hesychius), Arm. tik 'leather bag' is isolated. Obviously, the Indo-Europeans did not have a common term for 'goat', or perhaps they eliminated it as a consequence of some ecological change: at an early stage of colonization, the goat as destroyer of woods may have been useful, but once open wastelands had been created by impoverishment of the soil through primitive agricultural practice, the sheep, as a grass-feeder, definitely proved more valuable (Zeuner 1963:145-46).

Unfortunately, the counts of bones provided by archaeologists do not distinguish between sheep and goats and simply contrast the ovicaprid with the bovine elements in the herds; from these data, it appears that in the third millennium there were two coexisting and partly overlapping animal husbandry activities prevailing in Europe—cultures keeping flocks of sheep, which traded copper implements and ornaments with the Near East and Caucasus areas, and cultures concentrating on cattle breeding, with characteristic pottery styles and metal objects produced locally from their own ores (Murray 1970:111). Nevertheless, however valuable these data may be, and in spite of the problems they raise regarding definite cultures, e.g., in Switzerland, in the Middle and Lower Danube areas and in the Ukraine, they do not throw any light on the linguistic question.

The instrument of Indo-European mobility and a major asset to their conquering power is undoubtedly the horse. Apparently the oldest appearance of the domesticated horse is to be located in the southern Ukraine—originally dated around 3000 B.C. (Bökönyi 1973:238), it is now assigned to an earlier period, between 4400 and 3400 B.C., which coincides with the first invasion wave of Indo-European steppe pastoralists toward Europe (Gimbutas 1977:284). That the horse was, with the dog, man's closest companion on these moves appears both from the archaeological finds and from the lexicon: both *eḱwo- 'horse' and *ḱwōn-/ḱun- 'dog' are represented in all the major IE dialects, though their reflexes, such as Gk. *híppos* or Lat. *canis,* may sometimes present us with rather puzzling phonological problems. It is striking that, though the major implement used for horse-riding—namely, antler-cheek pieces with the attached bridle—is found in the earliest Indo-European settlements (Gimbutas 1977:281-82), no corresponding common lexical item has come down to us.[1] Neither is there a common Indo-European term for 'riding a horse', though 'riding a vehicle' is expressed by *weĝh-, documented in all the major Indo-European languages, also as the root for the common term for a wheeled vehicle. Cartwrights are presumably among the oldest craftsmen among Indo-Europeans, and their technical terminology goes back to the older periods of the speech community: words for 'wheel', *kʷelo-s/*kʷolo-s, reduplicated *kʷekʷlos and *retH-, both from verbal roots indicating motion, and both very old as evidenced by their areal distribution (see Table 1, p. 159); 'axle' (*aḱs-), 'yoke' (*yugom), etc. (Devoto 1962:236-37, 269-70). The problem, however, is what kind of vehicles are we talking about during the earliest Indo-European migratory movements? No doubt the first carts were drawn by cattle, but these were soon replaced by horses (Bökönyi 1974:249). The four-wheeled cart seems to have been the earliest vehicle: did it appear with the first Indo-Europeans or only at the turn of the third and second millennia B.C., followed by its variant with spoked wheels a few centuries later?[2] The latter dating is usually correlated with the first occurrence of the four-wheeled vehicle in the Uruk culture of Mesopotamia around the middle of the fourth millennium B.C. Military use is only documented since the twenty-eighth century B.C., and it will take until the fifteenth century B.C. before the Mitanni charioteers on fast chariots with two spoked wheels revolutionized the tactics of combat in the Middle East (Kammenhuber 1961:9-14). That this new instrument of victory was introduced by the Aryan aristocracy of Mitanni in Mesopotamia is most significant, for the improvement of the chariot appears to be an Indo-European achievement in the early Bronze Age, as is confirmed by Mycenæan data. This late date explains the absence of a common term for 'felly' or 'spoke', for example, though the correspondence between Gk. [w]ítus and Latin *vitus* points to the use of the wood of the willow for the rim of the spoked wheel. All these facts would tend to show that the horse

Table 1

Indo-European words for 'wheel'

Gmc.	OE *hwēol*	Baltic	OPruss. *kelan*	OCS *kolo*	A. *kukäl*
	OHG *rad*		Lith. *ratas*		Toch. B. *kokale*

Celtic OIr. *roth*

Latin *rota*

Greek *kúklos*

Avest. *čaxra-* : *raθa-* ('chariot')

Skt. *cakra-* : *ratha-* ('chariot')

was first used for riding and only later for drawing carts, but one question remains
to be clarified: how to account for the common Indo-European terminology if
the cartwright's trade postdates the first migrations by more than a millennium?

In order to appreciate the way of life of early Indo-European cultures in Europe,
it is also interesting to assess the relative importance of hunting in their daily diet;
bone finds provide valuable data which show considerable variation as to the
percentage of game versus meat of domesticated animals consumed by these populations. Thus, in the fourth millennium B.C., the Baden culture in Hungary shows
93.2 percent of bones of domestic animals versus 6.8 percent of bones of game,
mainly deer, but also aurochs and wild boar (Murray 1970:363), whereas the
older Altheim culture in Germany shows a considerable fluctuation depending
on the sites:

Bones of Animals	Domestic	Wild
Altheim	92.9	7.1
Altenerdingen	81.5	18.5
Pasternacker	51.7	48.3
Pölling	approx. 27.5	approx. 72.5

It stands to reason that in cases like this the ecology of the environment must be
greatly responsible for the discrepancies. The main wild animals involved are the red
deer, to a lesser degree the wild pig and the bear—which is in keeping with the
lexical data where the dialects of IE show two terms for 'deer', one (Gk. *élaphos*,
Lith. *élnis*, OCS *jeleni*, W *elain* 'doe', Eng. *elk*, Arm. *ełn* 'doe') presumably from a
root denoting the reddish color, and the other (Lat. *cervus*, W *carw*, OE *heorot*,
OPruss. *sirwis*) connected with the term for 'horn'. The bear must also have a
common IE name, but it was tabuized at an early date—hence, the Germanic and
Slavic substitutes for the correspondents of Skt. *ŕkṣa-*, Arm. *arj*, Gk. *árktos*, Lat.
ursus, OIr. *art*, and presumably Hitt. *ḥartagga-*. Striking is the practical absence of
bird remains, as the goose and the duck—for which the major Indo-European languages show a common term—were apparently hunted from time immemorial.
On the other hand, one site contains the bones of at least ten beavers, representing
6.8 percent of the total number of animals consumed there—the familiarity of early
IE with the animal being confirmed by the correspondence: Avest. *bawri-* : Lat.
fiber : Corn. *befer* : OHG *bibar* : Lith. *bēbrus* : OCS *bebru*. Unfortunately, such
data are not available for another important activity in the economy of the Early
IE cultures, namely, beekeeping. Although the PIE term for 'bee' is not known
(the root **bhī-* shared by Germanic, Celtic, and Balto-Slavic is presumably ono-
matopoeic), the occurrence of **melit-* for 'honey' in Greek, Latin, Celtic, Germanic, Armenian, Albanian, beside the use of **medhu-* 'mead'—the name of the

intoxicating drink made from it—for 'honey' in Balto-Slavic, guarantees that api-culture was part of the IE heritage. Acquaintance with the habits of the bees is documented since the end of the Neolithic—"it was not domestication, but simple exploitation of the guests by the host species," as Zeuner (1963:496) points out. Finding the bees was not a problem; their natural habitat stretched over most of the South Russian steppe to the greater part of Europe.

But if such were the main sources of food for these originally nomadic peoples of the steppe, what was their social organization? What were their beliefs?

Indo-European society, as far as we can judge, was agnatic and ethnocentric, its basic unit being the patriarchal, patrilinear, and essentially patrilocal extended family. Kindred was the foundation of its concentric structure, grouping the fami-lies in clans, claiming descent from a common ancestor, and the clans in tribes, presumably deriving their origin from some eponymous founder. Ethnic solidarity became especially manifest in contrast with outsiders—whether the Vedic term *arí*, which has been the object of such vehement polemic regarding its basic meaning,[3] expresses this awareness of an ethnic community, recognizing the same ancestry and practicing the same cults, is a moot question. The main point is the emphasis on the contrast *in*side versus *out*side which prevails at each level of the social struc-ture and conditions human relations. Inside his group, with his kith and kin, the Indo-European is safe; outside lurk the dangers. Inside his family, his clan, his tribe, he enjoys all the rights and privileges that pertain to free members of the community: 'to be free' is indeed to be one of the group, as the first element of Slavic *svoboda* 'freedom' and Skt. *svādhīna* 'free' indicates. These terms and other derivations from the reflexive pronoun stem **swe-* point to the status of the indi-vidual in the society: born in his proper social context, he will grow up into a free adult, receiving the love and affection people give to their own, as is evidenced by the Germanic term for 'free', related with Skt. *priyá-* 'loved', and the Greek *eleútheros* and Latin *līber* 'free', from the IE verbal stem **(H₁)lewdh-* 'to grow', which also yielded Lat. *līberī* 'children' and OCS *ljudŭ*, OHG *liut* 'people', as well as the name of the god of growth and fertility, Latin *Līber* and (maybe) ON *Lóðurr* (Polomé 1969:287-90; 1972:66-67; Benveniste 1973:262-72). The symbolism of the door, the persistence of the ritual separation of *in*side and *out*side in the sacralization of places, like sanctuaries, or later, cities, tend to show how this contrast pervades the conceptual world of the Indo-European and gives some validity to the view of Jost Trier (1942): "Am Anfang steht der Zaun. Tief und begriffsbestimmend durchwirken Zäune, Hegung, Grenze die von Menschen ge-formte Welt." Nowhere is this more obvious than in the field of the *sacred,* where the dichotomy involved placing *out of bounds to human beings* whatever was *consecrated to the deity.* In another context, the *ambiguous attitude toward out-siders* led the Indo-Europeans to treat them either as *enemies,* reduced to a state of servitude or, mostly in individual cases, to grant them most generously their *hospitality*—often a lasting pledge passed on to the following generation.

But if we consider the vertical structure of society, a question arises: was there a *hierarchy of social levels* in the original Indo-European society? Or did those families of pastoralists live more or less independently from each other, each clan respecting the grazing land of the other and the heads of the clan meeting only in case of emergency? Was there a clan of priests in charge of their religious activities, or were there only shaman-medicinemen, seers, or the like, to respond to their daily needs, in case of illness or death of people or cattle, to provide guidance in important decisions, to ward off ill-fortune, etc. Undoubtedly, there is strong evidence that historical Indo-European peoples had a tripartite social organization, described by Emile Benveniste and Georges Dumézil as consisting essentially of three functional classes:

1. The priests, in charge of the religious traditions of the community and entrusted with the performance of its rituals.
2. The warriors from among whom the "king" would usually emerge.
3. The clansmen—the pastoralists concerned with their living.[4]

One can, however, wonder whether such a neat discrimination between social levels already existed among the early Indo-Europeans of the fourth and third millennia B.C. It is, to say the least, astonishing that the Germanic tribes, for example, as they are described by the earliest sources, appear to have a rather egalitarian society, in which the leading men seem to be the clan elders whose council practically runs the show with the backing of the assembly of all the free adult males able to carry arms. As for religious activities, no mention is made of priests, but several of the sacred and magical functions are discharged by "holy women." Thus, in the tripartite system, the first function would be represented by these *seeresses,* whereas the *warrior* class would contain practically the *whole adult male population;* and the *aged,* the *women* and *children* would constitute the *third* group, working in the communal fields and tending the herds. It stands to reason that this cannot represent a genuine social hierarchy—but it could be objected that this reflects a special development of Germanic society due to the danger of living close to aggressive neighbors and the need to be constantly ready for combat. True—but, then, why does the type of society claimed for the Indo-European society develop in the same area after the same Germanic tribes have convinced the Romans of the futility of conquering their land and both have lived peacefully as neighbors for about a century?[5]

At any rate, even in the societies where the tripartite organization was well established from the earliest times on, the class status was not hereditary and there was no restriction on intermarriage, as several examples from Vedic times indicate (Altekar 1958:226). Moreover, even later, there was room for upward mobility within the framework of the three-generational unity of the lineage evidenced by the Germanic and Celtic kindred systems (Pearson 1973:159-60). Obviously, any societal framework is open for adaptation to changed conditions: with the urbanization of society and the development of new trades, some IE cultures added a fourth class to their social hierarchy to include all the artisans—hence, Avestan *hūiti* 'occupation, craft' and Gk. *dēmiourgoí* 'artisans'. Elsewhere, the fourth estate applied to people of the lowest category, originally *non*-Aryans, excluded from participation in the rituals, like the ancient Indian *śūdrás*. On the other hand, if the third functional class covers essentially the producers who ensure the survival of the society, the craftsmen can easily be included as a subgroup, just as the agriculturists have their place beside the original pastoralists in the same estate.

The beliefs of Early Indo-European society are difficult to assess, let alone retrieve. Undoubtedly, the ecology of their steppe environment must have influenced them. Their pastoral economy, and the problems and conflicts linked with it, were certainly reflected in their earliest myths, as recent research by Bruce Lincoln (1975, 1976, 1981) has confirmed. The dichotomy of the "holy" along the lines indicated by Rudolf Otto (1917) is definitely inherent to the terminology of the "sacred" analyzed by Baetke (1942), Benveniste (1973:445-69) and others; "divination," the interpretation of signs and omens, must have been common practice since time immemorial, as may have been some ritual procedures of sympathetic magic like invultuation or hoodoo. But more important is the problem of the Indo-European concept of the "supernatural." How did they visualize their gods? Were they really merely personified social processes as Meillet (1907) would have when he brilliantly analyzed the Vedic god Mitra as the divine symbol of the contractual agreements that are basic to all human relations—friendship, hospitality, marriage, etc.?[6] Are the gods the embodiment of the essential social functions? Does the internal structuration of the pantheon reflect the ideal human society in grandiose Dürkheimian terms? Or is the idea of "god" connected with celestial sacrality—with light and "transcendence," as the etymological link *dyeus* 'god (as celestial sovereign and spouse of Mother Earth)' : *deywos* 'god'/'divine' : Latin *diēs* '(light of) day' would suggest? Undoubtedly, celestial and atmospheric gods abound in the pantheon of the Indo-European peoples whether they be connected with the thunder or the wind or designate the sun, for example. Or is the universe full of magical forces, perhaps more powerful than the gods—impersonal powers that can adhere to any being or object, can be transferred and may prove either useful or dangerous, like the Melanesian *mana?*

It is doubtful that the nomadic Indo-European pastoralists developed much of a structured agricultural activity in which the regular rhythm of the seasons would have given rise to the development of the calendrical rites characteristic of organized religions with a specialized priestly caste (Titiev 1972). In a society like theirs, critical rites would be essential to counteract the personal emergencies, though, occasionally, the community as a whole might be affected, e.g., when a prolonged drought threatened the survival of their herds. The rituals performed under such circumstances would rather be the special function of seers, medicine-men, diviners, and such, than of a priestly hierarchy, though they may have included some "specialists" like rainmakers. But on the whole, their performance would be closer to what is traditionally labeled *magic.* Does that mean that we should follow those who see "magical potency" at work in the cosmos?

To be sure, it is attractive to project into Indo-European such Vedic concepts as *asu, ṛta,* and *māyā.* The "numinous" is intrinsically nameless and formless, residing in an invisible sphere; only its influence is felt to exist. By its own will, it projects itself into a sphere visible to Vedic man, where deities will perform their creative act. These deities *(Asuras)* are "charged with vital energy" *(asu)* and endowed with creative power *(māyā)* (Srinivasan 1975:141). Because of *māyā,* one of them wields sovereign power over the universe *(Varuṇa),* where he "enforces and upholds a self-operating cosmic power *(ṛta),* which establishes, governs and directs physical norms in worldly, human and ritual activities, causing these to appear as right and true." Dandekar, one of the main propounders of this view, shared to a large extent by Jan Gonda (1960:75-81), even goes so far as to claim that *asu* is the "primary and most basic religious concept of the early Vedic period," and he describes it as "a somatic magic potence [that] permeated through nature and the human world and thereby constituted the essential basis of their existence and functioning." Obviously, he identifies it with *mana,* when he adds: "The concept of an all-pervading somatic magic potence such as this is . . . common to the religious ideologies of many primitive peoples . . ." (1971:287). But Vedic *asu* as 'vital energy', just as Sumerian *me* (the impersonal, immanent 'divine power' of the earliest Mesopotamian religion), never occurs quite independently from personalized deities, so that if there is at all a power involved in Indo-European religion that is axiomatic to all that is supernatural, it should not be conceived as impersonal, but as depersonalized. It is, however, quite possible that "creative power" is no more than one of the attributes shared by a number of gods with a number of functional restrictions specifying their respective role in the creative act. Thus, after the searching analyses of Gonda (1972:27-28; 1974:197), Minard (1956: §809b), and Renou (1956:58; 1961:4), it seems fairly well established that *dakṣa* reflects Varuṇa's 'creative energy' and *kratu,* Mitra's 'power of deliberation'—Mitra conceptualizes, Varuṇa gives shape.

If, then, we are to consider that the Indo-Europeans had personalized gods, it is important to determine, as Mircea Eliade (1978:188-89) pointed out, to what extent "pastoral nomadism, vigorously reorganized for war and conquest, encouraged and facilitated the emergence of specific religious values." This task is made difficult by the fact that in their migrations and expansion, the Indo-

Europeans constantly came in contact with sedentary agricultural populations, which they subjugated and "absorbed" into their social structure, but this symbiosis must have created from the very earliest days the kind of tensions between heterogeneous and often antithetical orientations that Georges Dumézil (1970a: 65-76; 1973:7-16, 20-25) has illustrated in his comments on the Sabine War and the parallel conflict opposing the Æsir and the Vanir in Scandinavian mythology: on the one hand, a powerful leader and heroic fighters, who prevail through potent magic when sheer physical strength fails; on the other hand, wealthy agriculturists, who do not hesitate to use the lure of gold to corrupt their adversary, but are ultimately willing to compromise, so that from the merger of the two originally disparate elements a complete, viable, unified society results.

What was the situation prior to that "merger"? It has long been assumed that their oldest religious concepts were associated with nature and the cosmos—the supreme god being Father Sky (Vedic *Dyauṣ pitā*, Gk. *Zeūs patér*, Lat. *Juppiter*, etc.), whose main functions were sovereignty and creativity, the latter being manifested both in the cosmogony and his paternity in divine and human genealogies. As Eliade (1963:82-86) has shown, sky gods seldom maintain their cardinal role beyond the initial creative act, and often they yield their place to storm gods. It stands to reason that in the ecological milieu of the steppe where a long spell of dry weather can be disastrous for the grazing lands and endanger the cattle and horses, a deity controlling the thunder and unleashing the rains can be of prime importance, as it was for the Semites who invaded the fertile Sumerian alluvial irrigation lands of the south from semi-arid steppes in the northwest. Symbolically, the widespread mythological theme of the battle of the storm or thunder god with the monster that "imprisoned" the waters undoubtedly alludes to this ecological reality, but it would be simplistic to confine it to this naturalistic interpretation. As Norman Brown, in particular, has indicated (1978:31-32, 40-42), the myth has cosmogonic significance, marking the triumph of life over sterility and death—in particular, in the case of *Indra* and *Vṛtra*. Indra puts an end to inertia and transforms the "virtuality" of the world fashioned by *Tvaṣṭṛ* into the actuality of the cosmos. In other words, to quote Eliade (1978:207): "The world and life could not come to birth except by the slaying of an amorphous Being."

But, reverting to the original Indo-European religion, a number of important elements need to be considered, such as the prominent role held by the sun in prehistoric and protohistoric belief among the Indo-Europeans, though the Sun god seems to recede to a secondary position later on. Here again, an archaic society like the Germanic world could be mentioned with Caesar's reference to the sun cult and archaeological finds such as the sun chariot of Trundholm and the numerous Scandinavian rock engravings of the sun disk in the Bronze Age (Gelling and Ellis Davidson 1972:9-26, 140-45), contrasted with the total absence of reference to its cult in later Roman writers like Tacitus and the very episodic role played by *Sunna* in the Germanic tradition. Another cosmic hierophany would be the wind of the steppes, represented by the Indo-Iranian deity *Vāyu*, in which some want to see an incarnation of brutal violence, acting readily on its own, whereas its appearance in certain contexts rather suggests an "initial" god, like *Janus* or, to some degree, *Heimdall* (Dumézil 1970b:59, 90, 139; 1973:126-30). With supernatural beings whose mythology is limited to one Indo-European subgroup and partly of ambiguous interpretation, it is hardly possible to extrapolate anything valid into Indo-European. As for the fire, it seems that its domestic cult was already quite significant in early Indo-European times; it was believed to have been kindled by lightning and regarded, therefore, as of celestial origin. In Vedic, the god *Agni* is the embodiment of the sacrality of the fire, but that does not restrict his cosmic affinities and ritual activities. Just as his Iranian counterpart, *Atar,* is the son of Ahura Mazdā, Agni has *Dyauṣ* for a father, "born" in the sky; he descends in the form of lightning, but he is also in the waters—he is callĕd *āpam garbhaḥ* 'embryo of the Waters' and invoked as springing from the womb of the Waters (Eliade 1978: 208-9). On the other hand, he is also involved in an archaic cosmological idea, conceptualizing creation as the union of an igneous element (fire, heat, and human sperm) with the aquatic principle (the "waters," seat of all "virtualities")—an idea which will ultimately be elaborated in the speculations about the Golden Embryo *(Hiraṇyagarbha).* Nevertheless, he has no important mythology, but he is omnipresent in religious life; Agni is indeed the "messenger" through whom the offerings reach the gods. Therefore, he is the archetypal priest, but he is also *gṛhaspatiḥ* 'the master of the home', which indicates the prominent role he must have played from the very beginning. He keeps out the evil spirits, drives away sickness, protects against witchcraft—in a word, people are closer to him than to any other god, and they invoke him with full confidence. Again, of course, it remains rather speculative to assume that such a situation already obtained in early Indo-European times, but the striking correspondences between the implicit Roman theory of fires clarified by Dumézil (1970a:311-22) and the explicit Indian theory demonstrate the survival of Indo-European traditions. Again, a far echo comes from the Germanic world. Besides the two great celestial luminaries, the Germanic people, according to Caesar, worship *Volcanus,* i.e., the fire, and for centuries, they continued to kindle the New Fire at the winter solstice (de Vries 1956:360-61, 462); just as in Rome, the perpetual fire was put out and solemnly rekindled once a year, on March 1.

The Indo-Europeans must have elaborated an extensive mythology; their tradition was transmitted orally, and after some of them acquired the skill of writing, a taboo was maintained against putting down in writing their religious lore. Their gods were close to them, though their attitude toward them was ambivalent, characterized by: 1) awe, and 2) trust, tinged with a certain familiarity. The religious fear was inspired by their holiness, and the reserved attitude of the Indo-

Europeans was translated in their piety by a set of interdictions. As the gods were, however, accessible and interested in human affairs, the Indo-Europeans respected them for it, while giving them their full confidence, showing their feelings of trust and admiration for their deities in their prayers, their offerings and their entire cult. The cult was celebrated in consecrated enclosures, in the open—a technique developed at an early date by the Indo-Europeans seems to be the sacralization of space, for which they may have had special rituals. They did not build sanctuaries and made their offerings in the fire, a fact illustrated by the lexical correspondence: Hitt. *ḫašša*- 'hearth, fireplace' : Lat. *āra* (OLat. *āsa*) 'altar' : Skt. *ā́sa* 'ash(es)'; etc.

The Indo-European lexicon contains a number of archaic correspondences which reflect the old religious vocabulary. They include such terms as Hitt. *mald-* 'recite invocations' : Lith. *meldžiu, melsti* 'pray' (: OHG *meldōn* 'announce, reveal'); Hitt. *šaklaiš* 'rite, custom' : Lat. *sacer;* Hitt. *talliia-* 'solemnly call upon the gods' : ON *þulr* 'Kultredner'; etc. (Polomé 1975:660-62)—or designations for the "libation" (Skt. *juhoti* 'offers sacrifice' : Gmc. term for 'god' < **ǵhu-tó-m* 'to whom libations are poured'; Hitt. *šipant-*, Gk. *spondḗ* 'libation' : Lat. *spondeō*), the "ritual feast," the "sacrifice," the "prayer," etc. Particularly important is the act of speech, not only because of solemn verbal engagements (= 'vow', linked with the root **weg^wh-*, found in Lat. *uoueo*, Gk. *eúkhesthai*, etc.), but also as creative act, which may account for the glorification of the entity *Vāc* 'speech' in RV 10.125 as "the common foundation of all reality" (Dumézil 1970a:392). The root **k̑ens-* illustrates the ambivalence of speech and its power as an efficient but also scathing weapon, e.g., for the priest in a society where authority is still insufficiently established and people are more restless: *praise,* extolling their heroic deeds, enhances the prestige of the chiefs and the power of the gods; *criticism* can lash out at undeserved fame and bring down to size tyrannical usurpers or crush despicable arrogants. Such a society was disappearing in India (which accounts for the limited derogatory use of the Skt. *śaṃs-*), but it was undoubtedly still a prevailing type in the Celtic world where kings feared satirists (Dumézil 1969:103-8; Benveniste 1973:416-20).

The most important problem in connection with Indo-European religion is, however, the validity of the Dumézilian hypothesis of the trifunctional religious ideology for the earliest period, as a reflex in the world of the divine of the fundamental structure of the nomadic pastoral society. The problem is complex and fraught with controversial issues, but if we consider the fragmented and heterogeneous heritage of the Vedic Indians, of ancient Rome, and of medieval Scandinavia and Ireland, and the scattered elements provided by archaeology, votive inscriptions, runic formulae, onomastics, reports of ancient authors and early Christian missionaries, *capitularia* of Charlemagne, epic poetry and medieval historiography, and what not, it is undeniable that a set of striking correspondences emerges in which myths preserved in the *Rigveda* will find parallels in the legendary history of the kings of Rome as reported by Livy and in Scandinavian mythography in the collection compiled by Snorri Sturluson, as well as in some passages of the Irish epics. And, more important still, these traditions will be organized around a tripartite structure of the pantheon and of the corresponding society, the three social divisions—priests, warriors, and cattle breeders and agriculturists—corresponding to the three functional levels of the religious ideology—magical and juridical sovereignty; physical and martial force; fertility, health, and economic prosperity. With all its consistency, the system shows a definite flexibility, allowing for shifts and expansions according to local contingencies. Thus, the couple of sovereign gods Mitra-Varuṇa will be completed by associated deities like *Aryaman* and personified concepts such as *Bhaga* 'allotted fate', *Aṃśa* 'share', *Dakṣa* 'creative energy', which will specialize in certain aspects of the first function such as preserving the cohesive unity of the Aryan community and insuring its continuity, parceling out the goods, etc. (Dumézil 1977:86-114). On the other hand, in Scandinavia, the magical sovereign *Óðinn* will become essentially involved with war and the nobility—the *jarls*—on the second function level, while the fighting champion of the Æsir, *þórr*, will, as thunder god, control the fertility of the lands and become very close to the lower class—the *karls*. However, the preservation of the tripartite scheme—illustrated, for example, by the theme of the "three sins of the warrior" in the Indian, Iranian, Greek, and Scandinavian traditions (Dumézil 1970b:65-104) —indicated that the general structure of the trifunctional ideology must have been elaborated prior to the dispersal of the Indo-Europeans. This does not imply that it covers *all* the religious thought and speculation peculiar to the Indo-Europeans, nor that the complexity of religious practices and conceptions linked with the tripartite ideology had developed beyond the incipient stage. It stands to reason that when we compare Latin *iūs* with Avestan *yaož-dā* and Vedic *śám yóh* we can immediately measure the particular contribution of each society to the elaboration of the concept. Rome is a city of laws, and *iūs* defines the maximal area of action or claim resulting from the nature or conventional status of an individual or group; it is mutatis mutandis for the organization of society what Vedic *ṛta* is for the cosmos: the observance of rules contrasted with chaos. Rome establishes juridical ethics contrasting with the "frenzy" of the Barbarians, but they do not acquire a religious value. On the contrary, the Indo-Iranian world, stressing the religious consciousness of man, uses **yauš-* with a double polarity: 1) it maximizes a state (to be reached from a given state—whether mystico-ritual or physico-material)— hence, Avest. *yaož-dā* in the meaning 'sanctify'; 2) it brings back to normal, "restores" what is in an *impure or diseased* state—hence, Avest. *yaož-dā* 'restore ritually, purify', Ved. *śám yóh* associated with healing (Benveniste 1973:389-96; Dumézil 1969:31-45). The study of key words like Latin *fās, fētialis* versus Vedic *dhắtu*, Latin *augur, augustus* versus Vedic *ójas*, etc., provides additional illustration of this further elaboration of the basic ethico-religious concepts of the Indo-

Europeans within the sociocultural framework of the new societies they had shaped (Dumézil 1969:61-102; Benveniste 1973:407-15, 420-23).

Actually, it seems to me that the absorption of the sedentary agricultural populations of the conquered territories was a major factor in triggering the transformation of Indo-European societies. Obviously, their pastoral society could not coexist in complete independence side by side with the cultivators, and their economy and religion were bound to affect their mode of living and thinking in the new symbiosis. In the stabilized society, the tripartite system jelled into a hierarchized community in which a priesthood became the guardian of the ethnic heritage and a ruler emerged from the warrior group, while farming combined cattle and horse breeding with cultivation of grains and vegetables. Celtic society provides a good example of such an organization up to historical times. All through the Indo-European tradition, there are reminders of the major difficulty encountered in establishing an integrated society. Besides the Sabine War and the struggle between the Æsir and Vanir, one could mention the fact that the *Nāsatyas* were at first challenged by the other gods, because they had "mingled with men." They were even momentarily denied participation in the sacrifice ritual which was exclusively reserved for the Aryans—a fact that gains particular significance in light of their occasional mention in later literature as belonging to the *śūdras*, the very lowest level in the hierarchy, practically outside the organized Aryan society.

As attractive as this hypothesis may be, it is, however, fraught with problems: if the tripartite system became fully operative when symbiosis with agriculturists acted as a catalyst on the incipient ideology of the Indo-European pastoralists, why is it that the Mitanni Aryans show a completely developed trifunctional pantheon in the fourteenth century B.C. in Asia Minor, with gods like Mitra, Varuṇa, Indra, and the twin Nāsatyas? It must then be assumed that the development had already taken place in the staging area of the Indo-Iranian invasions, which only complicates the problem since we do not agree on the location of this area, nor on the kind of socioeconomic situation that prevailed there! On the other hand, how do we account for the Germanic situation, unless we admit that Caesar was "misinformed" and that Tacitus' Mercurius = *Wōðanaz*, Mars = *Tīwaz*, Hercules = **þunraz*, were already valid in the days of Ariovistus—disregarding the profound transformation of Germanic sociocultural and politico-economic life brought about by the Germanic wars of the reign of Augustus and intense trading and other contacts for more than a century along the Rhine-Danube *limes*.

Also, the fate of the Indo-European ideology in Anatolia remains puzzling if it predated the Indo-European moves toward this area, since nothing reminds us of the trifunctional pattern in the traditions of the Luwians, Hittites, and other Indo-Europeans of the Old Kingdom, which, otherwise, preserved quite a few archaic Indo-European features in its organization and in its language.

Anyhow, whatever the chronology of its elaboration, the tripartite ideology is definitely subjacent to a considerable number of myths and rituals in the Indo-Iranian, ancient Roman, Germanic, and Celtic world, and its prevalence is clearly evidenced by the ouster or radical transformation of such archaic Indo-European religious concepts as the sky god as creator, sovereign, and father: in India, *Dyauṣ pitā* has been driven out by Varuṇa, who appears to be threatened by the rising glory of Indra in the *Veda*. In Rome, *Juppiter* has considerably widened his dominion, becoming the symbol of the power and the mission of conquest of Rome. In the Germanic world, **Tīwaz* appears as: a) the equivalent of the Roman god Mars (hence, the survival of his name in *Tuesday*); and b) the protector of the assembly of the people in arms, the *þing* (hence, Ger. *Dienstag*); and c) a tribal god of the Saxons, also represented by a huge column, symbolizing the axis mundi, propping up the sky (de Vries 1957:10-26). Nevertheless, it is important to keep the whole matter in perspective. The trifunctional hierarchization of society and the corresponding tripartite ideology are only part of the total picture. They have to be viewed diachronically as part of a dynamic process of development: the staggered establishment of specific institutions keeps pace with the growing complexity in social organization and the stages of social evolution. In the older pastoral society, we rather expect *unranked* descent groups. As the community grows and *diversifies*, the extended family "swarms" for economic reasons; moving to establish new settlements leads to profound social changes with *ranked* descent groups and *full-time craft specialization* (Pfeiffer 1977:103). Therefore, in my opinion, the tripartite ideology is more recent than some of the purely pastoralist traditions that comparative mythology has been retrieving. It originated as the Indo-European community started breaking up—maybe after the departure of the Proto-Anatolians?

NOTES

1. The often alleged correspondence Gk. ἡνίαι 'reins': MIr. ē(i)si (plural) 'bridle', reflecting, respectively, **ansi(y)ā* and **ansi(y)o-*, would point to an original meaning 'halter' (Pokorny 1959:48; 'dem Zugvieh umgelegter Zügel'), as the further connection with Lat. *ānsa* 'handle', Lith. *ąsà* 'handle, slipknot', ON *ǣs* 'hole for the thong in a sandal' would also suggest. The derivation remains uncertain however (Chantraine 1970:413).

2. The early date of the arrival of the Indo-Europeans on the basis of their identification with the so-called Kurgan culture has also been challenged in recent work on the European Bronze Age (e.g., Milisauskas 1978:183-84; Coles and Harding 1979:6-8).

3. On the controversy between Dumézil, Thieme, and Gershevitch over the

interpretation of *ari-*, see Scott-Littleton 1973:186-92; cf. further Benveniste 1973:301-4. An extensive survey of the problem and the relevant literature is presented by Cohen in his forthcoming article on "Arya" in the *Journal of Indo-European Studies* (1981).

4. On the elaboration of this idea, see Scott-Littleton 1973:7-19, 49-53, 58-79; Rivière 1979:35-66. Cf. further Dumézil 1958; Benveniste 1973:227-38.

5. On the changes affecting the material civilization and social organization of the Germanic territories described by Roman authors from the time of Julius Caesar (51 B.C.) to the time of Tacitus (A.D. 98), cf. especially Thompson 1965: 1-71. See also Much 1967:154-60, 167-70, 201-11, 221-27, 236-37, 331-42.

6. Recently, the view of Meillet has come under criticism, especially by J. Gonda (1975:48-52). A review of the discussion is given by H. P. Schmidt (1978), who proposes a more general meaning 'alliance, allegiance'. B. Lincoln (1981: 54-55) derives *mitra-* from IE *mey-* 'join together, bind', and ascribes the meaning 'that which joins together' to the original form.

Postscript

After completing this study O. Szemerényi pointed out to me regarding my paper, "The Gods of the Indo-Europeans," *The Mankind Quarterly*, Vol. 21:2 (Winter 1980), pp. 151-64, that he had suggested new interpretations for a series of terms discussed here in his monograph, *Studies in the Kinship Terminology of the Indo-European Languages, with special references to Indian, Iranian, Greek and Latin*, in *Acta Iranica*, Vol. 16: *Varia*, Leyden: E. J. Brill, 1977, pp. 1-240.

Particularly important with regard to our discussion are the new etymologies proposed for the terms for 'free': IE *priyo-* (reflected by Goth. *freis*, OHG *frī*, etc.) originally designated 'people belonging to the same household' (as Ernst Risch suggested [*Museum Helveticum* 22 (1965), p. 194, fn. 4], the term was a derivative from *per-* 'house'; Szemerényi 1977:122-24). The IE reflexive *swe/o-*, contained in Slavic *svoboda* 'freedom', is considered by Szemerényi (1977:43-46) as a thematic adjective derived from *su-*, possibly the earliest expression for 'joint family, clan', so that it would originally designate 'people of the same ilk'. As for Gk. *eleútheros* : Lat. *liber*, Szemerényi (1977:109-11) believes they should be separated as Venetic (Cadore) *Loudera* proves that Lat. *liber* has to be traced back to *loudheros*, denoting a member of the 'people, nation', and as such free born, whereas Gk. *eleútheros* (Mycenæan *ereutero*) is to be compared with Hitt. *arawa-* 'free of impost'. However, Szemerényi becomes more difficult to follow when he assumes that: a) Mycenæan *ereutera* was borrowed from the more advanced Anatolian area via the Hittite abstract *arawatar* 'freedom of impost' (1977:116); and b) Hitt. *arawa-* 'free' has nothing to do with *ara-* 'companion, mate' and reflects *n̥-rǝ-wo- 'not giving' (not obliged to render any financial or physical service), versus IE *rē- 'give, bestow' (1977:115). These views tie in with his reinterpretation of the current connection of Indo-Iranian *arya- with the Anatolian terms: for Szemerényi (1977:144-48), Hitt. ara-, denoting a close relationship between equals, corresponds to Ugaritic áry 'kinsman' (: Egyptian íry 'companion') and must be a borrowing from a neighboring non-Indo-European language. This, in turn, implies that "part of the future Indo-Iranians which had *via* the Caucasus entered the peripheral area of the Near East acquainted itself with the important local term for 'kinsman, companion' and adopted it in the form arya-, which, transmitted to the kindred tribes further East, later became the overall term for their nationality" (Szemerényi 1977:148). What makes such a hypothesis rather disputable is that it postulates a rather uncommon pattern of name-giving for such a widespread ethnicon as *arya-, apart from the fact that there is still considerable disagreement as to the routes followed by the Indo-Iranians in their migrations. They may as likely have moved east of the Caspian Sea as via the Caucasus, and there is no evidence that the group branching off toward a dead-end in Mitanni served as a transmitter of Middle Eastern cultural features to the other tribes at any time.

BIBLIOGRAPHY

Altekar, A. S. 1958. Vedic Society. *The Cultural Heritage of India.* Vol. 1. *The Early Phases.* 2nd ed. Edited by S. K. Chatterji, N. Dutt, A. D. Pusalker and N. K. Bose, 221-32. Calcutta: The Ramakrishna Mission Institute for Culture.

Amiran, Ruth B. K. 1952. Connections between Anatolia and Palestine in the Early Bronze Age. *Israel Exploration Journal* 2:89-103.

Andrétéva, M. V. 1977. La culture de Maikop et les liens avec le sud. *Sovietskaya Archeologiya* 1:39-56.

Baetke, Walter. 1942. *Das Heilige im Germanischen.* Tübingen: J. C. B. Mohr (Paul Siebeck).

Becker, Carl J. 1961. Probleme der neolithischen Kulturen in Nordeuropa vom Anfang der Trichterbecherkultur bis zum Auftreten der Schnurkeramiker. *L'Europe à la fin de l'âge de la pierre,* edited by J. Böhm and S. J. De Laet, 585-94. Prague: Editions de l'Académie tchécoslovaque des Sciences.

Benveniste, Emile. 1954. Etudes hittites et indo-européennes. *BSL* 50:29-43.

———. 1962. *Hittite et Indo-européen.* Paris: Maisonneuve.

———. 1969. *Le vocabulaire des institutions indo-européennes.* Paris: Minuit.

———. 1973. *Indo-European Language and Society.* Translated by Elizabeth Palmer. Coral Gables, Florida: University of Miami Press.

Berciu, D. 1962. A Zoomorphic "Sceptre" Discovered in the People's Republic of Bulgaria and Its Cultural and Chronological Position. *Dacia* 7:397-409.

Bérézanskaia, S. S. 1971. A propos de l'horizon commun européen des cultures de la céramique cordée en Ukraine et en Biélorussie. *Sovietskaya Archeologiya* 4:36-49.

Bergsträsser, G. 1928. *Einführung in die semitischen Sprachen.* Munich.

Binchy, Daniel A. 1965. Bretha Déin Chécht. *Eriu* 20:22-48.

———. 1979. *Corpus Iuris Hibernici.* Dublin: DIAS.

Blanc, Haim. 1967. The "Sonorous" vs. "Muffled" Distinction in Old Arabic Phonology. *To Honor Roman Jakobson,* vol. 1, 295-308. The Hague: Mouton.

Bökönyi, Sándor. 1974. *History of Domestic Mammals in Central and Eastern Europe.* Budapest: Akadémiai Kiadó.

Bomhard, A. 1977. The "Indo-European-Semitic" Hypothesis Re-examined. *JIES* 5.1:55-99.

Bosch-Gimpera, P. 1961. *Les Indo-Européens: Problèmes archéologiques.* Paris: Payot.

Brjussow, A. Ja. 1957. *Geschichte der neolithischen Stämme im europäischen Teil der UdSSR.* Berlin: Akademie Verlag.

Brugmann, Karl. 1897-1916. *Vergleichende Laut-, Stammbildungs- und Flexionslehre der indogermanischen Sprachen.* 2 vols. 2nd ed. Strassburg: Trübner.

Buchvaldek, M. 1966. Die Schnurkeramik in Mitteleuropa. *Památky Archeologické* 57:126-71.

Burney, Charles A. 1964. The Excavations at Yanik Tepe, Azerbaijan, 1962. *Iraq* 26:54-61.

Campanile, Enrico. 1977. *Ricerche di cultura poetica indoeuropea.* Pisa: Giardini.

Campbell, J. A., M. S. Baxter and Leslie Alcock. 1979. Radiocarbon Dates for the Cadbury Massacre. *Antiquity* 53:31-38.

Cantineau, J. 1951-52. Le consonantisme du sémitique. *Semitica* 4:79-94.

Cardona, George. 1975. Review of Calvert Watkins' *Indogermanische Grammatik.* Vol. 3. *Formenlehre,* Teil 1. Heidelberg: Winter, 1969. In *IIJ* 17:103-11.

Caskey, John L. 1958. Excavations at Lerna, 1957. *Hesperia* 27:125-44.

———. 1971. Greece, Crete and the Aegean Islands in the Early Bronze Age. *The Cambridge Ancient History.* 3rd ed. Vol. 1, part 2. Edited by I. E. S. Edwards, C. J. Gadd and N. G. L. Hammond, 771-807. Cambridge: At the University Press.

Chantraine, Pierre. 1968-80. *Dictionnaire étymologique de la langue grecque. Histoire des mots.* Paris: C. Klincksieck.

Chard, Chester S. 1974. *Northeast Asia in Prehistory.* Madison: The University of Wisconsin Press.

Childe, V. Gordon. 1925. *The Dawn of European Civilization.* Reprint 1957. New York: Vintage Books.

———. 1926. *The Aryans: A Study of Indo-European Origins.* Reprint 1970. New York and London: Kennikat Press.

———. 1936. The Axes from Maikop and Caucasian Metallurgy. *Annals of Archaeology and Anthropology* 23:113-19.

———. 1948. *The Dawn of European Civilization.* 4th ed. New York: A. Knopf.

———. 1957. *The Dawn of European Civilization.* 6th ed. London: Routledge and Kegan Paul.

Chomsky, Noam and Morris Halle. 1968. *The Sound Pattern of English.* New York: Harper & Row.

Clark, Eve C. 1978. Locationals: Existential, Locative, and Possessive Construction. *Universals of Human Language.* Vol. 4. *Syntax.* Edited by Joseph H. Greenberg, 85-126. Stanford: Stanford University Press.

Clark, G. 1967. *The Stone Age Hunters.* New York: McGraw-Hill.

Clarke, David L. 1968. *Analytical Archaeology.* London: Methuen.

Colarusso, J. 1979. Typological Parallels between Proto-Indo-Europeans and the Northwest Caucasian Languages.

Coles, J. M. and A. F. Harding. 1979. *The Bronze Age in Europe.* New York: St. Martin's Press.

Crossland, R. A. 1971. Immigrants from the North. *The Cambridge Ancient History.* 3rd ed. Vol. 1, part 2. Edited by I. E. S. Edwards, C. J. Gadd and N. G. L. Hammond, 824-76. Cambridge: At the University Press.

Dandekar, R. N. 1971. Hinduism. *Historia Religionum. Handbook for the History of Religions.* Vol. 2. *Religions of the Present.* Edited by C. Jonco Bleeker and George Widengren, 236-345. Leyden: E. J. Brill.

Delbrück, Berthold. 1893-1900. *Vergleichende Syntax der indogermanischen Sprachen.* 1-3. Strassburg: Trübner.

———. 1889. *Die indogermanischen Verwandtschaftsnamen: Ein Beitrag zur vergleichenden Altertumskunde,* 11:v, 380-606. Leipzig: Abhandlungen der königlichen Sächsischen Akademie der Wissenschaften.

Denniston, J. D. 1950. *The Greek Particles.* 2nd rev. ed., 1966. Oxford: Clarendon.

de Saussure, Ferdinand. 1959. *Course in General Linguistics.* Edited by Charles Bally and Albert Sechehaye. Translated by Wade Baskin. New York: Philosophical Library.

Devoto, Giacomo. 1962. *Origini Indeuropee.* Firenze: Sansoni.

de Vries, Jan. 1956. *Altgermanische Religionsgeschichte.* Vol. 1. *Einleitung–Vorgeschichtliche Perioden–Religiöse Grundlagen des Lebens, Seelen- und Geisterglaube–Macht und Kraft–Das Heilige und die Kultformen.* 2nd ed. Berlin: Walter de Gruyter.

———. 1957. *Altgermanische Religionsgeschichte.* Vol. 2. *Die Götter–Vorstellungen über den Kosmos–Der Untergang des Heidentums.* Berlin: Walter de Gruyter.

Dolukhanov, P. M. 1979. *Ecology and Economy in Neolithic Eastern Europe.* London: Duckworth.

Dolukhanov, P. M., A. A. Semyontsov, Yu. S. Svezhentsev, V. I. Timofeyev, Ye. N. Romanova and N. S. Malanova. 1976. Radiocarbon Dates of the Institute of Archaeology III. *Radiocarbon* 18:190-201.

Dressler, Wolfgang U. 1969. Eine textsyntaktische Regel der indogermanischen Wortstellung. *KZ* 83:1-25.

Dumézil, Georges. 1958. *L'idéologie tripartie des Indo-Européens.* (Collection Latomus, vol. 31.) Brussels: Latomus. Revue d'Etudes Latines.

———. 1969. *Idées romaines.* Paris: NRF-Gallimard.

———. 1970a. *Archaic Roman Religion.* Translated by Philip Krapp. Chicago: The University of Chicago Press.

———. 1970b. *The Destiny of the Warrior.* Translated by Alf Hiltebeitel. Chicago:

The University of Chicago Press.

———. 1973. *Gods of the Northmen.* Edited by Einar Haugen. Berkeley and Los Angeles: University of California Press.

———. 1977. *Les dieux souverains des Indo-Européens.* Paris: NRF-Gallimard.

Dumitrescu, V. 1957. Le dépôt d'objets de parure de Hăbăşeşti et le problème des rapports entre les tribus de la civilisation de Cucuteni et les tribus des steppes pontiques. *Dacia* (N.S.) 1:73-96.

Dyson, Robert H., Jr. 1965. Problems in the Relative Chronology of Iran, 6000-2000 B.C. *Chronologies in Old World Archaeology,* edited by Robert W. Ehrich, 215-56. Chicago: The University of Chicago Press.

———. 1968. Annotations and Corrections of the Relative Chronology of Iran, 1968, Archaeological Seminar at Columbia University, 1966-67. *American Journal of Archaeology* 72:308-313.

———. 1973. The Archaeological Evidence of the Second Millennium B.C. on the Persian Plateau. *The Cambridge Ancient History.* 3rd ed. Vol. 1, part 2. Edited by I. E. S. Edwards, C. J. Gadd, N. G. L. Hammond and E. Sollberger, 686-715. Cambridge: At the University Press.

Ehrich, Robert W. 1963. Further Reflections on Archaeological Interpretation. *American Anthropologist* 65:16-31.

Eliade, Mircea. 1963. *Patterns in Comparative Religion.* Translated by Rosemary Sheed. Cleveland: Meridian Books (The World Publishing Company).

———. 1978. *A History of Religious Ideas.* Vol. 1. *From the Stone Age to the Eleusinian Mysteries.* Translated by Willard R. Trask. Chicago: The University of Chicago Press.

Emonds, J. 1972. A Reformulation of Grimm's Law. *Contributions to Generative Phonology,* edited by M. Brame. Austin: University of Texas Press.

Fairbanks, Gordon H. 1977. Case Inflections in Indo-European. *JIES* 5:101-31.

Fischer, U. 1958. Mitteldeutschland und die Schnurkeramik. *Jahresschrift für mitteldeutsche Vorgeschichte* 41/42:254-98.

Frankfort, H. 1928. Sumerians, Semites, and the Origin of Copperworking. *Antiquaries Journal* 8:217-35.

———. 1956. *The Art and Architecture of the Ancient Orient.* (Pelican History of Art.) Harmondsworth: Penguin Books.

Friedrich, Johannes. 1960. *Hethitisches Elementarbuch.* 1. *Kurzgefasste Grammatik.* 2nd ed. Heidelberg: Winter.

Friedrich, Paul. 1966. Proto-Indo-European Kinship. *Ethnology* 5.1:1-36.

———. 1970. *Proto-Indo-European Trees: The Arboreal System of a Prehistoric People.* Chicago: The University of Chicago Press.

Gamkrelidze, T. V. 1966. A Typology of Common Kartwelian. *Language* 42.1: 69-83.

———. 1975. On the Correlation of Stops and Fricatives in a Phonological System.

Lingua 35:131-61.

Gamkrelidze, T. V. and V. V. Ivanov. 1972. Lingvističeskaja tipologija i rekon- strukcija sistemy indoevropejskix smyčnyx. *Working Papers of the Conference on the Comparative Historical Grammar of the Indo-European Languages* (December 12-14, 1972), 15-18. Moscow: Akademija Nauk.

———. 1973. Sprachtypologie und die Rekonstruktion der gemeinindogermanischen Verschlüsse. *Phonetica* 27:150-56.

Garašanin, Milutin V. 1972. Les premières vagues indoeuropéennes en Grèce et dans les Balkans. *Acta of the 2nd International Colloquium on Aegean Prehistory*, 175-79. Athens: General Directorate of Antiquities, Ministry of Culture and Sciences.

Gelling, Peter and Hilda Ellis Davidson. 1972. *The Chariot of the Sun and Other Rites and Symbols of the Northern Bronze Age.* London: J. M. Dent.

Georgiev, G. I. and N. J. Merpert. 1966. The Ezero Mound in South East Bulgaria. *Antiquity* 40:33-37.

Georgiev, G. I., N. I. Merpert, R. V. Katincarov and D. G. Dimitrov. 1979. *Ezero.* Sofia: Bulgarian Academy, Archaeological Institute.

Ghirshman, R. 1954. *Iran.* Baltimore: Penguin.

Giedion, S. 1962. *The Eternal Present.* New York: Bollingen Foundation, Pantheon Books.

Gimbutas, Marija. 1956. *The Prehistory of Eastern Europe.* (Harvard University Bulletin, no. 20.) Cambridge, Mass.: American School of Prehistoric Research, Peabody Museum.

———. 1961. Note on the Chronology and Expansion of the Pit-Grave Culture. *L'Europe à la fin de l'âge de la pierre,* edited by J. Böhm and S. J. De Laet, 193-200. Prague: Editions de l'Académie tchécoslovaque des Sciences.

———. 1965. The Relative Chronology of the Neolithic and Chalcolithic Cultures in Eastern Europe North of the Balkan Peninsula and the Black Sea. *Chronol- ogies in Old World Archaeology,* edited by Robert W. Ehrich, 459-502. Chicago: The University of Chicago Press.

———. 1970. Proto-Indo-European Culture: The Kurgan Culture during the Fifth, Fourth and Third Millennia B.C. *Indo-European and Indo-Europeans. Papers Presented at the Third Indo-European Conference at the University of Pennsyl- vania,* edited by George Cardona, Henry M. Hoenigswald and Alfred Senn, 155-97. Philadelphia: University of Pennsylvania Press.

———. 1973. The Beginning of the Bronze Age in Europe and the Indo-Europeans, 3500-2500 B.C. *Journal of Indo-European Studies* 1:163-214.

———. 1977. The First Wave of Eurasian Steppe Pastoralists into Copper Age Europe. *Journal of Indo-European Studies* 5.4:277-338.

Glob, P. V. 1944. Studier over den Jyske Enkeltgravskultur. *Aarbøger for Nordisk Oldkyndighed og Historie,* 1-282.

Gonda, Jan. 1960. *Die Religionen Indiens.* Vol. 1. *Veda und älterer Hinduismus.*
(Die Religionen der Menschheit, vol. 2.) Stuttgart: W. Kohlhammer.
———. 1972. *The Vedic God Mitra.* Leyden: E. J. Brill.
———. 1974. *The Dual Deities in the Religion of the Veda.* (Verhandelingen der
Koninklijke Nederlandse Akademie van Wetenschappen. Afd. Letterkunde.
N.R. 81.) Amsterdam: North Holland.
———. 1975. Mitra in India. *Mithraic Studies,* edited by John R. Hinnells, 40-52.
Manchester: University of Manchester Press.
Greenberg, J. 1966. *Language Universals with Special Reference to Feature Hier-
archies.* The Hague: Mouton.
———. 1970. Some Generalizations Concerning Glottalic Consonants, Especially
Implosives. *IJAL* 36:123-45.
Gurney, Oliver R. 1979. The Symbolism of "9" in Babylonian and Hittite Litera-
ture. *Journal of the Department of English* (University of Calcutta) 14:27-31.
Gürtler, Hans. 1912. Zur Geschichte der deutschen -*er*-Plurale, besonders im Früh-
neuhochdeutschen. *PBB* 37:492-543.
Hajdu, P. 1972. The Origins of Hungarian. *The Hungarian Language,* edited by
L. Benkö and S. Imre, 15-48. The Hague: Mouton.
Hamp, Eric. 1973. Religion and Law from Iguvium. *Journal of Indo-European
Studies* 1:320-22.
———. 1976. Why Syntax Needs Phonology. *Papers from the Parasession on Dia-
chronic Syntax,* edited by Sanford B. Steever et al., 348-64. Chicago: Chicago
Linguistic Society.
Harrison, R. 1974. The Origins of the Bell Beaker Culture. *Antiquity* 48:99-109.
Haudry, Jean. 1977. *L'emploi des cas en védique. Introduction à l'étude des cas en
indo-européean.* (Les hommes et les lettres.) Lyon: Hermès.
Hawkes, C. F. C. 1940. *The Prehistoric Foundations of Europe.* London: Methuen.
Hencken, Hugh. 1955. Indo-European Languages and Archeology. *American
Anthropologist* 57.6, part 3. (Memoir No. 84.)
Hoenigswald, Henry. 1965. Indo-Iranian Evidence. *Evidence for Laryngeals,* edited
by Werner Winter, 93-99. The Hague: Mouton.
Hoffman, Karl. 1967. *Der Injunktiv im Veda.* Heidelberg: Winter.
Hoffner, Harry A. 1974. *Alimenta Hethaeorum.* (American Oriental Series, vol. 55.)
New Haven.
Hopper, P. J. 1973. Glottalized and Murmured Occlusives in Indo-European.
Glossa 7.2:141-66.
———. 1977a. The Typology of the Proto-Indo-European Segmental Inventory.
JIES 5.1:41-54.
———. 1977b. Indo-European Consonantism and the New Look. *Orbis* 26.1:57-72.
Humbach, Helmut. 1959. Aussage plus negierte Gegenaussage. *MSS* 14:23-33.
Jakobson, Roman. 1957. Typological Studies and Their Contribution to Historical

and Comparative Linguistics. *Selected Writings* I. Reprint 1962. The Hague: Mouton.

———. 1971. *Selected Writings* II. The Hague: Mouton.

Jakobson, Roman and Linda R. Waugh. 1979. *The Sound Shape of Language*. Bloomington: Indiana University Press.

Jettmar, Karl. 1972. Die Steppenkulturen und die Indoiranier des Plateaus. *Iranica Antiqua* 9:65-93.

Jucquois, G. 1966. La structure des racines en indo-européen envisagée d'un point de vue statistique. *Linguistic Research in Belgium,* edited by Y. Lebrun, 57-68. Wetteren: Universa.

Kalicz, N. 1963. *Die Pécelar (Badener) Kultur und Anatolien.* (Studia Archaeologica 2.) Budapest: Academiae Scientiarum Hungaricae.

Kammenhuber, Annelies. 1961. *Hippologia Hethitica.* Wiesbaden: Otto Harrassowitz.

Kiparsky, Paul. 1976. Oral Poetry: Some Linguistic and Typological Considerations. *Oral Literature and the Formula,* edited by Benjamin A. Stolz and Richard Shannon. Ann Arbor: University of Michigan Press.

Klaeber, Friedrich. 1950. *Beowulf and the Fight at Finnsburg.* 3rd ed. New York: Heath.

Klejn, L. 1969. Zum Problem der Aussonderung und Gliederung des Streitaxtkulturkreises. *Die neolithischen Becherkulturen im Gebiet der DDR und ihre europäischen Beziehungen,* edited by H. Behrens and F. Schlette, 209-14. (Veröffentlichungen des Landesmuseums für Vorgeschichte in Halle, 24.) Halle: Landesmuseum für Vorgeschichte.

Kortlandt, F. 1978. Proto-Indo-European Obstruents. *Indogermanische Forschungen* 80:107-118.

Kroeber, A. L. 1952. *The Nature of Culture.* Chicago: The University of Chicago Press.

Krzak, Zygmunt. 1976. *The Złota Culture.* Wrocław-Warszawa-Kraków-Gdańsk: Zakład Narodowy Imienia Ossolińskich Wydawnictwo Polskiej Akademii Nauk.

Kuhn, Adalbert. 1853. Über die durch nasale erweiterten verbalstämme. *KZ* 2:467.

Kuipers, A. 1960. *Phoneme and Morpheme in Kabardian (Eastern Adyghe).* The Hague: Mouton.

Kuryłowicz, Jerzy. 1975. *Metrik und Sprachgeschichte.* (Prace Językoznawcze, 83.) Wrocław: PAN.

———. 1976. The Linguistic Foundations of Metre. *BPTJ* 34:63-72.

Lanman, Charles R. 1880. A Statistical Account of Noun-Inflection in the Veda. *JAOS* 10:325-602.

Lanting, A. 1971. Corded Ware and Bell Beaker Culture. The Halle 1967 Symposium: A Review Article. *Helenium* 11:270-87.

Lehmann, Winfred P. 1951. The Distribution of PIE /r/. *Language* 27:13-17.

———. 1958. On Earlier Stages of the Indo-European Nominal Inflection. *Language* 34:179-202.

———. 1968. The Proto-Germanic Words Inherited from Proto-Indo-European Which Reflect the Social and Economic Status of the Speakers. *Zeitschrift für Mundartforschung* 35:1-25.

———. 1981a. The Genitive Singular Ending in *-syo:* How an Indo-Europeanist Works. *Kerns Gedenkschrift.* Amsterdam: John Benjamins.

———. 1981b. Review of *Universals of Human Language.* Vol. 4. *Syntax.* Edited by Joseph H. Greenberg.

Lincoln, Bruce. 1975. The Indo-European Myth of Creation. *History of Religion* 15:121-45.

———. 1976. The Indo-European Cattle-Raiding Myth. *History of Religion* 16: 42-65.

———. 1981. *Priests, Warriors and Cattle: A Study in the Ecology of Religions.* Berkeley and Los Angeles: University of California Press.

Machnik, J. 1966. *Studia nad Kultura ceramiki sznurowej w Malopolsce.* Wrocław-Warszawa-Kraków: Zakład Narodowy Imienia Ossolińskich Wydawnictwo Polskiej Akademii Nauk.

Mallory, J. P. 1973. A History of the Indo-European Problem. *Journal of Indo-European Studies* 1:21-65.

———. 1976. The Chronology of the Early Kurgan Tradition. *Journal of Indo-European Studies* 1:257-94.

Malmer, M. P. 1962. *Jungneolithische Studien.* (Acta Archaeologica Lundensia, Series in 8⁰, no. 2.) Lund.

Markey, Thomas L., R. L. Kyes and P. T. Roberge. 1977. *Germanic and Its Dialects: A Grammar of Proto-Germanic.* Amsterdam: John Benjamins.

Marshack, A. 1972. *The Roots of Civilization.* New York: McGraw-Hill.

Martinet, André. 1952. Remarques sur le consonantisme sémitique. *BSL* 49:67-78.

Masson, V. M. and V. I. Sarianidi. 1972. *Central Asia: Turkmenia before the Achaemenids.* (Ancient Peoples and Places.) New York and Washington: Praeger.

Meid, Wolfgang. 1978. *Dichter und Dichtkunst in Indogermanischer Zeit.* Innsbruck: Innsbrucker Beiträge zur Sprachwissenschaft.

Meillet, Antoine. 1907. Le dieu indo-iranien Mitra. *Journal Asiatique* 10:143-59.

———. 1923. *Les origines indo-européennes des mètres grecs.* Paris: Hachette.

———. 1936. *Introduction à l'étude comparative des langues indo-européennes.* 8th ed. Paris: Hachette.

Mellaart, J. 1958. The End of the Early Bronze Age in Anatolia and the Aegean. *American Journal of Archaeology* 62:9-33.

———. 1967. *Çatal Hüyük: A Neolithic Town in Anatolia.* New York: McGraw-Hill.

———. 1971a. Anatolia c. 4000-2300 B.C. *The Cambridge Ancient History.* 3rd ed. Vol. 1, part 2. Edited by I. E. S. Edwards, C. J. Gadd and N. G. L. Hammond,

363-416. Cambridge: At the University Press.

———. 1971b. Anatolia c. 2300-1750 B.C. *The Cambridge Ancient History.* 3rd ed. Vol. 1, part 2. Edited by I. E. S. Edwards, C. J. Gadd and N. G. L. Hammond, 680-706. Cambridge: At the University Press.

———. 1975. *The Neolithic of the Near East.* New York: Charles Scribner's Sons.

Mellink, M. 1966. The Art of Anatolia until c. 1200 B.C. *Art Treasures of Turkey: An Exhibition Circulated by the Smithsonian Institution 1966-68, Washington, D.C.,* 3-20.

Mellink, M. and J. Filip. 1974. *Frühe Stufen der Kunst.* Berlin: Propyläen Verlag.

Menghin, Oswald. 1936. Grundlinien einer Methodik der urgeschichtlichen Stammeskunde. *Germanen und Indogermanen. Festschrift für Herman Hirt.* Vol. 1. Edited by Helmut Arntz, 41-67. Heidelberg: Winter.

Merpert, N. I. 1961. L'Enéolithique de la zone steppique de la partie européenne de l'U.R.S.S. *L'Europe à la fin de l'âge de la pierre,* edited by J. Böhm and S. J. De Laet, 176-92. Prague: Editions de l'Académie tchécoslovaque des Sciences.

Mildenberger, G. 1961. *Mitteldeutschlands Ur- und Frühgeschichte.* Leipzig: J. A. Barth.

Milisauskas, Sarunas. 1978. *European Prehistory.* New York and London: Academic Press.

Miller, D. G. 1977. Some Theoretical and Typological Implications of an Indo-European Root Structure Constraint. *JIES* 5.1:31-40.

Minard, A. 1956. *Trois énigmes sur les cent chemins.* Vol. 2. (Publications de l'Institut de Civilisation Indienne, nr. 3.) Paris: E. de Boccard.

Mongait, A. L. 1955. *Archaeology in the U.S.S.R.* Reprint 1961. Harmondsworth: Penguin.

Montelius, Oscar. 1906. *Kulturgeschichte Schwedens.* Leipzig: E. A. Seemann.

Montler, T. 1980. Glottalized Consonants in Salish and Indo-European. *Working Papers in Linguistics.* Manoa: University of Hawaii, Department of Linguistics.

Much, Rudolf. 1967. *Die Germania des Tacitus erläutert.* 3rd ed. Edited by Wolfgang Lange and Herbert Jankuhn. Heidelberg: Winter.

Müller, Sophus. 1905. *Urgeschichte Europas.* Strassburg: Trübner.

Murray, Jacqueline. 1970. *The First European Agriculture: A Study of the Osteological and Botanical Evidence until 2000 B.C.* Edinburgh: University Press.

———. 1973. Einige Gesichtspunkte über die Beziehung zwischen Viehzucht und archäologischen Kulturen im Spätneolithikum in Europa. *Domestikationsforschung und Geschichte der Haustiere* (Internationales Symposion in Budapest 1971). Edited by János Matolcsi, 177-86. Budapest: Akadémiai Kiadó.

Nagy, Gregory. 1974a. *Comparative Studies of Greek and Indic Meter.* Cambridge, Mass.: Harvard University Press.

———. 1974b. Review of *The Language of Hesiod in Its Traditional Context,* by G. P. Edwards. Oxford: Blackwell, 1971. *The Canadian Journal of Linguistics* 21:219-24.

Neu, Erich. 1974. *Der Anitta-Text.* Wiesbaden: Otto Harrassowitz.
———. 1976. Zur Rekonstruktion des indogermanischen Verbalsystems. *Studies in Greek, Italic, and Indo-European Linguistics, Offered to Leonard R. Palmer,* edited by Anna Mopurgo Davies and Wolfgang Meid, 239-54. Innsbruck: Institut für Sprachwissenschaft.
———. 1980. *Studien zum endlosen "Lokativ" des Hethitischen.* (Vorträge und kleinere Schriften, 23.) Innsbruck: Innsbrucker Beiträge zur Sprachwissenschaft.
Neustupný, Evžen. 1973. Die Badener Kultur. *Symposium über die Entstehung und Chronologie der Badener Kultur,* edited by Bohuslav Chropovský, 317-52. Bratislava: Verlag der slowakischen Akademie der Wissenschaften.
Neustupný, J. 1966. From Indo-Europeans to Prehistoric Celts in Central Europe. *Rivista da Faculdade de Letras de Lisboa,* Series 3, no. 10, 3-32.
Norman Brown, W. 1978. *India and Indology: Selected Articles.* Edited by Rosane Rocher. Delhi: Motilal Banarsidass.
Normier, R. 1977. Indogermanischer Konsonantismus, germanische "Lautverschiebung" und Vernersches Gesetz. *Zeitschrift für vergleichende Sprachforschung* 91:171-218.
Oertel, Hans. 1926. *The Syntax of Cases in the Narrative and Descriptive Prose of the Brāhmaṇas.* Heidelberg: Winter.
Oldeberg, A. 1952. *Studien über die schwedische Bootaxtkultur.* Stockholm: Wahlström and Widstrand.
Otto, Rudolf. 1917. *Das Heilige.* Munich.
Palmer, L. R. 1955. *Achaeans and Indo-Europeans.* Oxford: Clarendon Press.
Passek, T. 1962. *Relations entre l'Europe occidentale et l'Europe orientale à l'époque néolithique.* (Les rapports et les informations des archéologues de l'URSS, VIᵉ Congrès international des sciences préhistoriques et protohistoriques.) Moscow: Académie des sciences de l'URSS, Institut d'Archéologie.
Pearson, Roger. 1973. Some Aspects of Social Mobility in the Early History of Indo-European Societies. *Journal of Indo-European Studies* 1:155-62.
Pedersen, Holger. 1931. *Linguistic Science in the Nineteenth Century.* Translated by J. W. Spargo. Cambridge, Mass.: Harvard University Press.
———. 1951. *Die gemeinindoeuropäischen und vorindoeuropäischen Verschlusslaute.* (Det Kgl. Danske Videnskabernes Selskab, Hist.-filolog. Medd., 32.) Copenhagen: Munksgaard.
Pfeiffer, John E. 1977. *The Emergence of Society: A Prehistory of the Establishment.* New York: McGraw-Hill.
Piggott, S. 1960. Neolithic and Bronze Age in East Europe. *Antiquity* 34:285-94.
———. 1962. Heads and Hoofs. *Antiquity* 36:110-15.
———. 1965. *Ancient Europe.* Chicago: Aldine Publishing Co.
———. 1968. The Earliest Wheeled Vehicles and the Caucasian Evidence. *Proceedings of the Prehistoric Society* 34:266-318.

Pilcher, J. R. and M. G. L. Baillie. 1978. Implications of a European Radiocarbon Calibration. *Antiquity* 52:217-22.

Pittioni, Richard. 1949. *Die urgeschichtlichen Grundlagen der europäischen Kultur.* Vienna: Franz Deuticke.

Pokorny, Julius. 1959. *Indogermanisches etymologisches Wörterbuch.* Bern: A. Francke.

Polomé, Edgar C. 1969. Some Comments on *Vǫluspá*, Stanzas 17-18. *Old Norse Literature and Mythology: A Symposium,* edited by Edgar C. Polomé, 265-90. Austin and London: University of Texas Press.

———. 1972. Germanic and the Other Indo-European Languages. *Toward a Grammar of Proto-Germanic,* edited by Frans van Coetsem and Herbert L. Kufner, 43-69. Tübingen: Max Niemeyer Verlag.

———. 1975. Old Norse Religious Terminology in Indo-European Perspective. *The Nordic Languages and Modern Linguistics* 2, edited by Karl-Hampus Dahlstedt, 654-65. Stockholm: Almquist and Wiksell International.

Renfrew, Colin. 1970. The Burnt House at Sitagroi. *Antiquity* 44:131-34.

———. 1971. Sitagroi and the Prehistory of South-East Europe. *Antiquity* 45:275-82.

———. 1973. *Before Civilization.* New York: A. Knopf.

Renou, Louis. 1956. *Etudes védiques et pāṇinéennes.* Vol. 2. (Publications de l'Institut de Civilisation Indienne, Nr. 2.) Paris: E. de Boccard.

———. 1961. *Etudes védiques et pāṇinéennes.* Vol. 8. (Publications de l'Institut de Civilisation Indienne, Nr. 14.) Paris: E. de Boccard.

Rivière, Jean-Claude. 1979. *Georges Dumézil: A la découverte des Indo-Européens.* Paris: Copernic.

Roman, Petre I. 1976. *Cultura Coţofeni.* (Biblioteca de Arheologie, 26.) Bucharest: Editura Academiei Republicii Socialiste România.

Rostovtzeff, M. 1922. *Iranians and Greeks in South Russia.* Reissued 1969. New York: Russell and Russell.

Sangmeister, E. 1976. Das Verhältnis der Glockenbecherkultur zu den einheimischen Kulturen der iberischen Halbinsel. *Glockenbecher Symposium, Oberried, 1974,* edited by J. N. Lanting and J. D. van der Waals, 423-38. Bussum and Harlem: Fibula-van Dishoeck.

Sangmeister, E. and K. Gerhardt. 1965. *Schnurkeramik und Schnurkeramiker in Südwestdeutschland.* (Badische Fundberichte, Sonderheft 8.) Freiburg i. Br.: Staatliches Amt für Ur- und Frühgeschichte.

Schmidt, Gernot. 1978. Über indogermanische nominale Relativkonstruktionen. *IF* 82:61-74.

Schmidt, Hans-Peter. 1978. Indo-Iranian Mitra: The State of the Central Problem. *Etudes Mithriaques.* Actes du 2nd Congrès International, Téhéran 1975 (Acta Iranica, vol. 17), 346-93. Leyden: E. J. Brill.

Schmitt-Brandt, Robert. 1973. *Die Entwicklung des indogermanischen Vokalsystems: Versuch einer inneren Rekonstruktion.* 2. *Verb. und erw. Ausgabe.* (Wissenschaftliche Bibliothek, 7.) Heidelberg: J. Groos.

Schuchhardt, Carl. 1935. *Vorgeschichte von Deutschland.* Munich and Berlin: R. Oldenbourg.

Scott Littleton, C. 1973. *The New Comparative Mythology: An Anthropological Assessment of the Theories of Georges Dumézil.* Rev. ed. Berkeley and Los Angeles: University of California Press.

Specht, Franz. 1947. *Der Ursprung der indogermanischen Deklination.* Göttingen: Vandenhoeck and Ruprecht.

Srinivasan, Doris. 1975. The Religious Significance of Multiple Bodily Parts to Denote the Divine: Findings from the *Rig-Veda. Asiatische Studien/Etudes Asiatigues* 29:137-79.

Strahm, Christian. 1969. Die späten Kulturen. *Die Jüngere Steinzeit,* Band 2, *Ur- und frühgeschichtliche Archäologie der Schweiz,* 97-116. Basel: Verlag Schweizerische Gesellschaft für Ur- und Frühgeschichte.

Šturms, E. 1961. Die Herkunft der Becher-Bootaxt-Kultur. *Bericht über den V. Internationalen Kongress für Vor- und Frühgeschichte, Hamburg, 1958,* 779-86. Berlin: Verlag Gebr. Mann.

———. 1970. *Die steinzeitlichen Kulturen des Baltikums.* (Antiquitas, Reihe 3, Band 9: Serie in 4to.) Bonn: Rudolf Habelt Verlag.

Sturve, K. 1955. *Die Einzelgrabkultur in Schleswig-Holstein und ihre kontinentalen Beziehungen.* Neumünster: Karl Wachholtz Verlag.

Sulimirski, T. 1970. *Prehistoric Russia: An Outline.* New York and London: J. Baker.

Swadesh, M. 1971. *The Origins and Diversification of Language,* edited by J. Scherzer. Chicago: Aldine-Atherton.

Szemerényi, Oswald. 1967. The New Look of Proto-Indo-European. *Phonetica* 17:65-99.

———. 1970. *Einführung in die vergleichende Sprachwissenschaft.* Darmstadt: Wissenschaftliche Buchgesellschaft.

Telegin, D. Ja. 1969. Das Mitteldneprgebiet und östlich anschliessende Ukraine in der Epoche des Neolithikums und frühen Metallzeit. *Zeitschrift für Archäologie* 3:1-15.

Thieme, Paul. 1960. The Aryan Gods of the Mitanni Treaties. *Journal of the American Oriental Society* 80:301-317.

Thomas, Homer L. 1967. *Near Eastern, Mediterranean and European Chronology.* 2 vols. (Studies in Mediterranean Archaeology: 17.1 text, 17.2 charts.) Lund: Studies in Mediterranean Archaeology.

———. 1968. Archaeological Implications of Near Eastern Historical Chronology. *Opuscula Atheniensia 8, Skrifter utgivna av Svenska Institutet i Athen,* 4°, 14:11-22.

———. 1977. The Dispersal of the Indo-Europeans and Concepts of Cultural Continuity and Change. *Ancient Europe and the Mediterranean: Studies Presented in Honour of Hugh Hencken,* edited by Vladimir Markotic, 181-88. Warminster: Aris and Phillips.

Thompson, E. A. 1965. *The Early Germans.* Oxford: Clarendon Press.

Titiev, Mischa. 1972. A Fresh Approach to the Problems of Magic and Religions. *Reader in Comparative Religion: An Anthropological Approach.* 3rd ed. Edited by William A. Lessa and Evon Z. Vogt, 430-33. (Reprinted from the *Southwestern Journal of Anthropology* 16[1960]:292-98.) New York: Harper & Row.

Todd, I. A. 1973. Anatolia and the Khirbet Kerak Problem. *Orient and Occident: Essays Presented to Cyrus H. Gordon on His Sixty-Fifth Birthday,* 181-206. (Veröffentlichungen zur Kultur und Geschichte des Alten Testaments.)

Traugott, Elizabeth Closs. 1981. From Propositional to Textual and Expressive Meanings: Some Semantic-Pragmatic Aspects of Grammaticalization. Paper presented at the 1979 MLA meeting in San Francisco.

Trier, Jost. 1942. Zaun und Mannring. *Beiträge zur Geschichte der deutschen Sprache und Literatur* 66:232-64.

Tringham, R. 1971. *Hunters, Fishers and Farmers of Eastern Europe 6000-3000 B.C.* London: Hutchinson University Library.

Vaillant, André. 1950. *Grammaire comparée des langues slaves.* Vol. 1. Lyon: IAC.

Vetter, Emil. 1953. *Handbuch der italischen Dialekte.* Heidelberg: Winter.

Vinogradov, A. P., A. L. Devirts, E. I. Dobkina and N. G. Markova. 1966. Radiocarbon Dating in the Vernadsky Institute I-IV. *Radiocarbon* 8:292-323.

von Gabain, Annaliese. 1974. *Alttürkische Grammatik.* 3rd ed. Wiesbaden: Otto Harrassowitz.

Waals, J. D. van der and W. Glasbergen. 1955. Beaker Types and Their Distribution in the Netherlands. *Palaeohistoria* 4:5-46.

Wackernagel, Jacob. 1896-1957. *Altindische Grammatik.* Göttingen: Vandenhoeck and Ruprecht.

———. 1926-28. *Vorlesungen über Syntax.* 2nd ed. Basel: Birkhäuser.

Watkins, Calvert. 1967. Language of Gods and Language of Men: Remarks on Some Indo-European Metalinguistic Traditions. *Myth and Law Among the Indo-Europeans,* edited by Jaan Puhvel. Berkeley: University of California Press.

———. 1969. *Indogermanische Grammatik III/1. Geschichte der indogermanischen Verbalflexion.* Heidelberg: Winter.

———. 1975. La famille indo-européenne du grec ὄρχις: linguistique, poétique et mythologie. *BSL* 70:11-26.

———. 1976. Towards Proto-Indo-European Syntax: Problems and Pseudo-Problems. *Papers from the Parasession on Diachronic Syntax,* edited by Sanford B. Steever et al., 305-26. Chicago: Chicago Linguistic Society.

———. 1978. In essar dam do á? *Eriu* 29:161-65.

———. 1979. NAMRA GUD UDU in Hittite: Indo-European Poetic Language and the Folk Taxonomy of Wealth. *Hethitisch und Indogermanisch,* edited by Erich Neu and Wolfgang Meid. Innsbruck: Innsbrucker Beiträge zur Sprachwissenschaft.

Weinberg, Saul S. 1965. The Relative Chronology of the Aegean in the Stone and Early Bronze Ages. *Chronologies in Old World Archaeology,* edited by Robert Ehrich, 285-320. Chicago: The University of Chicago Press.

West, Martin L. 1973. Indo-European Metre. *Glotta* 51:161-87.

Westphal, Rudolf. 1860. Zur vergleichenden Metrik der indogermanischen Völker. *KZ* 9:437-58.

Wetzel, G. 1969. Oderschnurkeramik und Einzelgrabkultur in Brandenburg. *Die neolithischen Becherkulturen im Gebiet der DDR und ihre europäischen Beziehungen,* edited by H. Behrens and F. Schlette, 101-113. (Veröffentlichungen des Landesmuseums für Vorgeschichte in Halle, 24.) Halle: Landesmuseum für Vorgeschichte.

Whitney, William D. 1896. *A Sanskrit Grammar.* 3rd ed. Boston: Ginn.

Winter, Werner. 1976. The Distribution of Short and Long Vowels in Stems of the Type Lith. *ĕsti:vèsti:mèsti* and OCS *jasti:vesti:mesti* in Baltic and Slavic Languages. *Recent Developments in Historical Phonology,* edited by J. Fisiak. The Hague: Mouton.

Woolley, C. L. 1928. Excavations at Ur 1927-28. *Antiquaries Journal* 8:415-48.

———. 1934. *Ur Excavations.* Vol. 2. *The Royal Cemetery.* London: Oxford University Press.

Young, T. Cuyler, Jr., and Louis D. Levine. 1974. *Excavations of the Godin Project: Second Progress Report.* (Occasional Paper 26, Art and Archaeology.) Toronto: Royal Ontario Museum.

Zeuner, Frederick E. 1963. *A History of Domesticated Animals.* New York: Harper & Row.